Super Bowl Monday

Super Bowl Monday

From the Persian Gulf to
the Shores of West Florida:
The New York Giants,
the Buffalo Bills, and
Super Bowl XXV

ADAM LAZARUS

TAYLOR TRADE PUBLISHING
Lanham • New York • Boulder • Toronto • Plymouth, UK

Published by Taylor Trade Publishing
An imprint of The Rowman & Littlefield Publishing Group, Inc.
4501 Forbes Boulevard, Suite 200, Lanham, Maryland 20706
http://www.rlpgtrade.com

Estover Road, Plymouth PL6 7PY, United Kingdom

Distributed by National Book Network

British Library Cataloguing in Publication Information Available

Library of Congress Cataloging-in-Publication Data

Lazarus, Adam.
  Super Bowl Monday : from the Persian Gulf to the shores of west Florida : the New York Giants, the Buffalo Bills, and Super Bowl XXV / Adam Lazarus.
    p. cm.
  Includes bibliographical references and index.
  ISBN 978-1-58979-600-3 (hardback) — ISBN 978-1-58979-602-7 (electronic)
  1. Super Bowl (25th : 1991 : Tampa, Fla.) 2. New York Giants (Football team)
  3. Buffalo Bills (Football team) 4. Football—United States—History—20th century.
  5. Persian Gulf War, 1991. I. Title.
  GV956.2.S8L4 2011
  796.332'648—dc22

                                                                    2011010710

Printed in the United States of America

For Sarah,
My love and my muse

Contents

Foreword

LYNN SWANN

If you are a sports fan who always wanted to know how a moment in the competitive landscape of championship sports came to be, then you have found your answer in *Super Bowl Monday*. The interviews conducted by Adam Lazarus, plus the revelations of key personnel through various books and stories, give you a 360-degree look at Super Bowl XXV. It is better than being in the locker room.

I have been fortunate to play and win four Super Bowls. Certainly being the MVP of Super Bowl X was a huge highlight. Also, I have broadcast several Super Bowls for ABC including Super Bowl XXV. In those telecasts, I always had the jobs of pregame reports or stories and interviewing the players and coaches of the losing teams. The NFL did not allow sideline reporters at that time.

For Super Bowl XXV, I found myself standing on the Giants' sideline as Whitney Houston was preparing to sing our national anthem. The Giants players all lined up with Bill Parcells standing on the left end, right next to me—the last formality before the players took center stage. With emotions running high under the security due to Desert Storm and F-16s flying low and loud, Parcells turned to me with a huge smile and eagerness, to say, "Swanny, this is what it is all about. This is the fuckin' best!"

At the end of a great contest, I was in the Buffalo locker room conducting live interviews for our world audience. Many players and coaches have been professional in discussing a Super Bowl loss. None was as gracious as kicker Scott Norwood. It was the first of many that night for Scott, and he gave lessons in class each time.

What I have just told you was a small part of the night from my viewpoint. Adam gives you the personal stories of all the key players.

Read *Super Bowl Monday* and you will feel that you now know the whole story of an American classic that continues to inspire a nation.

Lynn Swann
November 2010

Introduction

Every Super Bowl is special. A neck-and-neck game, such as the Steelers-Cowboys rematch in Super Bowl XIII, or a gripping finish, like Mike Jones' tackle at the end of the St. Louis Rams' win over Tennessee in January 2000, naturally establishes a permanent place in the game's mythology.

Super Bowl VI, between Dallas and Miami, was one of the worst playoff games during the entire decade of the 1970s: the Dolphins remain the only Super Bowl participant that failed to score even a single touchdown. Nevertheless, anyone present at that 24-3 Cowboy triumph witnessed arguably the greatest collection of talent in the history of professional football. Apart from the matchup of Hall of Fame head coaches (Tom Landry and Don Shula) and Hall of Fame starting quarterbacks (Roger Staubach and Bob Griese), eleven other starters in that game would eventually be enshrined in Canton, Ohio.

And through the course of five decades, the Super Bowl has featured moments that had nothing to do with football. Looking past the national crisis caused by Janet Jackson and Justin Timberlake's "wardrobe malfunction" in January 2004, political events and social issues have managed to seep into the story lines of past Super Bowls.

The New Orleans Saints' victory in Super Bowl XLIV was especially poignant considering the city was more than four years into the nightmare caused by Hurricane Katrina.

Nearly thirty years earlier, when the "Crescent City" hosted Super Bowl XV, the nation's attention was more fixated on the safe return of the hostages that spent 444 days in Iran than the impending Oakland Raiders–Philadelphia Eagles matchup on January 25, 1981. To honor the fifty-two Americans who had been released two days before the Raiders' 27-10 victory, the outside of the Superdome was adorned with an eighty-foot-long yellow bow.

That national pride would return to New Orleans in early February 2002. Fittingly, the red-white-and-blue-wearing Patriots from New England won Super Bowl XXXVI at the Superdome, five months after the tragic events that took place on September 11, 2001.

If these are the criteria that make the NFL's annual title game great, Super Bowl XXV, between the New York Giants and Buffalo Bills, had them all.

In terms of what took place on the field that particular day, January 27, 1991, there has never been a better contest. There were four lead changes. The game came down to the last seconds. The margin of victory was one point. There wasn't a single turnover. A seven-point underdog emerged triumphant.

With the Empire State showdown marking the Super Bowl's quarter century, silver anniversary, it was appropriate that a handful of pro football legends stood on the Tampa Stadium sidelines that day.

Two of the greatest pass rushers of all time, Lawrence Taylor and Bruce Smith, led their respective defenses.

Three (current or future) Hall of Fame head coaches, Bill Parcells, Marv Levy, and Bill Belichick, were the brains behind the game plans.

Several of the greatest players during their era starred for the Giants and Bills 1990 teams: Jim Kelly, Thurman Thomas, James Lofton, Andre Reed, Mark Bavaro, Carl Banks, Pepper Johnson, and Leonard Marshall. In all, thirty-four once-or-future Pro Bowlers competed in Super Bowl XXV: seventeen for each team if the injured Phil Simms is counted.

And with the Persian Gulf War—America's first true war since Vietnam—having officially begun ten days before the Giants and Bills kicked off in west Florida, Super Bowl XXV had a cloud of peril and uncertainty hanging above it like no other single-day event in the nation's sports history.

Still, for all the lines on a Hall of Famer's résumé, the back-and-forth excitement of a game that comes down to the last play, even the larger, far more significant non-football issues that might hover above a sporting event, Americans cherish the tales of redemptions and underdogs as much as anything. Why else are *Rocky, Hoosiers, Seabiscuit,* and *Major League* such compelling box office draws?

That is why the individual stories of New York Giants quarterback Jeff Hostetler and his teammate, running back Ottis Anderson, occupy special places in NFL history . . . and this book. That is also why the Buffalo Bills franchise's swift transition from laughingstock to dynasty, beginning in the late 1980s and into 1990, is central to the drama within *Super Bowl Monday.*

But an NFL team is comprised of dozens of players, coaches, trainers, administrators, secretaries, and so on. So while Hostetler, Anderson, Jim Kelly, James Lofton, and a few others are the "faces" of this book, inside these pages are any number of side stories and lesser-known tales.

The historic action that took place on the field that day is *the reason* for this book. But the men who carried out those graceful or superb displays of athleticism that evening are what I hope you will find most captivating.

Adam Lazarus
October 2010

Prologue

November 9, 1986

Week Ten of the 1986 National Football League season was a typical one for the New York Giants. Linebacker Lawrence Taylor guided the team to a shut-out of the Philadelphia Eagles through the first three quarters. The eventual league Most Valuable Player tallied three sacks and seven tackles in the NFC East showdown at Veterans Stadium. A pair of touchdowns by all-pro running back Joe Morris gave New York a seventeen-point lead late in the third quarter. And clutch passing by quarterback Phil Simms added just enough for the Giants to secure a 17-14 win over their division rival.

Equally routine that afternoon was the sight of Jeff Hostetler and Ottis Anderson watching most of the action from the Giants' sideline.

Few people possessed Hostetler's blend of intelligence and athleticism. Although six feet, three inches tall, 215 pounds, and blessed with speed and a strong throwing arm, brains were probably his greatest asset. After earning first-team academic all-American honors at the University of West Virginia, the finance major was nominated for a Rhodes scholarship.

Those physical and mental tools intrigued the Giants, who not only selected Hostetler in the third round of the 1984 NFL draft but also signed the twenty-three-year-old to a three-year, $1 million contract prior to his rookie season.

Regardless of his talents—and his comparatively large salary—in three years on the Giants' roster, Hostetler never dropped back in the pocket, never read the opposing defense's coverage to find the open receiver, and never threw a pass. Instead, Hostetler earned (very minimal) playing time only as a special teamer and, occasionally, an emergency wide receiver.

"What it made you feel like was that you weren't really part of the team. Here you are, you do all the work during the week and then come Sunday you stand there and watch," Hostetler said years later. "It was extremely difficult mentally because you know that if you had the opportunity to go out and perform and make some mistakes and learn from it that you could do that job. But to never have the opportunity was extremely frustrating."

By the middle of his second season, Hostetler could no longer take the inaction.

"I wanted desperately to get out on the field and get into the game, use myself up a little, so I asked if I could play on any of the special teams," Hostetler later wrote. "Then a couple of the wide receivers got hurt and we were running low on them in practice so I volunteered to run the plays. The coaches liked what they saw and they told [head coach Bill Parcells] that if they ever needed somebody, they could put me in as a receiver. . . . In the end, I got into quite a few games, which was better than just sitting on the bench eating my heart out."

And despite not doing so as a quarterback, Hostetler did make an impact for the Giants.

Midway through the second quarter of the Week Ten battle in Veteran Stadium, New York forced the Eagles to punt. Coach Parcells sent onto the field his return squad, of which Hostetler was a member. While both teams were lining up to start the fourth-down play, Eagles tight end John Spagnola—still discussing pass routes on the sidelines with his fellow receivers—forgot to fill his special teams duties as a blocker for the punt team.

"I knew they had only 10 men on the field," Hostetler said, "because there was no one on me. When I saw that, I hurried up and got down. I didn't want them to see me."

At the snap, Hostetler knifed through the line and deflected punter John Teltschik's kick. The ball went four yards past the line of scrimmage, giving the Giants offense great field position, inside Eagles territory. New York scored the game's first touchdown six plays later.

"It gets boring just sitting around," Hostetler said when reporters asked him that week about his non-quarterback role. "These things give me something to do. It gets me involved. At least I'm contributing somewhere."

But punt blocking and route running was not the pro-football future Jeff Hostetler had hoped for. Since childhood—playing two-on-two tackle football with his brothers, Ron, Doug, and Todd—he dreamed of commanding the huddle, scanning the field for receivers, and throwing the football to the open man.

"And I hope everyone remembers that," said Hostetler, addressing his desire to be the team's quarterback. "People ask me when I'm going to play. And I tell them I don't know. I know I can play. I just need the opportunity."

Like his teammate Jeff Hostetler, running back Ottis Anderson hungered for a chance to play. But at least Hostetler occasionally contributed to the Giants on special teams, as he did in the early November game against Philadelphia. On that day, Anderson never even set foot onto the field of play.

A month before their win over the Eagles, New York curiously acquired the eight-year veteran Anderson—a former all-pro and the eleventh leading rusher in NFL history—from the St. Louis Cardinals. But with Joe Morris in the middle of his second straight exceptional season, Anderson was not brought in to change the status quo. His role was expected to be that of a decoy or to occasionally spell Morris, who (at five feet seven inches and 190 pounds) was averaging more than twenty carries per game.

"The Giants told me they needed more production from the fullback position," Anderson later wrote, "though they knew I was a halfback. It was a way to quickly get me on the field and change their one-dimension offense, which was basically Joe Morris left, Joe Morris right."

Anderson carried the ball thirteen times for fifty yards in three games after joining the team; not bad for a soon-to-be thirty-year-old rusher still learning the playbook. But a nagging hamstring injury, which he suffered during his first appearance with the Giants, slowed his step.

And although, at first, he had been eager to leave the inept 1-4 Cardinals for the 4-1, perennially playoff-caliber Giants—"This is like a second chance in my life, a chance to play in the Super Bowl," he said when he met the New York press—his mood quickly soured. Only six carries in three games, then sitting out completely during the Giants' win in Philadelphia, left Anderson feeling lost.

"Embarrassed," he said, describing his mood a few weeks into his Giants career. "That's it. I get traded from a team that hasn't won a game to a team that has lost only once, and then this thing happens to my hamstring. So I'm more embarrassed than anything else. You can deal with frustration. People say don't worry, but you're a player. You want to produce."

New York's victory over the host Eagles that day pushed their record to 8-2, the team's best start since 1963. The Giants would not lose another game during the remainder of the regular season, earning home-field advantage in the playoffs. And once the postseason began, Bill Parcells' crew was even better. They obliterated Joe Montana and the San Francisco 49ers in the opening round 49-3, then shut out Joe Gibbs' powerful Washington Redskins to advance to the franchise's first Super Bowl. At the Rose Bowl in Pasadena, California, New York overcame a narrow halftime deficit to stomp the Denver Broncos and win Super Bowl XXI 39-20.

Anderson scored a somewhat meaningless two-yard touchdown in that Super Bowl win (the Giants already held a twenty-point lead with less than four minutes remaining in the game), but admitted the moment left him feeling "somewhat saddened, because I felt I was on a team that I didn't make a major contribution to."

"To be honest," he later said, "I didn't feel a part of that Giants team."

Neither did Jeff Hostetler. Playing wide receiver in a late-season game against San Francisco, the third-string quarterback injured his knee and was placed on injured reserve, leaving him ineligible for the postseason. From the sidelines of the Rose Bowl Stadium, in street clothes, Hostetler watched Phil Simms lead New York to the title by way of the most accurate passing performance in Super Bowl history. (The game's Most Valuable Player, Simms completed twenty-two of twenty-five passes for 268 yards and three touchdowns.)

As the weeks, months, and eventually years of being anchored to the sideline mounted—as did awareness that their ephemeral athletic gifts were being wasted—Hostetler and Anderson naturally connected.

"There was a pretty tight bond there as far as we both knew what we were going through and we were pulling for each other. There was a constant patting guys on the back and 'keep going, keep going' and 'it'll happen,'" Hostetler remembered. "I think having him there was a real positive for me because there was a guy there that had been playing and knew what it was like and then 'boom' the opportunities dried up and you weren't a contributor and you felt like you were on the outside looking in. . . . And that's frustrating, 'cause you didn't make it that far by being satisfied with just having a uniform on."

Week Ten of the 1986 National Football League season was *not* a typical one for the Buffalo Bills; and for reasons beyond simply posting a victory.

In their previous forty-three games, Buffalo had only six wins, by far the poorest record of any team during that stretch. They were the worst team in professional football.

"I went through the jokes," recalled Darryl Talley, a linebacker drafted by the team in 1983. "Like: Knock-knock.

"Who's there?

"Owen.

"Owen who?

"Oh-and-10."

The Bills did not start the 1986 season quite that horribly, as they had two years earlier. In fact, given the recent history, their 2-7 record practically constituted a hot streak. Still, those narrow wins over St. Louis and Indianapolis were not enough to save head coach Hank Bullough's job. One day after the Bills' early November loss to the comparably futile Tampa Bay Buccaneers, Bullough was replaced.

"We felt that new direction was needed," first-year General Manager Bill Polian told the press, "and we reached out to a man who had had an established head coaching career, who has helped build winners every place he has been in football."

That man was Marv Levy.

"I'm very excited and thrilled to be coming to Buffalo," said Levy. "I probably know the Bills better than any team in the NFL, by virtue of doing the preseason games. I've got a pretty good line on their personnel, their strengths and weaknesses."

Turning the Bills around would be a tall task for him, no matter how well he knew his new team. But Levy—a Phi Beta Kappa from Coe College, who earned a masters degree in English history at Harvard—approached the task with a scholar's lens.

"I think defensively, and statistics will bear this out, that there needs to be improvement, some of it from current players, some of it from development of current players," he told reporters. "Offensively, I see some good things, but it's very hard to divorce offense and defense from kicking."

But improvements to the defense and (especially) the kicking game would not stir up the excitement the franchise needed to please its loyal, yet starving, fans. And Levy knew that.

"It's a young team and I'm pleased to be coming to a team with an outstanding quarterback prospect."

That man was Jim Kelly, the team's gutsy, flashy, $8 million acquisition, who joined the Bills that season and immediately made a name for himself. In his NFL debut against the New York Jets, the twenty-six-year-old threw for 292 yards and three touchdowns. More so than his passing statistics, Kelly's scrambling ability and disregard for self-preservation—hanging in the pocket, he endured several hard hits from Jets defenders—endeared him to his teammates, his opponents, Bills fans, and the media.

"It's easy to lose perspective here. It's easy to get carried away. Let's just say, coolly and unemotionally, the National Football League debut of Buffalo rookie quarterback Jim Kelly was nothing short of sensational," *Sports Illustrated*'s Paul Zimmerman wrote. "Jim Kelly is Joe Namath with knees."

Even with super Namath, the Bills' abysmal record continued throughout the first two months of the regular season.

"I hate losing," Kelly said before the Bills' tenth game. "It hurts. It bothers me a lot. I've never been a loser. I've never been on a team with a losing record, not even in midget league, not in my whole life. We're a young team, so you have to expect us to lose some games. But it doesn't have to last. I can make this team a winner."

Once Levy took control of the team, Kelly's vow seemed reasonable.

"Marv had an immediate, positive impact on the team," said Kelly. "But it wasn't a case of coming in and running everybody into the ground, the way some new head coaches feel they have to do when they take over a losing program. In fact, the first thing Marv did was shorten practices saying it was quality that mattered, not quantity. . . . Marv came across as more of a college professor more than an NFL head coach, using a lot of big words and talking about a lot of historical figures whom most of us had never even heard of before."

Bills players crammed Levy's lesson plan that week, in preparation for their first exam, a November 9 home matchup with the Pittsburgh Steelers. Despite their own poor record (3-6), the Steelers came to Buffalo on a two-game winning streak. Chuck Noll's defense had not surrendered a touchdown in nine consecutive quarters, and with five touchdown passes from quarterback Mark Malone, the Steelers outscored their opponents 57-12 in the two wins.

Given the minor resurgence in Pittsburgh's passing game and the presence of Buffalo's skilled and exciting rookie quarterback, the game had the potential of becoming a shoot-out. Gusting winds on game day at Buffalo's Rich Stadium prevented that from happening. Garbage bags repeatedly swirled by the field of play, eventually blowing up and out of the stadium. When the referee executed the pregame toss to decide possession, the coin soared seven yards from where he was standing.

"I've seen hurricanes in Mississippi with less velocity than that," Bills center Kent Hull noted.

More than seventy-two thousand people braved the elements to see the Bills take an early lead.

Keeping his passes beneath the harsh wins, Kelly connected with wide receiver Andre Reed for a three-yard touchdown midway through the opening quarter. As the less-than-ideal passing conditions worsened, Levy suggested offensive coordinator Bob Leahy keep the ball on the ground. Buffalo's Robb Riddick carried out Levy's instructions, quickly racking up fifty yards and a touchdown late in the second period.

Buffalo's defense was even more impressive. With a sore knee limiting star defensive end Bruce Smith's availability, linebackers Darryl Talley and Ray Bentley anchored the defense and kept Pittsburgh without a single first down until two minutes before halftime.

"They were mixing up their defenses against the run," Steelers tackle Ray Pinner said, "but mainly they were just beating us one-on-one. We got stuffed."

With the score 13-0, the Bills charged out of the locker room after halftime, eager to preserve their lead and send the local fans home with a victory. However, within seconds of the start of the third period, one thought ran through the minds of every spectator present that day at Rich Stadium: "same old Bills."

Standing deep in his own territory, Bills wide receiver Eric Richardson settled under the second half kickoff. At the fifteen-yard line, Pittsburgh's

Rick Woods crushed Richardson, who fumbled. After it had been accidently kicked by a nearby official, Steelers linebacker Mike Merriweather picked up the football. A member of the return team, Steve Tasker, who had been cut by Houston and signed off waivers two days earlier, brought down Merriweather at the five-yard line, saving a touchdown.

As he jogged off the field—having just made his first significant special teams contribution to the Buffalo Bills—Tasker had one thought: "No wonder this team has been 2-14."

Pittsburgh needed just one play to cross the goal line and seconds into the half, the score stood 13-6. The ensuing Buffalo possession was similarly disastrous. Three plays by Kelly's offense failed to produce a first down, forcing Levy to send out his punt team. From his own twenty-four-yard line, John Kidd booted the ball downfield, only to see the unbelievably strong winds that blew in from Lake Erie stonewall the kick. The punt went five yards. Again, Pittsburgh took advantage of the Bills special teams mishap and quickly put another touchdown on the scoreboard.

At that point in the game, with just over ten minutes remaining in the third period and each team having recorded two touchdowns, the score should have been tied 14-14. But the wind affected more than just the punting game. Three of the four point-after-touchdown tries failed: one for Buffalo and both Pittsburgh attempts. Steelers holder Harry Newsome couldn't field either one of Dan Turk's long snaps.

"The ball was fluttering back," Noll said. "It was like a knuckleball and our catcher couldn't hang on to it. Our catcher didn't have a big enough glove."

Twenty-six-year-old kicker Scott Norwood ignored the kicking game conundrum when he trotted out to attempt a critical field goal. Kelly, Levy, and the rest of the sideline breathed a sigh of relief when his twenty-nine-yard try was good, making the score 16-12. With ten minutes remaining in the game, the task before Buffalo's defense was simple: keep Pittsburgh out of the end zone.

Pacing along the sidelines during the final minutes, Levy watched Buffalo's defense—which had been exceptional all afternoon—now surrender large chunks of yardage.

"I kept saying 'This can't happen. Not at the end. Please don't let them score,'" Jim Kelly said.

The Steelers drove from their own twenty-yard line to the Buffalo twenty-nine. With ten seconds showing on the clock, Malone surveyed the field and chucked a pass intended for Calvin Sweeney near the end zone.

"Mark throws it, he tries to throw it into the scoreboard end," Steve Tasker remembered. "Even on a good day, the wind knocks that down. And he threw it in a windy day and it had no chance. It ended up ten yards short from where it was gonna go and it goes right into Rodney Bellinger's hands."

At the two-yard line, Buffalo safety Rodney Bellinger intercepted the pass to secure the victory.

"We were relaxed, we were confident, even at the end," Bellinger said. "I attribute that to the new coach (Marv Levy). All the guys were loose. He wants to see us have fun and not be tight. I think the coaching change was a step in the right direction."

During his first postgame press conference, the ever-modest Levy deflected any praise.

"Thank God for 45 stout hearts and the north wind," he told reporters.

Levy didn't quite know his situation yet: there were only forty-three men on his roster, and the forty-seven-mile-per-hour winds were blustering in from the southwest.

1

Every Pennsylvania Boy Wants to Play for JoePa

With two athletically gifted older brothers, William Jeffrey Hostetler had learned to wait with patience and humility for his turn in the spotlight. The fifth child (third boy) of Norman and Dolly Hostetler, Jeff was born on April 22, 1961, in rural western Pennsylvania. A tough, hard-working farmer, Norm owned 120 acres off of State Route 601, where he raised dairy cows before a fire prompted him to switch exclusively to chickens. (Although their postal address was Holsopple, Pennsylvania, the family lived closer to the town of Jerome.)

In between feeding chickens and washing eggs, the Hostetler boys tossed around baseballs, footballs, or basketballs and watched Notre Dame football games on television. But because Norm and Dolly were Mennonites, they had not planned on sending the children to public school.

"Mom and dad prayed over the matter," recalled Ron, the eldest male. "They decided to see if the things they taught us would hold up (in public schools). It was a change that took a lot of thought, a lot of prayers. We thought it was God's will that we make the change."

Attending public school meant that the children could compete in team sports. Ron was the first in the line of Hostetler boys to excel in athletics at Conemaugh Township High School. In the fall of 1972, his senior year, Ron and the Indians posted a 9-0 record and a narrow second-place finish in the Western Pennsylvania Conference standings.

Those football skills impressed head coach Joe Paterno to invite Ron to play for Penn State University. Roughly a two-hour drive from the family farm, Penn State was close enough to home, and he enrolled there for the fall 1973 semester. Recruited to play quarterback, by the start of Ron's first season, Paterno moved the freshman to linebacker, where he would star for the Nittany Lions until a knee injury endangered his career. During the spring and summer of 1977, Ron, now a senior, worked his way back into shape. By August, he was ready to compete for one of the outside linebacker positions against the biggest threat to his reclaiming the starting job: his younger brother, Doug.

Even after Ron played his last game for Conemaugh in 1972, the following autumn, a Hostetler was under center for the Indians. A year younger than Ron, Doug followed his brother to Penn State in 1974. And, as he had with Ron, Joe Paterno soon converted the reluctant quarterback into a linebacker.

So when Jeff Hostetler entered Conemaugh High in the fall of 1975, his future had already been mapped out. He made the varsity as a freshman, then claimed his birthright as the Indians quarterback the following season. A linebacker on defense as well, the six-foot, 180-pounder earned all-county honors. Completing passes to another Hostetler boy, his younger brother, tight end Todd, Jeff guided Conemaugh to an 8-1 record as a junior and was again named an all-county quarterback. His senior year—the best time to impress college scouts handing out scholarships—was expected to be even better.

"I think he'll be the most sought-after player in the state," his head coach, Joe Badaczewski, said before the season opener. "He's got the size, the arm and the running ability they look for."

But a week later, Badaczewski moved Jeff to tailback so he could replace an injured starter. Todd Hostetler became the quarterback. With great speed and size, Jeff dominated as a runner and won the Southern Alleghenies Football Coaches Association award for Most Valuable Offensive Player. *Parade Magazine* also named him to their all-American team, as a linebacker. (A Californian named John Elway and a Pittsburgher named Dan Marino were named as the team's quarterbacks.)

The Indians again went 8-1 and Jeff played whatever role the coach asked of him in order to win.

"The fact that I was good at [linebacker] caused me a lot of grief as I got older and kept pushing to achieve my life's ambition—to be a winning quarterback."

Although most newspapers listed him as a linebacker, Hostetler did garner attention as a quarterback from many top college programs. The Hostetler legacy and his achievements as a sophomore and junior luckily overshadowed his yearlong sabbatical at running back.

Approximately fifty schools offered scholarships. He visited the campuses of Stanford University, Notre Dame, and the University of Pittsburgh. But everyone expected, given the family history, that he would be in Happy Valley for fall classes in 1978. The choice was not quite that simple.

"It came down to my determination to play quarterback," he remembered. "I didn't want to go to a school that wouldn't promise to let me play the position my heart was set on. It was something to worry about with Penn State, Joe Paterno or no Joe Paterno—or, maybe more to the point, because of Joe Paterno—because my brothers' experiences had taught me that promises made can be promises broken."

On February 21, 1979, Paterno drove through a snowstorm from State College to the Hostetler farm. Inside the family home, he shook hands with Norm and Dolly (for the third time in five years), then watched as Jeff and his parents signed the letter of intent.

"This is great," Paterno said. "I'm looking forward to seeing you and the family soon."

Exactly a month after the Penn State scholarship was complete, Jeff Hostetler was busy working at another family legacy: basketball. Ron and Doug had each been fine hoopsters for Conemaugh—big, tough, and strong, they could both rebound and score around the basket. As expected, Jeff soon starred for the Indians squad.

As a junior, he netted twenty-seven points (brother Todd tossed in twenty) and earned MVP honors in the Jaycee Holiday Tournament. The next year, Jeff and the Indians won the early season Mountain Cat Tip-Off Tournament and cruised through the regular season undefeated.

Victories over Mercyhurst Prep and Bentworth advanced Conemaugh to the semifinals of the Pennsylvania Interscholastic Athletic Associate (PIAA) Class A Championship Tournament. In the next game, their opponent was a high school from East Brady, Pennsylvania, a town about one hundred miles northwest of the Hostetler farm, and home to another family with a knack for churning out stellar athletes.

Twin brothers Dan and Kevin Kelly helped East Brady keep pace with the powerful Conemaugh team. A pair of free throws by Dan with just over a minute remaining evened the score at fifty-five. At the start of overtime, Dan gave the Bulldogs a one-basket lead. Then Jeff Hostetler dominated the extra period (he finished with twenty-eight points and twelve rebounds) to give Conemaugh a 63-57 win.

After the game, the Kelly clan—father Joe, the twins, Dan and Kevin, the older boys, Pat, Ed, and Ray, as well as college freshman James Edward "Jim" Kelly—met with Conemaugh's star forward.

"I was in the locker room after the game," remembered Dave Michaels, the Conemaugh Township baseball coach, "Jim Kelly and his father and brothers came in to congratulate Jeff. Jeff's father and brothers were there. I remember thinking how similar they were. Two very close families."

Joe Kelly's parents had died when he was two years old, and he was raised by nuns at a Pittsburgh orphanage. After spending time in the navy, he married Alice McGinn, then took up work as a machinist for Daman Industries, a steel mill repair company. The Irish Catholic family had six children, all boys.

"We all learned to be tough from the time we started talking," Jim Kelly later wrote. "That was the only way you could survive in our house."

The eldest boy, Pat, played linebacker for the University of Richmond and was selected by the Baltimore Colts in the fifteenth round of the 1974 NFL draft. The third Kelly boy, Ray, also played for Richmond, earning two varsity letters.

Jim Kelly was every bit as tough as his older brothers. Even when Jim was very young, his father knew that he was a special talent.

"He had something a little bit extra, more than the other boys," his father later said. "I felt that all he needed was a little push to become great."

Joe was often home during the daytime (prior to working the night shift), and Jim would come back from school to have lunch with his dad.

"I always told him, 'before you eat, you gotta throw so many passes, so many punts and so many kicks,'" Joe told NFL Films in 1996. "He had to keep doing it until he got it right. I kept at him every day. There was times he was getting mad at me and I knew it. He turned around and I knew he was saying something."

Although as a child and teenager, Jim hated this forced practice, he later said, "Looking back now, I'm really glad I had a father like mine."

Joe's training produced consecutive trips to the National Punt, Pass and Kick competition in 1970 and 1971. Jim was just as good at baseball and basketball. By age fifteen, he was ready to compete on the high school level, against kids older and bigger than he was.

The Bulldogs' sophomore quarterback (during Jim's freshman year, his brother Ray accounted for five touchdowns, six extra points, and a field goal in a rout of Shannock Valley), Kelly, and East Brady finished 7-2 in 1975. As a junior and senior, Kelly was the Little-12 Conference's best player, on both offense and defense. He capped off his high school career with a twenty-three-game undefeated streak. In the team's second consecutive bid for the conference championship—a 13-13 tie the year before meant East Brady had to share the honors with Clarion-Limestone—Kelly completed thirteen of seventeen passes for 155 yards and a touchdown.

"[East Brady] was a small town, I think we only had about thirty players on our football team. And in that community everything was about football, everything was sports. I think we only had about seven hundred people in our hometown," Kelly recalled. "But the bottom line is we had passion, we took it serious. We wanted to win, we were used to winning."

All that winning enticed powerhouse colleges programs—Tennessee, the University of Pittsburgh, Notre Dame—to court Kelly. But at the outset, only one school mattered.

"I wanted to play for Penn State, I wanted to play quarterback there. Penn State was my team. Where I'm from you're either Pitt or Penn State and I was always a Nittany Lion fan."

Paterno's assistant, J. T. White, handled Kelly's recruitment, visiting the boy's home and attending his high school basketball games. But Penn State's interest didn't exactly mesh with Kelly's boyhood dream. Paterno had already signed Terry Rakowski, from North Schuylkill, Pennsylvania, and Frank Rocco, from Fox Chapel, Pennsylvania, each a high school all-American quarterback. Content with his quarterback prospects, Paterno offered Kelly a scholarship as a linebacker.

"Well, look at it like this," Pat Kelly told his younger brother about a possible switch in positions, "I've been in football a long time and I've been on a lot of team planes. And I can tell you that the pretty flight attendants never ask where the linebackers are; they want to know where the quarterback's sitting."

Jim never again considered becoming a Nittany Lion.

"Quarterback was the only position for me. And nothing was about to change that. Not even a full scholarship offer from Penn State. I do give Paterno a lot of credit for being up-front with me *before* I signed on the dotted line. When talking to recruits, a lot of college coaches promise the moon, the stars, and the sun . . . and the kids end up being left in one big fog."

Jim Kelly was not the only western Pennsylvania boy during the late 1970s that didn't quite agree with the fabled Nittany Lions head coach.

Within a few weeks of signing the paperwork committing to Penn State, Jeff Hostetler received some off-putting news. *Sports Illustrated* had listed the nation's top ten recruiting classes. Penn State had been ranked fourth, behind the University of Southern California, Notre Dame, and Southern Methodist (who had just nabbed a pair of star running backs, the famed "Pony Express" backfield of Eric Dickerson and Craig James). One phrase in the summary of Penn State's class stunned the entire Hostetler family.

"Lots of big linemen, the nation's premier tight end, Mike McCloskey, a hot quarterback prospect in Todd Blackledge, and, of course, a future All-American linebacker, Jeff Hostetler."

Norm Hostetler compounded the confusion by telling reporters on signing day: "Jeff only wanted to go to college as a quarterback and Penn State is recruiting him as a quarterback. He has an understanding that they'll let him stay at the position as long as he wants to."

Hostetler was never guaranteed the quarterback's job, and appropriately, Penn State added depth to the roster by recruiting other quarterbacks, such as Blackledge, a top prospect from Canton, Ohio. Frank Rocco and Terry Rakowski—the quarterbacks who kept Jim Kelly away from Happy Valley—were also on scholarship. A crowded quarterback pool for the 1979 season, Hostetler's freshman year, made sense: Chuck Fusina, the Heisman Trophy runner-up a year earlier, had just graduated.

Paterno settled on junior Dayle Tate to run his offense, but each one of the underclassmen (except Blackledge) saw playing opportunities. Eventually,

Rakowski was switched to flanker and Hostetler competed with Rocco for the second spot.

"Jeff Hostetler isn't quite ready to run the show by himself," observed one Penn State beat writer. "It is quite revealing, though, that Paterno considers this young freshman capable enough of doing the backup work only two months after he arrived on campus."

An injured thumb bothered Tate late in the season, and Paterno switched back and forth between Tate, Rocco, and Hostetler. Rotating quarterbacks partly caused a disappointing 1979 season. Penn State finished 8-4, the single season between 1977 and 1982 that the school did not win at least ten games. Most disappointing was a 29-14 loss to rival Pitt, who the Nittany Lions routinely thumped. That day, Hostetler saw his most extensive action of the season, completing six of sixteen pass attempts for seventy-two yards and an interception. Another freshman quarterback from western Pennsylvania, Dan Marino, completely outplayed Hostetler that day at Beaver Stadium.

Both Penn State and Jeff Hostetler opened the next decade optimistic. A great spring convinced the coaching staff to give him the job for the 1980 season opener against Colgate, even though Paterno refused to announce his starter until the Friday before game day.

"At this stage, Jeff can do some things that will help us win the game," Paterno declared. "[But] any one of them could start and do a great job for us. It's going to be a long year and as much as we're going to ask the quarterbacks to do, all three will see plenty of playing time."

As Paterno hinted, the quarterback carousel continued throughout 1980. Although Blackledge posted better numbers against Colgate, and Rocco was not relegated to third string—"There's a lot of things about being a head football coach that you don't like. . . . I don't know if we're being fair to Frank," Paterno said on his weekly television show—Hostetler retained the starting job.

While Penn State fans booed during a late September loss to third-ranked Nebraska, Hostetler did not play well, completing just one pass, fumbling two snaps from center, and being sacked four times. After the loss, Paterno selected Blackledge to run the offense. The move seemed ingenious from the start, as the redshirt freshman accounted for all three touchdowns (including a forty-three-yard fourth quarter scamper to clinch the game) during Penn State's 29-21 road victory over ninth-ranked Missouri.

But Blackledge struggled with incompletions and interceptions during all but one of his starts. In early October, with the Nittany Lions behind 7-6 against Temple, Blackledge fumbled near the goal line (a few series after throwing an interception) and Paterno turned back to Hostetler. He rewarded the coach with six scoring drives. Hostetler accounted for two rushing touchdowns and completed seven of his ten pass attempts in the 50-7 comeback.

"I played extremely well and was told that I would start the next week against Pitt," he said, "and practiced that way until a day or two before the game and then was told that I wasn't gonna start but that I was gonna play a lot. And I never ended up taking a snap that game."

Penn State lost 14-9 to Marino's Panthers. A last-minute Nittany Lion drive ended when Blackledge, attempting to throw the ball out-of-bounds, was intercepted by Pitt's Carlton Williamson. Again, Hostetler expected a return to the lineup in the team's next contest.

"For the bowl game, I was told I was gonna start and practiced that way, and a day or two before the game, I was told I wasn't gonna start but I was gonna be playing an awful lot and the same thing happened: I didn't get to play."

Penn State defeated Ohio State in the Fiesta Bowl 26-10, largely because of clutch passes and runs by Blackledge. Watching virtually the entire game from the sidelines of Sun Devil Stadium, Jeff Hostetler decided it was time for him to leave.

"Joe had to make a decision, and he made it," Dolly Hostetler remarked a few years later. "It's just that he made the wrong one."

The mother of four Penn State varsity athletes, and now mother-in-law of a fifth one, did not have the most objective opinion. Blackledge would go on to lead the Nittany Lions to twenty-one victories during the next two years, win the Davey O'Brien Award (given to the nation's top quarterback), and deliver both Paterno and Penn State their first national championship in January 1983.

As much as it pained him, Jeff Hostetler chose to abandon his boyhood dream of playing football for the Nittany Lions.

It was probably the most difficult thing for me to do, to pull up and leave Penn State which I had a sister that was living up there—who married a player that I was a teammate of—I had all kinds of friends there, my two older brothers had gone there, and my younger brother was there on a baseball scholarship. So it was an extremely tough decision to make. But I knew the Lord had blessed me with an ability to play and I felt like he wanted to use me somewhere. And so I thought, "I have to go somewhere."

Jim Kelly moved past his Penn State disappointment and committed to the University of Miami in the spring of 1978. Lou Saban, former head coach of the Buffalo Bills and newly hired man-in-charge for the Hurricanes program, personally flew to the Kelly home to ensure the signing.

An injury to Kelly's ankle during training camp clinched the freshman's status as a redshirt during the 1978 season, although he did run plays with the first team in practice. Having been a focal point of a balanced offense at East Brady, Kelly was unaccustomed to Saban's run-oriented, option-style approach. The team's star running back "would constantly complain because I could never get outside fast enough to get him the ball for the option. I just didn't have the speed to keep up with him."

"What's wrong with you," the player once yelled at Kelly.

"Hey, I ain't no option quarterback," he replied.

"Well, if you want to be on this damn team, you better become one."

Kelly adhered to the player's order: the entire offense had been designed around the running back, who everyone called "O. J."

A year of experience sent Kelly into his second training camp poised to contend for the starter's job. Also to his advantage was a complete overhaul to the Hurricane's coaching staff. Saban left south Florida after just two seasons to take over the top post at West Point. The Hurricanes' athletic department did not look far for a new head coach, bringing in Miami Dolphins offensive coordinator Howard Schnellenberger and his pro-style, balanced offense.

Once Bear Bryant's top assistant at the University of Alabama—he famously recruited Joe Namath to Tuscaloosa—Schnellenberger worked in the pros under George Allen with the Los Angeles Rams and under Don Shula with the Miami Dolphins. In between, he had a brief stint as the head coach of the Baltimore Colts. In Baltimore, Schnellenberger learned a critical lesson in the nurturing of young quarterback talent.

"When I coached up there for one year, I had Marty Domres as the incumbent quarterback and Bert Jones as the [rookie] quarterback," Schnellenberger recalled. "And like a rookie coach, I started Bert Jones in the opening game. I knew it was a big chance, but we would make quicker progress with him than with Marty Domres as the quarterback. But it turned out just like I feared. The offense wasn't ready to win, the defense wasn't ready to win, and Bert Jones had a really rough start up there and I almost ruined him. . . . When I got to Miami and saw a great potential in Jim Kelly, I didn't want to screw that up again."

Schnellenberger—who left Baltimore two years prior to Bert Jones winning the 1976 NFL MVP Award—chose sophomore Mike Rodrigue to start the 1979 season at quarterback. Rodrigue directed the Hurricanes to three wins in the first seven games, a characteristically modest record for a program that struggled to succeed, both financially and in the standings. The combination of gorgeous south Florida weather, a monopoly held by Shula's two-time world champion Dolphins, and a historically mediocre product, meant the university's football program failed to attract fans to the Orange Bowl.

Since its inception, the program earned a handful of bowl appearances and produced great players and all-Americans, including future NFL stars Ted Hendricks and Chuck Foreman. But in fifty-two seasons, the Hurricanes did not have a signature win that vaulted the program to an elite standing.

That all changed on November 3, 1979. Nineteen-point underdogs, Miami traveled north to State College, Pennsylvania, for another difficult test against Joe Paterno's bunch. The Hurricanes had lost four consecutive matchups with Penn State, including a 49-7 drubbing two years earlier.

Schnellenberger knew that to have a chance, they would have to improvise.

"We felt we had to pass to beat Penn State . . . because we felt their secondary is not as strong as their front seven," the coach told reporters. "Because we felt we had to throw the ball, we went with Kelly, because he is our best thrower."

Penn State had expected to see the option quarterback Rodrigue under center. Schnellenberger didn't tell anyone of his intended lineup change, including Jim Kelly.

"Just a few hours before the game, he said 'I've decided to start you at quarterback today,'" Kelly said. "And the first thing I did was I went to the bathroom after I got done talking to him and threw up."

That unique pregame ritual would continue throughout the remainder of his college and professional playing career. Aside from the unpleasant visual image, Kelly's new warm-up routine had a surprisingly strong impact on his teammates.

"Schnellenberger was giving us our getting-ready-to-go-on-the-field speech and during the speech you could just hear Jim in the toilet puking his guts out," teammate Mark Rush remembered years later. "From that day on every game, we were not ready to go on that field until we heard Jim puke. Once he started puking, everybody would just start screaming 'all right, let's go, we're ready!'"

Kelly's howling heaves inspired the Hurricanes. On the first play from scrimmage, fullback Chris Hobbs caught a short pass and raced fifty-seven yards to set up a short field goal. Minutes later, Kelly converted a Penn State turnover into a touchdown pass to Jim Joiner.

Beneath a rainy, cloudy sky, Kelly took command of the offense, calling audibles from the sidelines, completing a slew of short passes, and ignoring the dislocated jaw that he suffered on the game's opening play. And although his brothers Dan and Kevin could not make the trip—they were playing Brockway for a Little 12 conference championship that same afternoon—forty-five friends and family members cheered Jim on from the Beaver Stadium stands.

Penn State's trademark ground game—they would run the ball sixty-five times for 248 yards on this day—narrowed the score to 13-10 at the half. But Kelly tossed two second-half touchdown passes to give "lowly Miami," as one newspaper noted, a 26-10 advantage.

"We're not a real good catch-up football team," said Paterno afterwards. "We used two tight ends and tried to control the football. We're aware of our limitations. I blame myself, not (quarterback) Dayle Tate. Maybe we didn't give him enough offenses to be a good football team."

With freshman Jeff Hostetler watching from the Penn State sidelines, Tate completed eleven of twenty passes for 109 yards and threw three interceptions. The Hurricane defense tossed a shutout in the second half to give the university a landmark victory.

"This day will go down in the history of Miami football as the day we turned our football program around," proclaimed Schnellenberger.

Jim Kelly, who completed eighteen of thirty passes for 280 yards and three touchdowns, was equally proud, of both the team's win and his own personal victory.

"Afterward, Paterno shook my hand, but he didn't say much. I think he just wanted to get off the field. Fast."

Victory over one of the most storied programs in college football did not transform Miami into a national power overnight. In fact, the Hurricanes were dismantled 30-0 in the next contest against Alabama—Kelly completed only two of fifteen passes—then suffered a 40-15 loss to Notre Dame in Japan. But they defeated rival Florida in the season finale and entered the off-season confident about the future.

Over the next two years, Kelly continued to develop physically. His best friend and roommate, Mark Rush, was the team's exercise/weightlifting dynamo, and his "contagious" attitude contributed to Kelly's increasing strength, size, and speed. But the aid of another mentor provided Kelly with the tools and knowledge to make the leap from talented underclassman to a polished and complete passer.

Just a month after Schnellenberger took over the team, he welcomed a critical new recruit to the Hurricanes program. But this was no teenage stud athlete; it was forty-four-year-old crew-cut-wearing Earl Morrall.

Morrall had played quarterback in the NFL for an incredible twenty-one seasons. The second overall pick in the 1956 draft out of Michigan State, he spent time, mostly as a backup, with San Francisco, Pittsburgh, Detroit, and the New York Giants. At age thirty-four, he found career rebirth in Baltimore during the 1968 season.

In that year's preseason, "something popped" in Johnny Unitas' elbow following a defender's hit on the reigning league MVP. Head coach Don Shula gave control of the offense to Morrall, who himself won the league MVP and quarterbacked the Colts to a 13-1 record and their famous doomed trip to Super Bowl III.

Shula left Baltimore to take over the Miami Dolphins in 1970. But two years later, he and Morrall (along with Schnellenberger, the Dolphins offensive coordinator) teamed up once again to replace a future Hall of Fame quarterback and guide a team to the Super Bowl. Bob Griese suffered a broken ankle in Week Five of the 1972 season, Morrall took over for the remainder of the regular season, and Miami won all eleven starts, including two playoff games. Griese returned to start Super Bowl VII for Miami, but the Dolphins' undefeated season might not have been "perfect" without the thirty-eight-year-old Morrall at the helm.

Morrall remained on the Dolphins' roster until 1977, then joined Schnellenberger as a volunteer coach in February 1979. And since Schnellenberger installed the Dolphins' pro-style attack, Kelly learned the playbook from a quarterback who ran that offense at the NFL level for nearly a decade.

"It was awesome," Kelly said.

> He played professional football, and that was something I always dreamed about. That was my goal, to be a quarterback in the NFL. And to have him tutoring the right things—put air under the football when you're throwing the deep pass, don't feel like you have to make the big play all the time, take what they give you—all the intangibles that you need to be a quarterback. And some of the things you need someone to tell you, how to study film. He prepared me for the next level early on in my college career.

That mentor-protégé relationship began to yield noticeable results in 1980. Miami opened up 5-0 before hitting a wall of three consecutive losses, each to a ranked opponent. The Hurricanes still finished 8-3, then defeated Virginia Tech in the Peach Bowl. The following season the team improved to 9-2. (The NCAA placed the school on probation because of a recruiting violation, making the team ineligible for a bowl game.)

That year, Kelly enjoyed another tremendous season as the team's star quarterback—and another sweet episode of revenge against Joe Paterno's Nittany Lions.

With Todd Blackledge becoming a fine college quarterback, Penn State improved to 10-2 following their disappointing 1979 campaign. And by late October 1981, the team was ranked first in the nation. On Halloween 1981, before a nationally televised audience, the two teams faced off again. But unlike the Hurricanes' 26-10 upset two years earlier, this time the game was in Miami at the Orange Bowl.

In the second quarter, Kelly and wide receiver Larry Brodsky hooked up for an eighty-yard touchdown that increased the lead to fourteen. With the score 17-0 early in the final period, Blackledge threw two touchdown passes to bring Penn State close—he would attempt forty-one passes and gain 358 yards for the normally grounded offense—but his interception with just over a minute left finalized another monumental win for Miami.

"In order for us to become a mature football program, we had to get into a game like this and win. The first Penn State game in 1979 was sort of like Cinderella. We kind of snuck up on them. That wasn't one of their best teams," Schnellenberger said. "But this was one of their finest teams. They had forewarning that we could play and I think they gave us their best shot."

Jim Kelly now had two wins over his personal rival. Most important to him, however, was knowing that he had brought life to the once-unheralded Miami program.

"People are going crazy down here," he said after the home victory, "and that is what everyone wanted to do—get the city excited about the team."

That excitement only swelled with the start of the 1982 season. Their team ranked fifteenth in the preseason polls, south Florida fans now spoke of a once inconceivable goal.

"Everywhere around the University of Miami, the talk is of a national championship for the Hurricanes this year," *Sports Illustrated* reported prior to the 1982 season. "Obviously the thought of a national title for the Hurricanes is utterly laughable, except for one thing: Everything coach Howard Schnellenberger has said his team would achieve since he arrived on the Coral Gables campus on Jan. 8, 1979 has been achieved."

Schnellenberger never predicted that a transcendent figure would help deliver his team from the wilderness. Nonetheless, he had such a player, a fact the national media had begun to recognize. Reporters, photographers, and camera crews hovered around Kelly during August and early September. The senior was the preseason favorite to win the Heisman Trophy.

A few weeks into the 1982 season, all the promise of a national title for the Hurricanes and college football's top individual prize for their quarterback quickly vanished. Miami lost the opener to Florida, then lost Kelly two weeks later: a defender planted him into the ground following a twenty-yard scramble late in the team's 14-8 victory over Virginia Tech. Surgery to reattach a separated acromioclavicular (AC) joint was performed the very next day and Kelly missed the rest of the season. Though respectable, the Hurricanes' 5-3 close to the season torpedoed any shot at a national championship.

"Unfortunately, we rode Jim's coattail way too hard and way too long," Mark Rush said. "We depended too much on him and when he did get hurt it just shocked everybody, of course: 'Now what are we going to do, our leader is gone, who are we gonna depend on?'"

Luckily for Miami fans and the returning varsity players, that question would be answered the very next year . . . and most of the next three decades.

With Bernie Kosar and Vinny Testaverde ready to fill Kelly's spot beginning in 1983, the Hurricanes found new and supremely capable leadership under center. Kosar would lead Miami to the national title in January 1984. Three seasons later, Testaverde, the Heisman Trophy winner, took the Hurricanes to the Fiesta Bowl, where the Hurricanes battled for (and lost) the national championship against Penn State.

Jim Kelly did not get to compete in either one of those thrilling national championship contests. The extremely premature end to the 1982 season also marked the end of his collegiate career. And, as a quarterback, such a serious injury to his throwing shoulder greatly jeopardized his professional prospects.

An entire team of people—doctors, trainers, teammates, family members— assisted Kelly in his efforts to regain his powerful throwing arm. And after several months, he did.

"I would drag his ass over to the rehab room with [Hurricanes trainer] Mike O'Shea and myself, twice a day even in the summertime," Mark Rush remembered.

> And sitting in our dorm room, just two chairs across from each other and he would slowly just throw a tennis ball back-and-forth to me, trying to get that range of motion. . . . I can remember finally being able to get back out on the field, down on our knees, we'd be like three yards apart and we'd just start throwing the football. Then we'd go back five, then we'd go back eight, then we'd go back ten. And then he was just zinging the ball, better than he ever did before. And it was such a nice feeling seeing him come back. We rehabbed him to death.

NFL coaches, scouts, and executives speculated—from afar and in person at workouts—about Kelly's value in the following April's draft. And although his arm was not completely healed by draft day, he assuaged any doubts.

During the first round of that now famous 1983 draft, six quarterbacks were selected: John Elway, Todd Blackledge, Tony Eason, Ken O'Brien, Dan Marino, and Jim Kelly. And each man would go on to experience his own unique professional football journey.

Eason helped quarterback the New England Patriots to Super Bowl XX and O'Brien earned a pair of Pro Bowl selections during a long tenure with the New York Jets. Ironically, Todd Blackledge enjoyed the least success of any members of the "Quarterback Class of 1983." As a Kansas City Chief,

Blackledge threw more interceptions than touchdowns and completed less than half of his pass attempts.

Elway was unhappy that the Baltimore Colts had selected him with the first overall pick and threatened to give up football to pitch for the New York Yankees. A week later, the Colts granted his wish and dealt the former Stanford quarterback to Denver.

Marino was similarly discontent on draft day, not because of *who* chose him, but rather *when* they had done so. By the impossible standards he had set as a freshman, sophomore, and junior, the Pitt quarterback was subpar as a senior. That perceived drop-off caused twenty-two teams to choose someone else. The Miami Dolphins finally selected Marino with the last pick of the first round.

And while Elway's and Marino's prolific careers each got off to a well-publicized rocky start, it was Jim Kelly who made the biggest splash.

Desperately in need of star power, the Buffalo Bills took Kelly with the fourteenth overall selection. Kelly would not, however, attend the team's training camp at Fredonia State College that July. Nor would he spend a single Sunday at Rich Stadium that autumn dressed in Bills red and blue.

Three months before Buffalo drafted him, Kelly was selected—in the fourteenth round—by the Chicago Blitz of the United States Football League, the professional alternative that attempted to outspend and out-flash the NFL's monopoly. (The Blitz waited fourteen rounds to choose Kelly because they expected him to join the NFL.) Officially founded on May 11, 1982, the new league opened play nine months later, and growing pains persisted from the outset.

Blitz General Manager Bruce Allen continued to pursue Kelly into May. So too did the Montreal Concordes (formerly the Alouettes) of the Canadian Football League. Kelly continued to listen.

"I always wanted to play in the National Football League. But there are other things you have to look at," he said a week after being chosen by the Bills.

Money was a factor for Kelly, as was a real disinterest in joining the small-market Bills.

"Buffalo would have two chances (twelfth and fourteenth), and I was praying they would pass on me both times. Everything I had heard about the team and the city was negative," he wrote years later.

Negotiations with the Bills dragged out into June, when Kelly's agents received a phone call. The USFL executives and owners were so eager to sign a big-name talent for their infant league, they offered Kelly, in addition to an enormous salary, the opportunity to join whichever team he wanted. Kelly— and Mark Rush, who was also allowed to sign with any team he chose—flew to Texas to meet with the owner of the USFL's Houston Gamblers.

"Jim and I always wanted to try and play [professional] football together," Rush said. "And of course he was drafted by Buffalo, I was drafted by Minnesota, we're living in Florida: who the hell wants to go to the cold weather?"

The opportunity to play in Texas (and the Astrodome, where weather would *never* be a factor) clinched it. On June 9, Kelly inked a multimillion-dollar deal with the Gamblers. Giving this young quarterback with western Pennsylvania roots an outrageously lucrative contract to spurn the NFL and join an upstart league sounded like a familiar tale.

"His signing is the equivalent of Joe Namath signing with the American Football League. In fact, Jim's a much better player. Namath's college statistics can't compare. Jim did more in three years than he did in four," boldly proclaimed the Houston owner, Jerry Argovitz. "We had Jim Kelly rated as college football's top quarterback even before the NFL draft. We like everything we see about him. This signing has impact."

An organization named the Gamblers seemed an appropriate one for Jim Kelly to join after leaving Miami. An expansion team, Houston would not play its first game until late February 1984. (As part of its early appeal, USFL games were played in the spring, opposite the NFL's fall schedule.) Having seen no playing time since the injury to his throwing shoulder in September 1982, Kelly would go nearly eighteen months without taking an in-game snap. The stability of the newfound league as well as the quality of play (and his teammates) were also issues that Kelly had to consider.

"There are risks in what I'm doing, but I made up my mind," he said upon signing his contract. "Everybody has to take a risk once in his life. But I'm happy I did and I won't regret it."

Jeff Hostetler also took an enormous risk leaving Penn State in January 1981, another decision that he would not regret.

"Our family had a meeting with coach Joe Paterno to inform him of our decision. Joe tried to change Jeff's mind, but his decision is final," Norm Hostetler told the *Harrisburg Patriot*. "Because of all our past connections, it was an extremely difficult thing to have to do. But we felt that Jeff will not get his chance here."

Family had played a central role in Jeff enrolling at Penn State. And in his second college search, again a fellow Hostetler pointed him in the next direction.

"My older brother Doug was recruited by West Virginia when he was coming out of high school," said Hostetler. "After he had graduated [from Penn State in 1979] he was in sales and he was traveling and he had always gone down through Morgantown and told me I have to go down and take a look. And he is the only reason I went down to take a look."

Jeff had actually been to Morgantown the previous fall. In late October 1980, Penn State traveled south along Interstate 68 to play at newly opened Mountaineer Stadium. Hostetler relieved an injured Todd Blackledge in the second half and preserved a 20-15 victory over first-year head coach Don Nehlen's team.

"It was a cold, miserable, wet day," he remembered. "It was a big day for us and I had a big part in it. I remember walking down through their stands in order to get to their locker room—because the stadium still wasn't completed—so we had to walk through the stands to get down to the locker room. And I can remember the fans yelling at us and saying stuff to us. And I can honestly remember thinking, 'Wow, is this great. This would be a great group of people to play for. They just absolutely loved their Mountaineers."

Although he weighed opportunities from Ohio State, Michigan State, Maryland, and nearly transferred to Pitt (where, by Hostetler's senior season, Dan Marino would have just left), West Virginia soon became an easy choice. Only eighty miles south of the family farm near Holsopple, Morgantown was a short drive for the Hostetlers each Saturday afternoon of the college season.

Teammates immediately welcomed their new quarterback. Linebacker Darryl Talley had been a junior when Hostetler and the Nittany Lions defeated the Mountaineers in 1980. Now he was elated to have Hostetler playing for, rather than against, West Virginia.

"Jeff came in the game after I knocked Todd [Blackledge] out and proceeded to beat us," Talley said about the 20-15 loss to Penn State in which he also recorded two sacks and recovered a critical fourth quarter Hostetler fumble. "And then the following year, he came to school at West Virginia. I'm thinking to myself, 'Why the heck did you come to school here now? Why didn't you come last year? We could have beat Penn State!'"

The transfer meant that Hostetler would not be allowed to play during the 1981 season. West Virginia already had a starter in place, senior and Phi Beta Kappa candidate Oliver Luck, so playing time would have already been limited. He spent that fall practicing with the team and going to classes. Suffering no drop-off as a result from the transfer, Hostetler earned a 4.0 his first semester, virtually the same grade-point average he achieved during three semesters at Penn State.

Coach Don Nehlen viewed Hostetler as a worthy replacement for Luck, and not just in order to keep the team GPA steady.

"He was our scout-team quarterback [in 1981] and we knew we had a big league quarterback," said Nehlen, who would become Hostetler's father-in-law within three years. "The great quarterbacks, when they walk in the other guys know 'we're gonna get it done.' And that's what Jeff brought to the table. And our kids knew that long before he was even eligible. They knew that when he was on the scout team."

After West Virginia won the Peach Bowl in December, Hostetler was ready to assume command of the team. He made it through spring camp with the quarterback job (as well as a sore knee) and started the season opener at Oklahoma.

The Sooners were coming off a down year (7-4-1), but since 1970, Oklahoma had lost only one non–Big 8 Conference game at Norman. In the previous meeting between the two schools, the Sooners crushed West Virginia 52-10. Head coach Barry Switzer was already a college football deity, having won back-to-back national championships in the mid-1970s.

Even after the Sooners scored a pair of first-quarter touchdowns, Hostetler was unconcerned by the Oklahoma mystique. Trailing 14-0 at the start of the second period, he tossed two touchdown passes and marched his team into the locker room at halftime ahead 20-14.

The teams traded blows throughout the second half. With eight minutes remaining in the fourth quarter, Hostetler hit Rich Hollins on a forty-two-yarder, then connected with Wayne Brown in the back of the end zone. Hostetler's fourth touchdown of the day put the Mountaineers ahead for good.

"The Oklahoma game resonated coast-to-coast," Nehlen said three decades later. "All of a sudden people started to say, 'Hey, who are these guys?'
And that was the beginning of West Virginia's run at being a very highly
respected football program."

The win kicked off a great year. An 8-2 regular-season record earned a trip
to the Gator Bowl: never before had the university appeared in consecutive
bowls. Although Hostetler's passing statistics (47 percent completion percentage, 1,916 yards passing, ten touchdowns) didn't earn him votes in the
Heisman Trophy race or consideration as an all-American, he had become the
team's unquestioned leader. According to Darryl Talley,

> Jeff was a great football player, because in my opinion, he was what he thought a
> quarterback was supposed to be. He was tough, he was smart . . . he would lead
> a lot by example by saying, look, I'm willing to sit there and take these shots if
> you guys are willing to catch the ball down the middle of the field at the spot
> where I have to throw it. That I think endeared him to his offensive linemen
> because he was like one of the linemen. Back then, it didn't seem like he wanted
> a whole lot of publicity around him. He just wanted to go out and do his job
> and win football games.

By 1983, both West Virginia and Jeff Hostetler peaked. Winning their
opening six games—including a victory against archrival Pitt—gave way to
a number four ranking in the national polls. Hostetler became prominently
mentioned as a Heisman candidate. Impressive passing numbers contributed to the attention. So did the school's aggressive media campaign, which
painted him as the boy next door that just happened to be a football star.

The cover of the team's media guide featured Hostetler dressed as a gun-
toting cowboy beside a white stallion. Billboards along the interstate praised
his intimidating play. And a record—entitled "Old Hoss, the Ballad of Jeff
Hostetler" and set to the theme song from the television show *Bonanza*—was
distributed to radio stations across the region. (One lyric, sung in a distinctive
West Virginia twang, glorified that "Ole Hoss, Ole Hoss can really get those
first downs. He's got the arm, he has the range to be end zone bound.")

The media blitz worked.

"He is more handsome than his pictures suggest. The nose, so prominent
in the photographs, becomes part of a more attractive package when you see it

in conjunction with the carved cheekbones and toothy grin," wrote one Philadelphia reporter. "[His] strong arm has led the West Virginia University football team to a No. 4-ranking in both wire service polls and a No. 1-ranking
in the hearts of the residents of this rugged little city. Hostetler's biography is
as all-American as his looks. He is a 4.0 finance student. He dates the coach's
daughter. He does not curse . . . he does not drink, either, not even beer."

The victory in early October over Pitt helped the Mountaineers achieve
their highest-ever ranking in the national polls and enabled Hostetler's rise in
the Heisman race. Defeating the Panthers snapped a seven-game losing streak
with their rival, but to fully establish themselves as the best team in the region,
they would have to exorcize a much bigger demon.

The Mountaineers' seventh game of the 1983 season was against Penn
State in Happy Valley. Every year since 1959, West Virginia had played
against, and lost to, the Nittany Lions. The most recent loss fit the norm: a
24-0 shutout at home. Jeff Hostetler started that game, squandering the opportunity to show up the coach and quarterback that sparked his departure
from State College. Adding insult to injury—he badly sprained his knee in the
first quarter—three turnovers by Hostetler yielded three Todd Blackledge-
led touchdown drives.

Paterno's team went on to win the national title at the end of that season.
A year later, the number-four ranked Mountaineers held similar aspirations.
Like Jim Kelly—who twice toppled Penn State in critical, program-defining
wins—Hostetler was desperate to craft a victory over Paterno's Nittany Lions.

> I still had friends at Penn State, and they told me the coaches had gone all out—
> at my expense—to fire up their team. The whole week before the game, they'd
> played that Heisman Trophy promo song (the one written to the "Bonanza"
> tune) over the PA system. They plastered the locker room with the West Vir-
> ginia cover shot of me in the cowboy suit with the white horse. I cringed when
> I heard that. By the time the week was over, the Nittany Lions were chomping
> at the bit to play, if only because it meant they wouldn't have to hear that song
> anymore. I'd always known that song would come back to haunt me—and it
> did.

Before a record crowd of 86,309, Hostetler completed his first seven passes,
avoiding would-be tacklers all afternoon, and keeping the score tight.

"We had him pinned in a few times," said defensive tackle Greg Gattuso. "But he kept getting away."

Ahead just 21-17 in the third quarter, the Nittany Lions defense tightened up and kept West Virginia's offense out of the end zone the rest of the game. A late touchdown by freshman D. J. Dozier sealed Penn State's 41-23 win.

"Later my family came over," he wrote. "I think it was hard for them, because they wanted that win even more than I did. My brothers especially— even Todd, who was playing baseball then at Penn State—had wanted to see a Hostetler beat the Lions and show Paterno the error of his ways."

Two road defeats in the final four games cost West Virginia their shot at the best season in school history and an appearance in one of the big-stage bowl games. Still, an 8-3 record earned a spot in the Hall of Fame Bowl in late December. Cold winds and the Kentucky defense handcuffed the Mountaineers in the first half: Hostetler misfired on his first ten attempts.

"Nothing seemed to go right in the first half," he said. "But I'm proud that the team had the confidence in me and the coaches stuck with me."

To jump-start the team, Nehlen opened the second half with a successful onside kick, and minutes later, Hostetler found Rich Hollis for a sixteen-yard touchdown pass that evened the score at ten. Playing in his final college game, Hostetler set up the go-ahead score, keeping the ball on the option, to charge thirty-seven yards to the Kentucky two. On the next play, he hit Rob Bennett for the winning score. After the game, Norm Hostetler told reporters that his son battled through the fourth quarter with a concussion.

Hostetler had now given the Mountaineers a pair of bowl appearances, eighteen wins in twenty-four games, and consecutive top-twenty finishes in the national poll.

Not winning the Heisman Trophy didn't bother the modest Hostetler. He claimed his share of personal accolades that year. The first team academic all-American won the Hall of Fame Bowl MVP for his gritty performance in the win over Kentucky and earned spots on both the Blue-Grey Bowl and the Hula Bowl rosters.

During his week in Honolulu for the Hula Bowl, Hostetler received word that the Pittsburgh Maulers of the USFL selected him with their first "territorial" draft choice. A less-than-impressive financial offer from the Maulers quickly caused Hostetler to abandon any considerations of playing USFL games just a few dozen miles from his birthplace in western Pennsylvania.

As a finance major graduating in a few months with a 3.92 grade-point average, Hostetler could afford to be selective about his future. That spring, the University of West Virginia's Finance Department nominated Hostetler for a Rhodes scholarship. He turned down the prestigious honor—"a great educational experience, but it would not have fit with pro football. Too much time lost"—to pursue his dream of quarterbacking an NFL team.

That dream started to materialize in early May when the New York Giants selected Hostetler with their third-round choice. (Boomer Esiason, who went to Cincinnati in the second round, was the only quarterback taken ahead of Hostetler.)

"I didn't know anything about the Giants, had no idea. Hadn't talked to them at all before the draft. I didn't have any idea. And so I actually didn't even know who their coach was. So when I got told that I was going there I didn't know what their quarterback situation was or anything so I was kinda in the dark with it."

Phil Simms was the Giants incumbent, but injuries, inconsistent play, and a complicated relationship with head coach Bill Parcells sidetracked his career. Scott Brunner took over when Simms was injured or ineffective, only to be traded to Denver a week before the 1983 draft. The other veteran vying for playing time was Jeff Rutledge, a former Los Angeles Ram for whom the Giants gave away a fourth-round pick.

"I thought that it was a great opportunity once I found out that they had a couple quarterbacks there, but nobody had been there playing and had the job locked up. So I thought this would be a great opportunity to at least see the field."

A month after marrying coach Nehlen's daughter, Vicky, Hostetler signed with the Giants in June. The new Hostetler family was even more delighted when Giants coach Bill Parcells refused to cave to the New York media, who speculated that the quarterback position belonged to Simms.

"After all our changes, wouldn't it be crazy for me to say someone who has hardly snapped the ball in three years, 'You have the job?'" Parcells asked reporters. "That's not the way things are going to work this year."

Training camp was wide open: Simms, Hostetler, and Jeff Rutledge each believed they could win the job. By the first exhibition game, Parcells decided that Simms and Rutledge would split time and Hostetler should watch from the sidelines.

"He's not ready, and I told him so. I don't want to throw him to the wolves."

No one could blame Parcells for that decision. Simms and Rutledge were each five-year veterans; Hostetler was a rookie. Except the next week, Parcells told him that he would play the game's last ten minutes against Indianapolis. He never took a snap. He never took a snap the following week against the Jets. And in the final preseason game against Pittsburgh, he watched the entire game from the sidelines.

"It was Penn State all over again," Hostetler later said.

Being told he would play in the exhibition portion of his rookie season irritated Jeff Hostetler. But keeping a rookie quarterback on the sidelines—even during the preseason—is not unheard of. And Parcells' reasoning was sound: four months removed from college and with only a few weeks of training camp, he simply wasn't prepared. He didn't take a single snap at quarterback in 1984.

Not playing the next season also bothered Hostetler. But away from Giants Stadium and the team's practice facilities, far greater concerns held his attention. In June 1985, Vicky Hostetler gave birth to the couple's first child. The following morning, the entire family was stunned to learn that Jason Hostetler suffered from pulmonary stenosis: one of his heart valves was too narrow to pump a sufficient amount of blood from the heart to the lungs.

Doctors performed surgery on the one-day-old child and over the next eleven months, he endured four more operations to correct the problem.

"Now he's doing real well. He has a lot of fun, and he's becoming more active. The doctors are pleased with the way he's doing. Only time will tell if everything will be good," Hostetler said when Jason was seventeen months old. "This puts everything in perspective. I know what my priorities are— what's important and what isn't. That little boy is important. This makes you realize how lucky you really are and how trivial all the other little worries and disappointments are."

Compared to the painful uncertainties caused by Jason's health crisis, not seeing action as a quarterback during those first two seasons was "trivial." But by 1986, with Jason's health improving, Hostetler was once again ready to focus on football. Contributions on special teams (blocking that punt against Philadelphia) and as an emergency wide receiver seemed to make his coaches take notice. Bill Parcells personally told him he would compete for the job as Simms' backup.

Unfortunately, his fourth season in the NFL, 1987, got off to the worst start yet. A bruised kidney suffered in a preseason game against Cleveland landed him in the hospital, then on the injured reserve list for a month. Jeff Rutledge retained the second-string job.

"I knew it was do-or-die when I went to camp in 1988," Hostetler said. "I had worn Giant blue for four years, and when Bill Parcells said again that he wanted to know what I could do, I figured I would have to show him something or make room for someone else.

"I had a good preseason camp, and they told me I had earned the No. 2 job. They were keeping [Rutledge], too, at least for now. But I was officially the backup to Phil. At least I was moving in the right direction. It wasn't where I wanted to be, but maybe I was on my way at last."

Hostetler finally earned a chance at quarterback later that season. In a November loss to Philadelphia, Eagles defensive end Reggie White slammed Simms' left shoulder into the ground, forcing him out of the game. With Jeff Rutledge on injured reserve, Hostetler was the only other quarterback on the roster. In his first prolonged quarterback action in fifty-nine months, Hostetler struggled, tossing a pair of interceptions, including one in overtime that set up Philadelphia's game-winning score.

With Simms still sidelined, Hostetler started the following week against New Orleans.

"If Hostetler plays," Parcells said, "we will use our full game plan. He should be able to handle our offense by now."

Despite that statement, the Giants utilized a conservative, run-heavy approach to hide the inexperience of their quarterback. On one of the few pass plays, Hostetler tossed an eighty-five-yard touchdown to Stephen Baker, giving New York a 7-6 lead early in the second period.

Still, Parcells chose Jeff Rutledge (who was activated from the injured list the day before) to begin the third quarter. On the opening two plays of the second half, New Orleans sacked Rutledge, who fumbled the ball each time; he finished the game with an interception and virtually identical statistics to Hostetler. The Giants eked out a 13-12 victory.

"The reason I changed quarterbacks is that I felt Rutledge had a bit more experience. I thought Hostetler did a good job and I told him that."

Hostetler, infuriated at having been removed, lashed out to reporters after the game, saying, "I'm hot, did you ever see anything like that?" Once again, false promises bothered him more than did watching from the sideline.

"I'm through here," he told reporters. "[Parcells] told me that I had done a good job, but that he wanted to make a change. He said he'd get me back in there. But he didn't say anything to me after that."

Hostetler instructed his agent to demand a trade. Giants General Manager George Young consulted with the head coach.

"George asked me, 'You want to keep him?' I said, 'Of course," Parcells responded.

With unrestricted free agency for NFL players still several years away, Hostetler needed Parcells and the Giants. And with starting quarterbacks made of mere flesh and bones, the Giants and Parcells needed Hostetler.

"The rule of thumb is, people don't get rid of good players. This isn't fantasy football. That's for the fans," Young later said. "The best thing to do is pick the young players and develop them the way you want."

The Giants were not going to trade him. That didn't stop Hostetler from storming into Bill Parcells' office.

"I went in and Bill and I had a knock-down, drag-out discussion and it wasn't very friendly. But it was a situation where I got off my chest what I wanted to say. And if you know Bill, Bill's not going to sit there and take anything; he had his comments to say," Hostetler said years later. "I left there and was coming out to practice later in the day and he comes up beside me and says 'You feel better?' And I just looked at him. And from that point on, I knew exactly where I stood with him and he knew where he stood with me."

"I thought he was a bright young guy," Parcells said two decades later. "I think Jeff as a young player was a little sensitive and certainly frustrated. Because he was there a long time and he really wasn't getting an opportunity to play and as any competitive guy would be he wanted that opportunity. I understood his sentiments, but yet, we weren't in the habit of trying to get rid of good players."

Hostetler set aside his frustration from the New Orleans game—what he called "the lowest point of my whole football career, lower than the Fiesta Bowl"—and returned to the Giants, awaiting his next chance to play. It came a year later.

With Simms injured in the first quarter of a game against Minnesota, Hostetler contributed to a Giants comeback victory: his mobility outside of the pocket produced key first downs. Simms remained inactive for the Giants' next game at Phoenix and Hostetler made his second start in six years. Unlike the Saints episode a year earlier, Parcells did not experience any "gut feeling" that prompted him to make a halftime switch. Hostetler scrambled for two touchdowns and again converted several first downs through the air in the 20-13 win. New York improved to 8-1.

"I thought Jeff handled the game well," said Parcells. "We ran the ball real good. We played within ourselves."

Although Simms returned for the next week, Parcells and the Giants players had a growing trust in Hostetler.

"I think our guys have confidence in me now. Before [the Cardinals game] some of them said that you've waited a long time, so take advantage of it," he said afterwards. "I'm just trying to get the job done. Maybe I've helped myself for the future, knowing the team has confidence in you and you're able to perform better. You expect to win."

That confidence grew much more the following autumn.

Three consecutive victories to open the season established New York as the early front-runner for the 1990 NFC East title. In Week Four against Dallas, Simms' three touchdown passes built a 24-10 advantage early in the fourth quarter. Parcells surprised the Cowboys, his offense, and especially his second-string quarterback, when he inserted Hostetler to close out the game.

"I wanted him to run the offense without running out the clock," Parcells said. "I wanted him to drive the ball down the field and try to score."

A fifteen-yard run along with a twelve-yard pass completion pushed the Giants into Dallas' red zone. With less than ten minutes remaining, Hostetler capped off an eight-play, sixty-six-yard drive by eluding Cowboys defenders Ken Norton Jr. and Tony Tolbert, then racing into the end zone for a twelve-yard touchdown.

"I think [Parcells] was testing me, I think he was testing my preparation, he was testing me whether I was ready to go at a moment's notice."

Two weeks later, Hostetler was again thrust into the Giants lineup, and this time with three full quarters remaining. On the final play of the first period, two Phoenix Cardinals high-lowed Simms, knocking him out with an injured ankle. Hostetler took over and produced a short scoring drive that put New

York in front 10-3, five minutes before halftime. But after that field goal, neither the Giants offense nor the defense could do anything right, and Phoenix surged to a 19-10 edge with just over five minutes remaining in the game.

Shaking off four sacks as well as a fumble and an interception (both of which preceded Cardinals scores), Hostetler floated a perfect post-corner touchdown pass to a diving Stephen Baker. Trailing 19-17, the defense then forced a punt with one minute to play. Two completions by Hostetler moved New York from their own twenty-nine-yard-line into field-goal range. On the game's final play, the Giants kicker nailed a forty-yarder to complete a spectacular comeback.

"I thought it was an outstanding comeback and a great job by Hostetler," Parcells said. "I'm glad he's been around for the time he has because I don't know if a guy with less experience could have done what he did."

Once again the following Sunday, Simms was under center when the Giants took on Washington.

Although being relegated to second-string and not playing on Sundays bothered, even angered, Hostetler, he could understand it. For nearly seven full seasons, the Giants had thrived under Simms, who won fifty of eighty-three starts from 1984 to 1990, a stretch in which New York earned five play-off berths and a Super Bowl title.

"I didn't have a guy in front of me that was stinking out the place," he said. "[Simms] was throwing the lights out of the ball, playing really, really well. So there just weren't the opportunities there that you normally get as a backup quarterback."

Not being given opportunities to take snaps—even in practice—was Hostetler's true frustration. He knew that the first, and really the only, objective of the Giants coaching staff was to prepare the team to win football games. And if the Giants believed Simms gave the team their best shot at victory, then he was the logical choice to quarterback every down. Still, to best serve the team—and himself—the backup felt he needed *some* level of regular participation.

During the first six seasons of his NFL career, Hostetler played only four games at quarterback. And aside from the outrage that seeped through after being pulled at halftime against New Orleans in 1988, he quietly endured his frustration.

"Jeff is the kinda guy that he is such a competitor, he said, 'Coach, I don't even have to shower, I never get in. I don't do anything. It's just murder,'" Don Nehlen remembered.

But twice in 1990, he had tasted the so-called crunch time of the fourth quarter. And now, near the end of that season, Hostetler's patience quickly evaporated.

"Seven, eight weeks go by and I've just had it. You think about it, six-and-a-half years, how long [that] is, over two thousand days. I remember coming home after a Friday practice, no reps again. I sat down at the dinner table with my wife," he said about reaching his breaking point after six painful years as the team's backup. "I can remember telling her, 'That's it, I'm done; I'm absolutely done. I've had it. End of the year, we're moving; we're taking everything. I'm done with football.'" Hostetler said later.

"I felt like I'd finally reached the end, I felt like I had reached the bottom. There wasn't any further that I could go. And I felt disappointed. I felt empty."

2

Quarterback Lack

Very early into an eighth decade of professional football, the collective body of New York Giants fans had been familiar with cruel and crippling home losses. Members of the older generation lamented losing to Johnny Unitas' Baltimore Colts at Yankee Stadium in the 1958 NFL Championship Game. But at least that one was somewhat honorable. The overtime defeat clinched professional football's unyielding place in American culture.

The franchise's transition to brand new Giants Stadium in October 1976 also came with home-field frustrations. "Big Blue," as the team was sometimes called, lost their first three home contests, the last two by shutout. By the time of the "Miracle at the Meadowlands" (the Philadelphia Eagles impossible last-second victory in 1979), New York had been so bad at home that such an absurd, fluke defeat was almost laughable.

"Laughable" also describes that 38-12 rout by Washington in October 1987. Instead of the defending Super Bowl champions, scab, replacement players filled in for the striking NFL Players Union. New York lost a third home game in twenty-two days. Most horrified fans stayed home anyway, electing not to watch the faux-Giants drop to an 0-4 record.

Any history-conscious New Yorker who walked into the East Rutherford, New Jersey, stadium on Saturday, December 15, 1990, had to be aware of the team's occasional brush with embarrassing or painful home losses. But when the Giants sulked off the Meadowlands AstroTurf later that afternoon, their fans had never known anything like this.

Following a remarkable 12-4 regular season in 1989, the Giants squandered home-field advantage in their first-round playoff showdown with the wild-card Los Angeles Rams, losing in overtime. At the start of the next year, the team held high hopes, which they fulfilled through two-and-a-half months. A wonderfully balanced New York team won each of the first ten games of the 1990 season.

Sitting out all of training camp to protest his contract did not keep linebacker Lawrence Taylor from reclaiming his position as the league's best outside linebacker. He posted three sacks in the season opener against Philadelphia—just five days after returning from his holdout—then recorded another and returned an interception for a touchdown the following week at Dallas. The thirty-one-year-old did not need a preseason to knock the dust off his revolutionary pass-defense skills. With Taylor, Leonard Marshall, Carl Banks, and Pepper Johnson, the Giants featured the best and most feared front seven in the NFL. By Week Eleven, the "Big Blue Wrecking Crew" ranked first in the conference in yardage and points allowed and were ranked first in the NFL in rush defense. The only team to allow fewer yards (fifty-five) and points (one) was the Miami Dolphins, who the Giants dominated 20-3, in late September.

Throughout the 1980s, the Giants defense had largely overshadowed the offense. But at the start of the new decade, New York's scoring attack seemed every bit as potent. After ten games, quarterback Phil Simms was the league's number-one-rated passer, the running attack averaged over 120 yards per contest, and with only ten turnovers in ten games—the lowest in the NFL—the Giants embodied head coach Bill Parcells' ideal offense.

By the start of Week Twelve (the team's bye came in early October), every aspect of the Giants 1990 team seemed flawless. Even Sean Landeta's punting was tops in the NFL.

"Each week, you get another win and you get hopeful," Parcells said at a Monday press conference prior to the eleventh game of the season. "If someone said you're going to lose five of the next six games but win the division, I'll take it."

A month after Parcells made that comment, he and the Giants were on target for that exact scenario.

In a rematch at Philadelphia, the Giants suffered their first loss of the season, as elusive quarterback Randall Cunningham scrambled and passed the

Eagles to a decisive 31-13 victory. A road loss to one of the league's best—and a team that had swept New York in both games the previous two seasons—didn't crush morale. Neither did a narrow 7-3 defeat the following week against San Francisco. After traveling cross-country to battle the reigning two-time Super Bowl champion 49ers, the Giants came up on the short end of a physical defensive melee. Apart from a two-minute stretch in the second period, the game was scoreless.

Consecutive losses raised questions, but at 10-2, with a three-game lead in the NFC Eastern Division, and a roster full of veterans—most of whom already owned Super Bowl rings from the 1986 season—panic never entered Parcells' mind.

"There's a lot of things unsettled right now," he said a few days after returning from San Francisco. "Things will change a lot. A loss, or two or three, in the middle of the season, really, will not be how you're judged. You're judged not by the middle of the season but by the end."

Judgment of the Giants' end-of-the-season prospects continued to dim the following Sunday. In Week Fourteen, they returned to the Meadowlands for a game against the Vikings and what was a showdown of two teams headed in opposite directions.

Minnesota had lost six of their first seven games before an impressive resurgence. During a perfect November in which they crushed the 9-1 Chicago Bears by four touchdowns, the Vikings arrived in East Rutherford at 6-6. With Herschel Walker and a fantastic defensive line that included all-pro Chris Doleman, Henry Thomas, and undrafted rookie (yet future Hall of Famer) John Randle, the Vikings had remarkably climbed into the playoff picture.

With a two-game losing streak and the division title at stake, coach Parcells had plenty on his mind that week. He didn't need a serious personal health crisis to drain both his physical and mental strength. But he got one. Near midnight on Saturday—a little more than twelve hours before kickoff—Parcells checked himself into Morristown Memorial Hospital in New Jersey. The pain from dislodged kidney stones had become unbearable. Although doctors insisted he stay longer, Parcells checked himself out at 9 a.m. the next morning and, equipped with a supply of Demerol, he rode to Giants Stadium, where he fell asleep on the trainer's table.

"[Parcells said to me] I'll go as long as I can," team physician Dr. Allan Levy told reporters. "This is just about the greatest pain you can have, but he couldn't take very much to kill the pain. He wanted to be able to think during the game."

Assistant coaches ran the pregame activities and spoke to the team in the locker room. Ten minutes before game time, Parcells gingerly took his place on the sideline and watched, understandably without his usual fire and gyrations.

"He didn't make any moves to show he was hurt," said Ed "Whitey" Wagner, the team's equipment manager, who routinely stood next to Parcells on the sideline, "but I knew it was like a knife sticking in him."

Parcells' pain only increased as he watched his team continue to wipe away all memories of a perfect 10-0 start. Four minutes into the action, Doleman sacked Phil Simms in the end zone for a safety, and by the middle of the second quarter, New York trailed 12-3. The Meadowlands crowd repeatedly booed, especially at the sight of Minnesota stuffing a Giants running back on a key fourth down and short. (The Vikings then drove seventy-six yards for the game's first touchdown.) New York eventually crawled back into the game late in the second period, as a rushing touchdown narrowed the score to 12-10.

A third consecutive week of trailing at halftime—this time at home against a .500 team—generated palpable frustration in the locker room. Especially for a prideful, once-dominant defense that surrendered 175 first-half yards to the league's seventeenth-ranked offense.

"We didn't tackle anybody and we didn't cover anybody in the first half," said defensive end Leonard Marshall.

"We weren't aggressive, we let their offense set the tempo," added linebacker Steve DeOssie.

Those plain facts infuriated Lawrence Taylor.

"We're not physical enough," he shouted at halftime. "I'm going to start playing the way we're supposed to play. If anybody wants to come along, fine."

In the second half, Taylor led and the Giants followed. Behind 15-10 late in the third quarter, Taylor and the Giants pass rush forced quarterback Rich Gannon into a premature throw, which Greg Jackson intercepted. Four plays later, the Giants added a field goal. Taylor and rookie Mike Fox opened the ensuing series with a sack of Gannon. Then, a lunging tackle from Taylor, followed by defensive lineman Erik Howard's quarterback sack on third down forced a punt. The offense capitalized on the momentum, as Ottis Anderson closed out an eight-play drive with a two-yard touchdown run.

Now ahead 20-15, the Giants continued to apply pressure. With under six minutes remaining, Taylor breached the Vikings offensive line and grabbed the legs of Gannon, who was barely able to get rid of the football. Linebacker Gary Reasons intercepted the wobbly pass inside Minnesota territory. The Giants added a short field goal to clinch the victory and the division.

"He's a one-man wrecking crew," Gannon said. "He just took over the fourth quarter. L. T. was the difference. We couldn't stop him."

Taylor accounted for twelve tackles, 2.5 sacks, and one forced fumble.

"We'd gotten away from our basic objective, to win the division," Taylor told reporters. "We were thinking about 16-0, about the Super Bowl. We had to get back to basics."

Halting the losing skid to secure the NFC East title seemed to cure many of the Giants' ailments, but not those that pained Parcells, who checked back into the hospital hours after the win to undergo surgery.

"I just remember watching him on the sidelines that day," Parcells' personal secretary Kim Kolbe said years later, "I couldn't believe that he was out there coaching. And then I just remember him getting in a [state trooper's car] right after the game and going to the hospital."

The defense atoned for the poor efforts against Philadelphia and a disappointing first half against Minnesota. And while the offense had managed only two touchdowns in the previous ten quarters, rookie Rodney Hampton's presence (he rushed for 105 yards on twenty-one carries) behind their once–Super Bowl MVP quarterback Phil Simms, gave New York a formidable backfield.

"We've taken two steps [making the playoffs and winning the division]," Parcells said. "Maybe we can take another one. We still got some work left."

Losers of the previous six Super Bowls, the American Football Conference (which had won eleven of the first thirteen post-merger Super Bowl titles) could no longer claim status as the league's dominant faction. Worse yet, the margin of defeat during the AFC's losing streak had been twenty-six points.

The second half of the 1980s suggested that the AFC was the lesser conference. And the 1990 NFL season continued to promote that myth.

By the midway point, Week Nine, the National Football Conference boasted two undefeated teams, the Giants and 49ers, as well as Mike Ditka's 8-1 Chicago Bears. And with the intimidating Philadelphia Eagles and Washington Redskins (Super Bowl champions just three years earlier) still in the playoff hunt, the NFC was as strong as ever.

Most AFC players and coaches scoffed at the idea of a conference gap.

"I don't think there's any difference between the two conferences. It's not like the players come from a different talent pool," said Bills wide receiver James Lofton, a former Raider who had also spent nine seasons with the Green Bay Packers.

Lofton was right. Great players and great teams still resided in the so-called inferior AFC. Denver's John Elway and Houston's Warren Moon operated prolific passing attacks, as did Boomer Esiason of the Cincinnati Bengals, who came very close to an upset win over San Francisco in Super Bowl XXIII. And the Miami Dolphins, coached by Don Shula, had put together a simple-yet-proven formula for success: Dan Marino plus a stout defense yielded wins.

But no team in the AFC was better than the Buffalo Bills.

Marv Levy's November 1986 victory over Pittsburgh—the product of "45 stout hearts and the north wind"—was the first of many. And as much as Levy's craftiness keyed the Bills' turnaround, good fortune was also a factor.

There had been nowhere to go but up when Levy took over the Bills in the middle of 1986. Talented, young defenders, Darryl Talley and Bruce Smith, along with rookie offensive linemen Will Wolford and Kent Hull gave the Bills a solid foundation up front. With second-year wide receiver Andre Reed and former all-pro running back from Notre Dame Greg Bell, the Bills did not lack skill players. And the inevitable demise of the United States Football League during the summer of 1986 gave Levy and the Bills what they needed most: a quarterback, a star, and a leader.

As he predicted, Jim Kelly had no regrets over choosing the USFL over the Buffalo Bills in June 1983. A multimillionaire at age twenty-three, Kelly enjoyed every bit of his new celebrity, driving a cherry-red Corvette Stingray to bars, restaurants, and publicity events all across town. He quickly validated his large salary and larger brashness. The expansion Gamblers, coached by Jack Pardee, won the Central Division in the spring of 1984. Kelly was unquestionably the league's finest passer, throwing for 5,219 yards and forty-four touchdowns during the eighteen-game regular season. He won the league MVP that season and was equally superb in 1985.

Despite the exciting brand of scoring-heavy football, USFL franchises could not draw enough spectators to stay financially sound. In February 1986, Kelly's Gamblers merged with the New Jersey Generals. Moving to the tristate area meant that the familiar comparisons only continued.

"For a new league, Kelly is the kind of guy you want," Jerry Argovitz re-stated. "He's like Namath—working class, talented, antiestablishment."

A reputation as a "playboy" furthered the parallels. Much like Namath, who once famously sported shades and a fur coat on the sidelines, Kelly almost always wore sunglasses, except underneath his helmet. And the first official act as a member of his new team was to fly to New York City and interview sixty finalists for the Generals cheerleading squad.

Before he ever threw a pass for owner Donald Trump's team, the league suspended operations and granted its players the right to negotiate contracts with the NFL for the 1986 season. By August, Kelly and the Bills—who still owned his exclusive draft rights—agreed to terms, thirty-nine months after his selection in the 1983 draft.

Bills fans didn't care that he previously chose Houston over Buffalo. Nor were they bothered by his less-than-optimistic outlook—"they need more than a quarterback in Buffalo"—for the previously 2-14 team. The day he arrived in town, hordes of Bills fans cheered and chanted his name as his limousine pulled up to the Hilton Hotel for an introductory press conference. Four thousand season tickets were sold the week his signing was announced. Even New York Governor Mario Cuomo phoned during the press conference to welcome him to town.

According to his former head coach Howard Schnellenberger, Kelly had already been a "messiah" to the University of Miami's program. His impact on the short-lived Houston Gamblers franchise was similar. Buffalo expected nothing less.

"I can remember the very first game, we played the Jets, in 1986, the home opener, and people had been talking about getting twenty thousand, thirty thousand people in the stands, and, shoot, we had eighty thousand. They wasn't there to look at me," remembered Bills center Kent Hull. "They were there to watch Jim Kelly. He was the savior of that city. That city had just gone through a terrible ordeal where Bethlehem Steel had laid off thirty thousand people in one year. . . . The best way to rally everybody is to find some simple thing everyone enjoys and they all come together. And that happened to be Jim Kelly and the Buffalo Bills."

Kelly's addition was critical, both on and off the field. But Levy and General Manager Bill Polian knew they needed to revamp the roster. By the middle of his first full season, Levy had received a pair of outstanding linebackers. In the first round of the 1987 draft, Buffalo selected Shane Conlan, a captain of the Penn State team that won the national championship that January.

In case one first-round rookie linebacker from a premier college football program wasn't enough for Levy to mold the Bills defense, Polian brought in another six months later. Cornelius Bennett, the top linebacker taken and second overall pick in that 1987 draft, went to the Indianapolis Colts. Well into the start of the regular season, the two sides could not agree to a contract, and in late October, Bennett was dealt to the Bills as part of a three-way trade that sent all-pro running back Eric Dickerson to the Colts. Bennett signed with Buffalo and was on the field eight days later, sacking John Elway during a 21-14 win over Denver.

A steep price had been paid to acquire Bennett. In addition to parting with running back Greg Bell, the Bills dealt away their first-round selections in the 1988 and 1989 drafts. But Polian was shrewd and knew that first-round picks don't build dynasties.

"It's all about the entire process—not just the first round," Polian would later say at the end of three decades as an NFL general manager.

In April 1988, Polian's big-picture thinking yielded one of the greatest "steals" in the history of the NFL draft.

Running back Thurman Thomas had been a phenom at Oklahoma State. As a freshman, he rushed for 206 yards and two touchdowns against Kansas State, and topped the 100-yard mark two more times that season. In that year's Gator Bowl, the eighteen-year-old from Houston posted 155 yards on thirty-two carries, scored a rushing touchdown, and even threw a touchdown pass in the Cowboys' 21-14 comeback victory over South Carolina. He was named the game's Most Valuable Player.

Tremendous numbers the next season (three 200-yard games, 1,553 yards rushing) brought on talk of Thomas becoming the first sophomore to win the Heisman Trophy. He finished tied for tenth place in the voting, far behind Bo

Jackson of Auburn. An off-season knee injury suffered while playing pickup basketball set back his growth as an upperclassman. Luckily for the Cowboys, head coach Pat Jones had recruited a capable replacement that spring: a grossly undersized player from Wichita, Kansas, named Barry Sanders.

Thomas struggled most of the 1986 season with the sore knee, enabling Sanders to see significant playing time as a freshman. Oklahoma State finished with a very disappointing 6-5 record and no bowl appearance. A year of rest and rehab rejuvenated Thomas for his senior season, and in 1987, the Cowboys finished 10-2, losing only to powerhouses Oklahoma and Nebraska. And although Sanders would go on to post the greatest season ever by a running back in the history of college football a year later (2,638 rushing yards, thirty-nine touchdowns), Thomas relegated him to second-string.

Ten 100-yard rushing games, including an incredible 293-yard performance against Iowa State, again put Thomas in the Heisman conversation. He didn't garner nearly enough votes to contend, but in his collegiate finale, Thomas proved he belonged among the nation's elite. On an absurdly snow-covered field in El Paso, Texas, he scored four touchdowns in a Sun Bowl victory over Don Nehlen's West Virginia Mountaineers. During the 35-33 victory, Thomas touched the ball on more than half of the Cowboys' offensive plays and accumulated more than half of the team's total offense.

"He ended his career the way he began it as a freshman—standing on a platform a champion and a most valuable player," Pat Jones told reporters.

Despite all his college accomplishments, which also included the Senior Bowl MVP, Thomas tumbled on draft day. The once-torn anterior cruciate ligament in his left knee reportedly scared off many teams. As six running backs were selected ahead of him, ESPN cameras filmed Thomas fall asleep on his couch back in Texas.

Spurred on by assistant coach Elijah Pitts—a backup in Vince Lombardi's Hall of Fame backfield of Jim Taylor and Paul Hornung—Marv Levy and Bill Polian hoped Thomas would fall to them.

"This is the best back in the draft and he is a difference maker," Polian told owner Ralph Wilson. "But it will be a gamble and it's your money."

"Ah hell," said the sixty-nine-year-old. "Life's a gamble, go ahead and do it."

By Week One of his rookie season, Thomas paid out. In the season opener at Rich Stadium, Thomas scored a first-quarter touchdown to give Buffalo a

10-0 lead over Minnesota, a team that lost the previous season's NFC championship by seven points. In the fourth quarter, the Vikings cut the lead to three points with less than four minutes to play. But a twenty-eight-yard burst from Thomas gave the Bills a first down, and eventually a 13-10 win. He finished the day with eighteen carries for eighty-six yards and a pair of receptions, earning NFL Rookie of the Week honors.

"Thurman is the ideal back you want to have in any offense: very bright, very intelligent," Bills offensive coordinator Ted Marchibroda said years later. "When he came into preseason camp [as a rookie], he never missed an assignment: he knew all his assignments already. He was the complete back. He could run, he was an outstanding pass receiver, he had foot speed, everything."

Despite the influx of young talent, Levy had been cautious about his team and the fans expecting too much too soon. Asked in preseason about the possibility of a division title in 1988, Levy responded:

"What would they be hanging their hats on, a 7-8 record [the previous season]? We've yet to prove we're a good team. Last year we proved we're not a lousy team. There is no one step. You get better little by little. It's a sophisticated process."

The process needed less time to take effect than he realized. Following the Thomas-aided win over Minnesota, Buffalo won ten of the next eleven games and clinched the AFC East title. They repeated as division champions the following season. By 1990, a third division title seemed not only a certainty but also a prelude to greater achievements.

"Hopefully . . . Jim [Kelly] can have an All-Pro year and help lead us to the Super Bowl," Andre Reed said prior to Week One. "With our talent and him as our quarterback, anything else would be falling short of our potential."

By mid-November, the Bills had only one blemish on their record, an early season loss to the Dolphins in the hot south Florida sun. A victory over the defending AFC Champion Denver Broncos followed a month later by a 42-0 slaughtering of Cleveland—in front of the "Dawg Pound"—solidified Buffalo as the class of the conference. And to show any disbelievers who thought they simply beat up on "second-rate" AFC teams, Buffalo defeated the Eagles 30-23 on the first Sunday of December.

That win, just a week after Philadelphia ended the New York Giants' perfect 10-0 record, was Buffalo's most impressive. The defense withstood a twenty-three-point barrage (highlighted by a miraculous ninety-five-yard touchdown pass from quarterback Randall Cunningham) to keep Philadelphia scoreless throughout the game's final twenty-four minutes.

But offense separated Buffalo from the Eagles that afternoon . . . and separated the Bills from the rest of the NFL.

Coached by Buddy Ryan, architect of the fabled 1985 Chicago Bears defense, the Eagles featured one of the finest defensive lines ever assembled. Future Hall of Famer Reggie White, all-pro defensive tackle Jerome Brown, and pass-rushing specialist Clyde Simmons each relentlessly pressured quarterbacks. Complimented by linebacker Seth Joyner and ball-hawking Eric Allen—arguably the league's top cornerback—the Eagles accumulated more turnovers and sacks during the previous two seasons than any other team in the NFL.

But not a single Eagle sacked quarterback Jim Kelly in their December 1990 matchup, and Buffalo's lone turnover didn't even cost them a possession. (An interception was negated when Thurman Thomas deflected Joyner's attempt to lateral the ball, and the Bills recovered the fumble.)

Fluke plays such as this one were not necessary for the Bills to ground out yardage, first downs, and points. At 9-2, they were averaging more than twenty-eight points per game, far better than any other team in the league. Prior to the Philadelphia game, Kelly paced the AFC in completion percentage, Thomas led the entire NFL in total yardage, and receiver Andre Reed was in the midst of a second straight all-pro season.

The Bills featured the most balanced, yet supremely explosive attacks in the league. It was also, coincidently, the most unique and unconventional offense seen in decades.*

The Bills flirted with a fast-paced approach early in the 1989 season. Trailing by eleven points late in the fourth quarter in the opener against Miami, a pair of touchdowns—orchestrated via the no-huddle—spurred the Bills to victory. Using the offense throughout the second half a week later against the

---

*The Bills were not the only team in the mid-1980s that ran a no-huddle offense. The Cincinnati Bengals operated without a huddle just a year before, in 1988. The Bills attack was much different. In their offense, minimizing time in between plays was just as important as not using a huddle. As James Lofton said in 2010, "No one had ever run it at that fast of a pace. It was our objective to try and run a play every 22–24 seconds. . . . I don't think that Jim [Kelly] ever got enough credit for being the field general that he was. I look at what Peyton Manning is doing now—Jim Kelly was doing that in 1990."

Broncos didn't produce another comeback and convinced Levy that the no-huddle was not reliable.

"If you think you're going to win games doing that right out of the box, it will win you one and lose you two," Levy told reporters after the loss to Denver. "You make a garrison try at it and it looks exciting, but it's desperation football. It pays off on rare occasions, but not on frequent occasions."

But Kelly lobbied the coaching staff for more opportunities to perfect the no-huddle. In Week Three, the Bills played Houston in the Astrodome. Running a perpetual "two-minute" offense, Kelly posted five touchdowns and 363 yards passing—the best performance of his short career—as the Bills triumphed in overtime 47-41. (The Bills eventually dubbed this offense the "K-Gun," a salute to their tight end Keith "Killer" McKeller.)

By their first-round playoff game against Cleveland, the no-huddle was ready for an extended test. The Browns boasted the second-best defense in the conference, and on that day inside Municipal Stadium by Lake Erie, the unit surrendered just forty-nine rushing yards on eighteen carries.

The absence of a ground attack did nothing to slow down the Bills offense. In fact, it worked to their advantage.

"They chose not to feature the running game," Browns linebacker Clay Matthews said afterward. "Instead they spread us out and confused us. We were out of sync. They created some matchup problems."

The greatest matchup problem quickly became Cleveland's entire defense versus Thurman Thomas. In his second NFL season, Thomas emerged as an every-down, multitalented player. He finished the regular season sixth in the NFL in rushing yards, but 669 additional yards on sixty receptions meant the NFL lead in total yards from scrimmage. (He would win that title four consecutive years, a record that still stands.)

So when running lanes did not open up early in the playoff battle against Cleveland, Thomas tied a playoff record, catching thirteen passes for 150 yards and two touchdowns. Every member of the Buffalo passing game benefited from Thomas' omnipresence. In the first half, receivers Andre Reed and James Lofton each caught long touchdown passes from Kelly, who finished the day with over 400 yards passing.

Spreading out the Browns defense added a new wrinkle to the Bills attack. But the pace of the Bills offense handcuffed their opponent. Buffalo ran virtually every play without a huddle. The unorthodox strategy not only prevented the defense from catching its breath in between plays, it also kept the Browns coaches from making instantaneous substitutions to both the lineup and the defensive strategy.

Across a frozen though snowless field, Kelly repeatedly traded scoring drives with his former Miami Hurricane teammate, Browns quarterback Bernie Kosar. Two minutes, forty-one seconds remained in the fourth quarter when the Bills offense, behind 34-30, took the field. Quick passes from Kelly and the subsequent catch-and-runs by his marvelous receiving corps moved Buffalo into scoring position. With three seconds left, Kelly attempted to squeeze a pass by Clay Matthews into the hands of Thurman Thomas. Although he had struggled all afternoon to cover the elusive second-year back, on the final play Matthews cut in front of Thomas and intercepted the pass at the one-yard line.

"There was an important lesson that we did learn as a result of that loss and of that hectic fourth quarter on the scarred grass of grimy old Cleveland Stadium," Levy wrote. "As we walked off the field immediately after the game, however, we were all too distraught to reflect upon any educational benefits that could be derived from that unhappy ending. Many months later it would hit us, and when it did take hold, it would be a revelation that helped inspire a decision that would lead to energizing the Buffalo sports scene as never before."

That revelation resurfaced sometime the following summer, and by opening day of the 1990 season, Levy slowly implemented the K-Gun strategy as the standard offense. Executing the no-huddle during the first series of the season opener against Indianapolis, Kelly ran ten plays (nine-for-nine on pass attempts) that covered seventy-six yards. After that opening drive, the Bills put away their new toy.

"We used it sparingly in the ball games. But the guys liked it," Marchibroda said. "Then we finally went to it exclusively 100 percent against Philadelphia. We were playing Philadelphia [in 1990] and we thought we needed an element of surprise to beat them, because they had a strong defense. So we went with the no-huddle exclusively in that ball game and as a result we scored twenty-four points in the first quarter. As a result, we got hooked."*

---

*Marchibroda had flirted with the no-huddle as a standard offensive strategy two years before he joined the Bills staff. After Philadelphia Eagles head coach Marion Campbell was fired prior to the last week of the 1985 season, Marchibroda—the team's offensive coordinator—installed a no-huddle offense for the season finale against Minnesota. According to Mark Kelso, who was a member of that

Operating without a huddle meant that the quarterback selected the plays, a facet of the game now regarded as a relic from a previous era. But apart from calling his own plays—a dream for any quarterback—Jim Kelly delighted in the new game plan: using the K-Gun a year earlier against Houston and Cleveland, he combined for nine touchdowns and 768 yards passing. The rest of the offense shared Kelly's enthusiasm.

"Everybody liked it," Ted Marchibroda said. "Jim really liked it and he was made for it. But the other thing was that the guys that really liked it were the offensive linemen. Because they could see the defensive linemen tiring. And it gave them a definite edge."

The additional and now standard use of the no-huddle instantly generated results against the Eagles. Requiring just two plays (and forty-five seconds), the K-Gun posted a lightning-quick touchdown. By the end of the first quarter, Buffalo held a 24-0 lead. And although the Bills needed a pair of second-half field goals by kicker Scott Norwood to solidify a 30-23 win, the K-Gun had arrived.

"It was a miserable day for football," reported the *New York Times*, "with a cold and steady rain leaving a light coating of ice on the roads outside Giants Stadium and chilling players and spectators inside."

The stage for a December 15, 1990, showdown between the 11-2 Giants and 11-2 Bills bothered those spectators much more than it did the men on the field. Standing on the sidelines beneath cold drizzling rain, Marv Levy told an assistant: "I don't care, whatever, just go play. Whatever it is. You're supposed to play in whatever kind of weather. That's the way this game is meant to be played: outside."

Giants fans discouraged by the weather—more than thirty thousand already-sold tickets went unused—missed a promising start. New York took the opening kickoff and marched downfield. A forty-one-yard run along the sideline by Rodney Hampton, combined with a series of short ground gains neutralized the nasty elements. On the eleventh play of the drive, Simms

---

1985 Philadelphia team, "That's where [the Bills no-huddle offense] originated." The Eagles won 37-35, scoring more points that day than the franchise had in any game since 1981.

handed the ball to Ottis Anderson, who plowed into the end zone to cap the seventy-one-yard drive.

Eighty-eight seconds—instantaneous compared to the Giants drawn-out, seven-minute possession—rolled off the clock before the K-Gun evened the score. Largely the result of a forty-eight-yard catch-and-run by Thurman Thomas, Buffalo reached New York's six-yard line. There, Kelly fired a quick strike over the middle and watched Andre Reed finish off the short touchdown pass. The Bills scored an opening-drive touchdown for the fifth consecutive week.

Buffalo continued exclusive use of their no-huddle offense and less than a minute into the second period, they were in the end zone again. Kelly and Reed hooked up for a thirty-six-yarder to set up Thomas' tenth rushing touchdown of the season. The Bills had run seventeen plays, amassed 152 yards and a pair of touchdowns, all while running a few minutes off the game clock.

"On both drives, it was obvious the Giants' defense was confused," said Kelly. "Especially their linebackers, who didn't seem to know exactly where to line up and looked awkward in their movement at the snap. After all the scoffing they had done about the no-huddle, I think we caught them off guard with it. It seemed like we were one step ahead of them in everything we did."

When asked earlier that week about the unconventional and seemingly dynamic K-Gun, the Giants did not express much concern.

"We're not going to have trouble," Parcells said. "Huddle or no huddle, the offense has to play the defense. Execution is what counts."

"I guess a lot of teams aren't prepared for the no-huddle," cornerback Mark Collins added. "They think it won't happen to them. But we'll be ready. Jim Kelly will be looking at us to see what we're doing, but we'll be looking at him."

Barely a quarter into the game, New York had looked unprepared and overconfident. Despite the three-week slump that detonated a perfect record and sent the team into a tailspin, the Giants still owned the league's top-ranked defense in both points and yards allowed. More important, they had already proven capable of completely shutting down explosive offenses packed with all-pro talent. New York crushed the Dolphins in September 20-3, limiting Dan Marino to paltry figures: 115 yards passing, two interceptions, and no touchdowns. Ten weeks later, they held Joe Montana to 152 yards on twenty-nine pass attempts, completely shut down the 49ers' running game, and forced nine punts.

Two seemingly effortless touchdowns by Buffalo now overshadowed those previous achievements, and defensive coordinator Bill Belichick angrily corralled his unit for discussion. Crouching along the sideline with a dry-erase board against his knee, Belichick shouted out reminders and adjustments to the defense. Fortunately, Belichick and the players processing his instructions on a nearby bench had plenty of time: Phil Simms was in the middle of constructing another trademark time-consuming scoring drive.

The defense retook the field and, behind 14-10, received a lucky break.

At his own twenty-one-yard line, Bills quarterback Jim Kelly unloaded a short pass to Andre Reed, who caught the ball, gained a few yards, and set up an important third and short. Kelly stayed upright long enough to dump the pass off to Reed, thanks to solid protection from his offensive line.

But while Kelly read his options and prepared to release the ball, left tackle Will Wolford engaged the Giants' Leonard Marshall, whom he successfully rebuked at the line of scrimmage. On Wolford's right, guard Jim Ritcher also did his job, stymieing a blitzing Carl Banks. Ritcher so overpowered Banks that he hurled him toward Will Wolford. Banks crashed into Wolford, who stumbled backward and fell onto the left leg of Jim Kelly.

"I just turned around and it seemed like there were people laying everywhere," Kent Hull remembered. "It was pretty scary."

Absorbing the blow from his three-hundred-pound tackle caused Kelly to tumble to the turf where he writhed in pain. Carefully, the Bills training staff escorted their three-million-dollar-per-year quarterback to the sidelines. Soon he was loaded onto a utility cart and taken for X-rays.

Injury to a quarterback equipped with the leadership qualities and athletic abilities possessed by Jim Kelly would severely hamstring any team. But Kelly was more than just the team's passer. In the newly installed—and now thriving—K-Gun offense, he called all the plays. And after nearly four full seasons as the team's starter, Kelly operated the offense with a few personalized tweaks not in the playbook: specific terminology for audibles, "dummy" calls, and hand signals to his skill players.

"Jim's like the NBA player who wants the ball at the end of the game," Marchibroda noted. "He's our Michael Jordan, our Magic Johnson. And that, first and foremost, is why the no-huddle has been so successful for us."

Veteran Frank Reich filled Kelly's place as the K-Gun's conductor/quarterback. The University of Maryland product had been an efficient backup the year before, winning three starts with Kelly sidelined due to injury. But without the league's top-rated passer, every Buffalo offensive series during the second and most of the third quarter went fruitless: punts—not points—concluded each drive.

With the K-Gun now surprisingly silenced, the Bills were vulnerable. And although New York's offense was not nearly as potent at the Bills, quarterback Phil Simms had produced a pair of early, lengthy scoring drives. Still, after cutting the lead to 14-10 in the second period, the Giants offense also faltered and under familiar circumstances.

Less than three minutes had rolled off the second-quarter game clock when Simms, unable to find an open receiver, tucked the ball under his shoulder and hurried upfield. One of the least mobile quarterbacks in the league, the eleven-year veteran was easily brought down at the line of scrimmage by Bills Leon Seals and Cornelius Bennett.

"That's when I hurt [my right foot]," he told reporters. "Then it started hurting more and more and at halftime they taped it up."

The play had occurred on third down so Parcells sent out the punt team. Because the Bills pieced together a short drive to close out the first half, Simms did not miss a snap. At the half, inside the locker room, trainers applied tape to stabilize the foot. On the Giants' next possession, Simms returned to the huddle, and after five consecutive handoffs, the Giants coaching staff deemed him healthy enough to throw. Simms completed his first attempt since the injury, an off-balanced toss to Dave Meggett that gained nine yards. He landed awkwardly on the slick, rain-soaked AstroTurf and fell to the ground, clutching his leg.

"I was turning to throw to my right. It felt like someone had shot me. I heard it click, or whatever," Simms said. "When I walked off the field, I thought it was OK. It was numb, but I thought once the numbness wore off, it would be all right. But once the numbness went away, there was a lot of pain."

As Simms hobbled off the Meadowlands field, Jeff Hostetler jogged past him and into the Giants' huddle. The thirty-year-old—who told his wife just a few weeks earlier that 1990 would be his last of seven increasingly frustrating NFL seasons—had been given one more opportunity. And it came under less-than-ideal circumstances.

"It was a tough situation to come into and not one of the most favorable ones, especially with the weather. I don't remember [ever] being as cold as I was before the second half."

Under Hostetler, the Giants scored three points to cut into Buffalo's lead. Matching his second-string quarterback counterpart on the following series, Frank Reich pushed the Bills near the Giants' goal line, and on the first play of the fourth quarter, Scott Norwood's twenty-nine-yard field goal made the score 17-13.

With an entire quarter remaining, New York would see several more opportunities to make up the small deficit: They failed each time.

Early in the final period, Hostetler drove the Giants to the thirteen-yard line, where a holding penalty, followed by a shotgun snap over the quarterback's head—"My hand was wet and numb," center Bart Oates admitted—sabotaged the drive. The next series also looked promising. Hostetler hooked up with Stephen Baker to produce an apparent first down at the Buffalo twenty-two. An offensive pass interference penalty during the play negated the gain. The Giants punted two plays later.

"We were moving the ball," Hostetler said. "Then we'd get in scoring range and do something stupid."

With seventy seconds remaining, the defense forced a Buffalo punt, giving New York one final opportunity to take the lead. Hostetler completed three consecutive passes to reach the Bills' twenty-six-yard line, then spiked the ball, stopping the clock. With no time-outs and a few seconds remaining, the Giants' options were limited.

"We were running seam patters, and the (Bills) were just sitting back there waiting for them," Hostetler said. "In that case, it was best to just try to get it into the end zone."

Second and third down shots toward the goal line came up incomplete and on fourth and ten, Hostetler's pass to rookie Troy Kyles fell to the ground—final score: Bills 17, Giants 13.

"If you told me before the game," Parcells told reporters, "that we were going to have the ball 38 minutes, we would have half the penalties the other team had, we would not miss any extra points or field goals, we would run the ball for 157 yards, we would complete over 55 percent of our passes, we would hold them to 65 yards rushing and we would give up one sack for no yards lost, I would say we would win the game."

Penalties and several miscues—including two dropped interceptions near the Buffalo goal line by Lawrence Taylor—caused woes for Parcells' team the entire day. Most troublesome, however, was the New York running game's inability to gain critical yardage when called upon. Rodney Hampton gashed the Bills for 105 yards on twenty-one rushes, but the Giants were left with third and short or fourth and short on nine separate occasions. They could not gain the first down on six of those tries.

"Not making those first downs was a kick in the face, because we've been so successful with it in the past," said Ottis Anderson, who, despite his early touchdown, finished the game with five carries for zero net yards.

"We've been pathetic. We haven't done anything in the last four, five weeks on short-yardage," offensive coordinator Ron Erhardt said after the loss. "Third down has been a killer. Every time it seems like a different thing, a guy missing a block or a penalty or whatever. We could change our offense and start doing other things, but you like to be able to run from your strength."

Despite comparable offensive woes (after Kelly's injury, the offense managed only four first downs), that Saturday was sweet for Buffalo. Victory had preserved the Bills' one-game edge in the race for both the division title and home-field advantage in the AFC playoffs. The win also improved their record to 3-0 in December, the critical final month of the regular season in which the team had poor records during recent seasons. (The previous three years, Buffalo finished 1-3 in December.)

Also, any panic over Kelly's injury was slightly muted by the win. The defense's performance convinced both themselves, and the rest of the National Football League, that the K-Gun comprised only one-half of their attack.

"After Jim was hurt we were determined not to let the game slip away," Darryl Talley said. "I think that was the best half of defense we played this year. Guys making plays—coming up with big plays at the times we needed them."

Reich did not have Kelly-like passing stats (eight completions in fifteen attempts for ninety-seven yards), and his teammates acknowledged a significant talent and experience disparity. But his forty-three-yard connection to Don Beebe was the play that set up Norwood's key fourth-quarter field goal. (Had it not been for Norwood's three-pointer, the Giants could have attempted a go-ahead field goal during their two possessions near the Bills' goal line.)

"I don't think Kelly's loss will hurt the team," said James Lofton.

Even the outlook for Kelly was promising. Team doctor Richard Weiss declared the prognosis excellent and expected a return by the postseason.

Phil Simms' right foot caused much more stress for his team. Giants orthopedic surgeon Dr. Russell Warren said the injury "looks significant" and Simms left East Rutherford that day on crutches. By Tuesday, doctors put him in a cast for four weeks, and the team placed him on injured reserve, meaning he was ineligible until the NFC Championship Game.

Giants coaches and players expressed sadness over losing their leader, the man who had started all but five of the team's previous ninety games. But confidence in Simms' replacement, Jeff Hostetler, circulated throughout the locker room.

"A lot of people outside of our locker room didn't realize that everyone was rooting for Jeff Hostetler," Carl Banks said years later. "He stood in special teams huddles; he ran scout team in practice. The guy did everything. He was everyman's man."

Head coach Bill Parcells also publicly endorsed his de-facto starter.

"Anytime you lose your starting quarterback, it's a big loss. But it's part of the game, and you can't dwell on it. I think Jeff can fill in very ably and I think he will."

Hostetler naturally remained skeptical. He had heard all that before.

3

Scuds, Patriot Missiles, and the K-Gun

For nearly a quarter of a century, the city of Buffalo had waited for this moment: a chance to see its beloved Bills compete, at home, for a championship. Twenty-four years, two weeks, and six days had passed since the Bills faced Kansas City for the American Football League championship, a title Buffalo claimed each of the previous two seasons. And, as if to set a trend that would last for the rest of the century, the Bills lost that title game when the Chiefs marched into War Memorial Stadium, lovingly referred to as "the "Rock Pile," and massacred Buffalo 31-7. Four turnovers combined with a porous run defense did in Joe Collier's squad. And two weeks later, the Chiefs, not the Buffalo Bills, appeared in the first-ever AFL-NFL title showdown, the game soon to be dubbed the Super Bowl.

Over the next three decades, Bills fans—wrapped up so passionately in their team's fortunes each frigid Buffalo winter—would not be deprived of thrills. Throughout the 1970s, Orenthal James "O. J." Simpson donned the Buffalo colors and dazzled pro football fans with his electric moves and lightning fast feet. And in the early 1980s, ultra-successful head coach Chuck Knox—previously a miracle worker with the Los Angeles Rams—teased Buffalo with back-to-back playoff appearances, only to make little noise in the postseason.

Through all those years, however, the Bills never earned a trip to the Super Bowl, the game they had just missed reaching on New Year's Day 1967.

"We haven't been that close since," Gary Pufpaff, a Buffalo-area teacher, football coach, and wistful Bills fan said in January 1991. "There has been a buildup from that day, and the Super Bowl is the piece de resistance."

Within two years of hiring Marv Levy, Buffalo was competing for that title. They lost the 1988 AFC Championship Game, on the road against the Cincinnati Bengals, and suffered a frustrating wild-card loss the following year. But Buffalo's Januaries were now filled with more than just snow. Talk of the Bills playing in a Super Bowl swirled through the air in western New York. And by Christmas 1990, the Bills and their fans did more than simply dream of playing in the Super Bowl. They expected it.

The Bills' 17-13 regular-season victory over the Giants in December 1990 had been merely a prelude to the most critical game of the season: a rematch against Miami with the division title awarded to the winner. A third consecutive AFC East crown was not nearly as important to the Bills as the other prize on the line in the season's second game against the Dolphins. Home-field advantage came with the conference's top seed in the playoffs.

Chilly temperatures and nearby Lake Erie–effect winds and snow made Rich Stadium intimidating to any opponent who came to Buffalo in winter. So did the Bills' record of twenty-two wins in the previous twenty-four home games.

Defeating Miami would secure the added bonus of a first-round playoff bye. An MRI of Jim Kelly's ailing left leg revealed a partial tear to both the medial collateral ligament and knee cartilage. Doctors deemed him able to "practice in three weeks and play in four." The bye in the opening round meant that Kelly would be able to return in time for the start to Buffalo's postseason. Until then, Frank Reich quarterbacked the team.

Before a record crowd (80,235) at Rich Stadium, the Bills squashed Miami 24-14, as Reich played "a near-perfect game," according to Dolphins head coach Don Shula. He completed fifteen of twenty-one attempts and tossed a pair of touchdowns. But Thurman Thomas' performance was the main reason why Bills fans triumphantly stormed the field and tore down the goalposts. The recently named pro-bowl starter ran for 154 yards on thirty attempts. And despite muscle spasms in his lower back in the fourth quarter, he carried the ball on seven consecutive plays, the last one a thirteen-yard touchdown that pushed the Buffalo lead to 24-7.

"[He] ran as hard as I've ever seen him run," center Kent Hull said. "When that happens, I think the offensive line plays a little harder. There's a guy who weighs 190 pounds taking on the big guys. When we see that we've got to go get after somebody."

A meaningless regular-season finale against Washington coupled with their bye during the opening wild-card round gave the Bills three weeks to rest and prepare for whoever their opponent would be in the second round of the playoffs. Coincidentally, that team turned out to be the Miami Dolphins.

"If we get complacent and think we're going to beat them because we beat them before, or they're not going to want to play because of the cold weather, we won't win," guard Jim Ritcher said. "It's as simple as that. Miami's too good a team to be complacent about. The fact we beat them in the last game is going to give them a lot of incentive to play harder."

The season's third showdown went much like the second: a ten-point victory by Buffalo during a cold winter day at Rich Stadium. Apart from a hefty brace on his left knee, Jim Kelly showed no signs of the recent injury. Kelly completed a twenty-yarder to Thomas on the game's opening snap, ran two more quick plays, then hit Andre Reed for a forty-yard touchdown. Less than two minutes into the game, Buffalo led 7-0.

In freezing temperatures, the offense was practically flawless, racking up nearly five hundred total yards and eight scores (five touchdowns, three field goals). Miami's offense was equally stellar, however, recording twenty-four first downs (the same number as the Bills) and only sixty-three total yards fewer than Kelly, Thomas, and the K-Gun.

Early in the final period, Marino's passing cut the Buffalo lead to 30-27. Thomas then scored his second rushing touchdown to create a ten-point cushion. On the ensuing kickoff, Miami fumbled the football, which kicker Scott Norwood recovered. Thirty-eight seconds later, Kelly hit Reed for a touchdown, effectively sealing the win.

"We simply came out and executed," Thomas said. "We felt as a team that a lot of people thought we were going to come out flat. We wanted to show everyone that even with the week layoff, we were still going to come out and do the things we've been doing all season."

This time, following the crucial win over Miami, Bills fans didn't even think about storming the field. To avoid another incident, the Bills' front office chose not to sell beer and brought in hundreds of police officers and security guards. Upon the game's end, mounted officers and a pack of twenty-four Doberman pinschers, rottweilers, and German shepherds surrounded the playing surface. There was good reason to keep fans from toppling the goalposts: eight days later, Rich Stadium would be the site of the AFC Championship Game.

"Nobody was going to storm the field today," said Orchard Park resident Tom Wolff. "But if we win next week and the Bills are going to their first Super Bowl ever . . . that could be different."

Bills fans, like Town of Tonawanda resident Doug Pagano, were rightfully ecstatic following their team's triumph: "I've been watching the Bills since I was a kid and for me, this year's team is burying a lot of bad ghosts from losing teams in the past."

Despite the optimism and excitement that flowed throughout western New York, few Americans—even the die-hard, long-suffering Bills fans who had just witnessed their team's great victory—would rejoice in unbridled celebration that evening.

While the Bills were busy churning out their victory over Miami, 533 U.S. senators and members of the House of Representatives sat in the Capitol building in Washington, D.C. Before them was House Joint Resolution 77, a bill authorizing the use of military force against Iraq. In the narrowest such vote since the War of 1812, the bill passed, first in the Senate, 52-47, then in the House, 250-183.

"We have now closed ranks behind a clear signal of our resolve to implement the United Nations resolutions," President George H. W. Bush told the American people. "Those who may have mistaken our democratic process as a sign of weakness now see the strength of democracy. . . . Throughout history, we have been resolute in our support of justice, freedom, and human dignity."

For months, Americans were aware of, but not overly concerned with, a bubbling conflict in the Persian Gulf. Iraq had invaded its neighbor Kuwait on August 2, 1990. Since that date, U.S. naval groups had been in the area, while the president and his foreign allies condemned Iraq's dictator, Saddam Hussein. At least officially, this was not yet a war.

"This will not stand, this aggression against Kuwait," Bush declared in August, just before he launched Operation Desert Shield.

Over the ensuing months, Hussein remained defiant. His troops refused to let approximately one thousand Americans in Iraq and Kuwait—and hundreds more from other nations—evacuate. (Some of those hostages were used by Iraqi military personnel as human shields. A handful of them were eventually freed when Muhammad Ali, the famous boxer, met with Hussein in Baghdad. Hussein said he released them out of respect for Ali, a hero to many Islamic Arabs.) Hussein also openly boasted about his country's nuclear aspirations.

"We don't underestimate the military might of the United States, but we belittle its evil intentions," Hussein declared to his people during a speech in late November. "If Allah wills that war should take place, the Americans will find that their Stealth plane is seen even by the shepherd in the desert, and is also seen by Iraqi technology."

That same day, the United Nations Security Council voted to impose upon Iraq a January 15 deadline: either Hussein withdrew his troops from Kuwait or the Unites States and its allies would remove them.

Hussein scorned the deadline, declaring to his people and troops via radio broadcast "the mother of all battles is under way." He urged them to prepare for a battle "of justice against vice, of the believer against the infidels." Given the power by Congress, President Bush declared war. Operation Desert Storm had begun and at 7 p.m. EST on January 17, the United States launched air attacks and missile strikes on Iraq and occupied-Kuwait.

"We're using force and we're not going to stop until he pulls out of Kuwait," Bush insisted.

The president quickly backed up his stern words by authorizing the call-up of one million army reservists and national guardsmen and guardswomen. Those potential reinforcements were added to the tens of thousands of men and women already serving in the Persian Gulf.

One of those soldiers already stationed in Saudi Arabia was Conway Bailey. That October, Bailey left his post as deputy warden at the Jessup Correctional Institution in Maryland to return to active duty as a member of the 260th Armored Division, Army Reserve Unit of Baltimore. A chief warrant officer, Bailey's platoon supplied ammunition to military units throughout Saudi Arabia.

Age forty-four, Bailey had already served two tours in Vietnam a decade and a half earlier.

"I was a lot more frightened [in Saudi Arabia]," he recalled. "I kept comparing Saudi with Vietnam. I kept expecting things to happen that didn't. In Vietnam, the danger was real. In Saudi Arabia and Iraq, it was more imagined. You sat around and wondered what could happen."

Conway Bailey wasn't the only member of his family who sat around wondering what *could* happen. In his hometown of Baltimore, Conway's daughter, Conya, and his ex-wife, Thelma, also feared the worst. And in Buffalo—while he practiced, studied, and watched film to prepare for the biggest game of his life—Conway's eldest son, Carlton Bailey, prayed for his father's safety.

"I knew that things were happening, and I may not ever see him again, and the love that I had for my dad was going to be gone," Carlton said years later.

Although Carlton's parents divorced when he was in high school, Conway stayed a part of his son's life. He guided and mentored his son in addition to rooting him on during football games, first at Baltimore's Woodlawn High School, then at the University of North Carolina.

"He was always supportive, always a positive type person," Bailey said about his father.

Despite playing most of his collegiate career as a nose tackle, Bailey possessed great speed and agility; in addition to football, he had been a hurdles champion in high school. A ninth-round draft choice of the Bills in 1988, Bailey cracked the team's starting lineup two seasons later, at the same time his father was called back into military service.

"It's kind of hard not to think about it when one of your loved ones is over there," Bailey said the week of the AFC Championship Game. "It's real hard. But in the latest letter I received from my father, about two weeks ago, he said, 'Do the best you can and don't worry about me.' He said to take care of things here and get to the Super Bowl, and he'll take care of things there."

To get to the Super Bowl, Bailey and the Bills would have to defeat the Los Angeles Raiders. During the Bills' weeklong preparations for the Raiders—whose high-powered running game featured not one, but two, former Heisman Trophy–winning running backs, Marcus Allen and Bo Jackson—Carlton Bailey did his best to follow his father's orders.

"He hasn't missed a beat, he hasn't missed a call, he hasn't missed a down," Darryl Talley said of his defensive teammate. "So that shows he's concentrating exactly on what he has to do. That takes discipline—a whole lot of discipline."

"In one of the letters I wrote to him, I said that, hopefully, when I'm on the field, I can make a big play not only for the team or myself, but for him," Bailey told a reporter that week. "Whether we win or not, I'm going to put forth the extra, extra effort. And that way, when he's reading a newspaper article about our game, he can be that much more proud."

While Bailey—and teammates Eddie Fuller (stepfather), John Hagy (nephew), Keith McKeller (father-in-law), and Scott Norwood (brother-in-law), who also had relatives serving in the Persian Gulf—tried to focus on football, the Bills' front office prepared for the biggest sporting event in the history of western New York.

Not only had the Bills franchise never reached a Super Bowl, virtually no member of the front office had, either. Among the team's key decision makers, only head coach Marv Levy and his two top assistants, coordinators Ted Marchibroda and Walt Corey, ever participated in the Super Bowl. (Despite eighty-eight combined years of professional football, Levy and Marchibroda each had just one Super Bowl experience, in 1973 as assistant coaches for the Washington Redskins; Corey was a reserve linebacker for the 1966 Chiefs but did participate in Super Bowl I.) Not one member of the Buffalo roster had ever reached the Super Bowl.

By contrast Al Davis' Raiders—victors in three of the previous fourteen Super Bowls—assembled a squad filled with championship game heroes. Future Hall of Fame defensive end Howie Long and Super Bowl XVIII MVP Marcus Allen starred for Los Angeles. Even journeyman starter Jay Schroeder had taken a few significant snaps (subbing briefly for injured quarterback Doug Williams) as the Washington Redskins backup quarterback in Super Bowl XXII.

More pressing than the Raiders overwhelming edge in experience was the welfare of Buffalo's defense.

Aside from a marginal effort during the second half of the Giants' victory, the Bills offense had been spectacular all season, even without Jim Kelly. In two matchups with Miami—the only meaningful games the Bills played during the previous month—Buffalo totaled sixty-eight points and 922 yards against a defense that finished second in the AFC. Given that they were averaging more points per game (26.8) than any other NFL team, the Bills expected a tremendous offensive output each week.

Buffalo's defense had been comparably steady all season. But the unit anchored by all-pro Bruce Smith and a trio of outstanding linebackers, Shane Conlan, Cornelius Bennett, and Darryl Talley, faltered in the playoff rematch with Miami. Dan Marino torched the Bills for 322 yards and three touchdowns.

Familiar Buffalo weather—wind and cold rain freezing into snow—contributed to defensive woes. The AstroTurf at Rich Stadium became very slippery and, as one reporter noted, "was more suitable for skiing than football."

"It was horrible," said Bruce Smith, who the Dolphins frequently occupied with two, sometimes, three blockers. "We couldn't pass rush. We couldn't turn the corner."

With a similarly miserable forecast for the AFC Championship Game, Smith and the Bills would again be tested. Although they defeated the Raiders in Week Five, a twenty-four-point fourth quarter was needed to do so. And in that 38-24 win, the Raiders actually outgained the Bills in both rushing and passing yards; disturbing statistics given that dynamic runner Bo Jackson did not even suit up. That week, Jackson was hitting cleanup and playing left field for the Kansas City Royals.*

On game day, an entirely different set of concerns permeated the locker room, the city, and the entire nation. Again, war pushed football onto the back burner.

Iraqi forces launched Scuds—long-range, surface-to-surface missiles—at Israel and Saudi Arabia on Friday, then resumed their attacks late Saturday evening. At least seventeen were reported injured in Tel Aviv and Haifa. The United States struck back, with its own new weapon: the Patriot missile, a seventeen-foot-long, twenty-one-hundred-pound surface-to-air missile that soared three times the speed of sound. In its first-ever combat test, the Patriot was used to intercept airborne Scuds.

---

*Jackson injured his hip the week prior to the AFC Championship Game and would never play professional football again. However, the extent of his injury was not immediately known. Raiders head coach Art Shell said two days before the game, "He's doubtful, but you never know. If I think he can go, he'll go." Sunday morning, he was expected to dress. He did not. Regardless, another installment of his "Bo Knows" Nike campaign advertisements ran twice during the television broadcast.

Following Iraq's strike on Friday, Israel accepted the use of American technicians—they had preferred to employ their own technicians—along with two additional batteries of Patriots. Another battery was positioned in central Saudi Arabia.

"We're going to have to go in [Iraq and occupied Kuwait] and chase them out," said twenty-four-year-old Sergeant John Marion of Carthage, North Carolina. "It's real scary. It's going to be the unknown."

Days before this escalation of warfare, the executive offices of New York State's Erie County began preparations for an enormous rally to celebrate the Bills and rile up Buffalo's rabid supporters. It had been scheduled to take place on January 18, the Friday before the championship game against Los Angeles. More than seven thousand people were expected to attend. The County Office Building Plaza was to be strewn with red and blue decorations, and police planned to close off Franklin Street so fans could chant and cheer when the players arrived.

But two days before the rally, it was canceled. Instead, a noon prayer service took place at St. Paul's Cathedral, a block away from where the exuberant party was supposed to be staged.

"There is a time and a place to celebrate," Buffalo's deputy mayor, Sam Iraci, announced. "And a time and a place to reflect. This is a time to pray for the people over there, rather than celebrating for ourselves. We'll have time to celebrate."

Bills General Manager Bill Polian and two injured players attended while the rest of the team was at practice. "Once the game starts, I'm sure it's going to be just as rowdy as ever," said sidelined wide receiver Don Beebe. "When they get back home, I'm sure it's going to be back to thinking about the war and the Middle East."

The thought of tens of thousands of "rowdy" fans preoccupied with anything—especially a football game—other than the war bothered some Americans. Many citizens preferred that the playoffs be postponed indefinitely.

"I can't even believe they're going to have the game this weekend," said a spokesman for Erie County Executive Dennis Gorski, the man whose office planned, then canceled the Bills' pep rally. "It's good for morale, but . . . it's too fresh."

Throughout the entire week, NFL Commissioner Paul Tagliabue listened to debates on the issue and sought input from each of the league's owners and NBA Commissioner David Stern. The White House also weighed in.

"Our attitude is that the business of the nation has to continue and should continue, and we are conducting this war with a high degree of public support," Press Secretary Marlin Fitzwater stated. "We don't see any need why people should disrupt their lives any more than necessary. The President's attitude is that the games should go on."

Even if it didn't quite fit his job profile, Bush's secretary of Housing and Urban Development took to serving as an informal liaison between Tagliabue and the White House. As a six-term member of the U.S. House of Representatives, Jack Kemp had been a faithful public servant to New York's thirty-first, thirty-eighth, and thirty-ninth districts. He was also the only man to ever quarterback the Buffalo Bills to a championship.

Kemp played seven of his twelve professional seasons in a Bills uniform, and won both the regular-season and championship game MVP in 1965. That year, Buffalo won a second consecutive AFL title, defeating Sid Gillman's San Diego Chargers. (Each of Buffalo's championship-game victories came against San Diego and Gillman, who cut Kemp in the middle of the 1962 season because he believed that the Chargers "could not win consistently with Jack.")

The seven-time all-star retired from football in 1969, the AFL's final season, and transitioned into politics. After twenty-eight years as a congressman, he joined President Bush's cabinet in 1989.

With Kemp's assurances from the "highest levels of the Defense Department," Tagliabue elected to proceed with the championship games.

"We can't be paralyzed as a nation for the situation," he announced, "and can't act out of fear. We have to maintain appropriate respect for the situation, and keep appropriate proportion. So we've decided to play the games, but we're going to follow events right up until the kickoffs. There could be a change at any moment."

Just after 1 p.m. EST, the Bills sprinted out of the tunnel and onto the Rich Stadium turf. The crowd of 80,324 erupted as the starting offense lineup was announced over the public address system. And for all those who felt conflicted about cheering, arguing, and pleading over a trivial sporting event in times of war, the game was not a contest for long.

On his sore knee, Jim Kelly jogged onto the field, through blustering forty-mile-per-hour winds. Running the no-huddle, Kelly breezed into the Los Angeles red zone. In less than two minutes, Buffalo gained fifty-five yards on five plays. The bewildered Raiders defense needed a time-out.

"I really think they weren't prepared for it," Thomas said about K-Gun. "We've been running it for a long time now, and you would think the (Raiders) coaches would know that's what got us this far and would prepare for it. But it seemed they didn't prepare for it until we got down there deep in their territory when they called the timeout."

The time-out did not cool off Buffalo's torrid start. Within four plays, a catch-and-run by James Lofton gave the Bills a seven-point advantage.

The Bills appeared incapable of making a mistake. At the start of Lofton's touchdown play, Kelly dropped the shotgun snap—which was nearly recovered by a Raiders defensive lineman—picked up the ball, whirled around, and rolled to his right, where he spotted an open Lofton at the Raiders' seven-yard line.

"First I thought I'd just fall on the ball," Kelly said afterwards, "but then I decided that the line had given me such good protection I'd try to do something. I found James free on a break and tossed him the ball."

Ahead 7-0, Bills kicker Scott Norwood toed the ball downfield to Raiders return man Jaime Holland. Holland raced upfield, escaped the grasp of a Bills defender, then was clobbered and pinned to the ground by Carlton Bailey at the nineteen-yard line.

"I was going to do whatever it took—sacrifice my body, knocking myself out—to put the extra edge in there for my pops," said Bailey.

Surprisingly, the Raiders—a run-oriented team—countered with back-to-back passes and on just two plays charged into Buffalo territory. The Bills defense settled in and did not allow another first down on the drive and forced the Raiders to attempt a forty-one-yard field goal.

"This is going to be a great game, Dick," color analyst Bill Walsh told the audience and his partner, Dick Enberg, during NBC Sports' television broadcast. "These teams are really playing well, but they're opening up everything, throwing that ball."

Walsh may have chiseled Joe Montana, Jerry Rice, and a handful of other raw players into Hall of Famers during his tenure as architect of the 1980s San Francisco 49ers dynasty, but he was dead wrong that afternoon. Once Jaeger's field goal sailed through the upright, *that* was the extent of Los Angeles' scoring.

The K-Gun needed just five plays on the ensuing drive to put another touchdown on the scoreboard. The Bills defense then matched Kelly's score with one of their own. Linebacker Darryl Talley stepped in front of a Schroeder pass and charged into the end zone for a twenty-seven-yard touchdown return. Still in the first quarter, Buffalo led 21-3.

"I don't think they knew what hit 'em from the opening bell. We knew that if we won that game, we're going to the Super Bowl," Talley recalled years later. "And I was just somewhere different that day, I guess. Cornelius [Bennett] came up to me on the sideline and he says 'I've seen you play before, but I ain't never seen you do the things you're doing today on the field. What's going on, I ain't never seen you play like this.'

"'This is a chance to go to the Super Bowl. Don't you understand what's on the line here. . . . I've got my one chance to go and I've got to do everything I can think of to get there.'"

Talley did do everything: he finished with four tackles, two interceptions, and spent the rest of the afternoon charging up the Bills' sideline.

"I was on everybody, yelling at everybody, shouting 'Come on! Let's go! Let's go! We gotta do this!' And we never let up."

The second quarter proved just as rich for Buffalo, and just as harrowing for the Raiders. A short touchdown run by Kenneth Davis, Thomas' backup, increased the Bills' lead to twenty-four points. And when Kelly threaded a pass downfield through double coverage to Steve Tasker, setting up a first and goal, the game was officially a blowout.

Bills fans at Rich Stadium could now relish every moment of the decades-overdue victory. But for millions of television viewers across the nation, Buffalo's championship coronation was abruptly halted.

"We understand there are some important developments in the Gulf crisis," Dick Enberg told the audience. "We go to NBC News and Garrick Utley."

"Yes Dick," said Utley, "We're going right to Saudi Arabia, there appears to have been a missile attack against the big base there. We're going to [Saudi Arabia] to get the situation."

The screen cut to a fairly young, handsome man standing on a rooftop at night, shouting out orders to a camera crew.

"Get us up in audio," he said, waving his arm up and down.

"Please, get us up," he repeated, pointing to someone offscreen.

The reporter readjusted a tiny microphone attached to his vest.

"Hello, New York, this is Saudi Arabia. This is not a drill," he said as he shot a look off into the pitch-black horizon.

"Hello, New York, this is Saudi Arabia. This is not a drill," he repeated. Now he waved a gas mask in front of the camera.

The man was Arthur Kent, a thirty-seven-year-old Canadian-born television journalist. During the ensuing weeks, Kent's name, and the powerful image of him standing on that hotel rooftop would become inextricably linked to the Persian Gulf War.

"We're firing Patriots. We've got flares and we've got sirens.

"Let's go, focus," he shouted.

A harried Kent turned back into the night, then frenziedly recoiled and ducked.

"There goes a Patriot. Let's go!"

"Arthur Kent, you are now live from Saudi Arabia, tell us what has happened" said Utley. The scene viewers had just watched was taped footage from a few minutes earlier.

There was no update from Kent.

"We apparently do not have audio, from Arthur Kent," said Utley, only adding to the hectic drama. "But just to recap quickly, a few minutes ago, a number of Patriot missiles—those are the U.S. antimissile missiles—were fired from the big base there in Saudi Arabia—apparently, against incoming missiles from Iraq. We will bring you further details as soon as we get them from Arthur Kent on the scene there. Now back to the game and Dick Enberg."

"Boy, Garrick, that's sobering news from the Middle East," said Enberg, resuming the live action from Orchard Park, New York. "Boy, the perspective changes so dramatically when we get the real important news of this day."

During the newsbreak, Kenneth Davis scored his second rushing touchdown in less than six minutes. Buffalo now led by the absurd score of 34-3, barely a quarter-and-a-half into the game. Cornerback Nate Odomes then picked off Jay Schroeder on the Raiders' following offensive snap. Kelly's K-Gun soon scored their fifth touchdown, thanks to another Los Angeles turnover gift.

"The Buffalo Bills and their fans can start thinking seriously about Super Bowl XXV. But we have other, more serious thoughts, as we have another NBC News report coming up shortly," said Enberg, during a brief Thurman Thomas rush. "So we'll leave Rich Stadium in Buffalo. We turn you now to NBC News and Garrick Utley."

Utley handed off the scene to Saudi Arabia: Kent's audio had been connected.

Garrick, very suddenly, we heard the loud boom, the report of the firing of a Patriot antimissile missile. Suddenly flares were flying, sirens started to sound, and we realized that we were under the most intense air-raid warning that we have witnessed since the beginning of Operation Desert Storm. You'll remember that three nights ago, an incoming Iraqi long-range missile—thought to be a Scud or an improved Scud missile was intercepted and destroyed just about seventeen thousand feet above our position here by one of those Patriot missiles. Tonight, we've seen four separate launchings.

With sirens blaring in the background, Kent continued to narrate the action.

"What will be happening now is that on the air base and here at our location in this hotel, people will be heading for the shelters. They will be on maximum, MOP-alert, which means they will be donning their chemical warfare protective suits and clothing, which we're keeping close at hand here. But we would remind you that we have decided, as we have in past, that we will continue broadcasting to you through these attacks."

"Well Arthur, tell us, the people going into the bunker, are they being told to do so by the military and, if so, should you be going now? " Utley asked.

"In all likelihood, Garrick" responded Kent, "that would be a wise course of action if we were not concerned with making sure that we were broadcasting to you. But we've handled this kind of threat before. We're dealing with conventional warheads as we've seen in Israel and those of us here feel we should stay at our post."

"Arthur, Arthur," Utley interrupted. "Thank you very much. Go, go into the bunker with the others. We have your videotape report from earlier on. We'll get back to you and you can come back and report on the latest events there. But go now into the bunker."

Kent and his crew remained atop their hotel roof throughout the evening as the periodic air attacks continued.

The Raiders' defensive woes—they yielded a playoff record 387 yards in the first half—were compounded by complete ineptitude on offense: three punts, three turnovers, and a measly 108 yards of offense (more than half of which came during the Raiders' first two offensive plays).

"We had the kind of day where it seemed we couldn't do anything right," said Schroeder. "It was a heck of a time to have a game like that."

Eventually, the first half came to a merciful end, and both teams headed toward the locker room.

"With an insurmountable lead of 41-3," NBC's Bob Costas told his viewing audience, "they are thirty minutes of football from the Super Bowl."

Any halftime interpretations of the first-half action by NBC's studio analysts—Paul Maguire and Will McDonough joined Costas in the New York studio—was completely unnecessary. Instead, the millions watching the game at home listened more intently to additional updates from Kent live in Saudi Arabia, a taped interview with the commander of the Allied Forces, General Norman Schwarzkopf, and a detailed report from the Pentagon by NBC News' Fred Francis. It was easy for viewers to forget that an entire half of football remained.

The Bills outscored Los Angeles 10-0 once the third period began and sent the Raiders back to warm and sunny California with the most lopsided playoff defeat since the AFL-NFL merger in 1970. The 51-3 drubbing was a true team effort: the offense scored seven times; the defense scored seven turnovers. And in the most prominent, most crushing triumph in Buffalo Bills history, Carlton Bailey paced the team with seven tackles, most of them on special teams.

"They told me the game was being televised over in Saudi Arabia," said Bailey, "and hopefully, [my father] had an opportunity to watch the game. Hopefully, I made him proud."

4

A Young Man's Game

When you've got a young kid on that sideline who's hungry and trying to play, you keep him off the field, whatever it takes because if you come out you'll be on the bench.

—*Running back Willard Harrell's advice to St. Louis Cardinal teammate Ottis Anderson, circa 1981*

For more than a decade, Ottis Anderson never needed to look over his shoulder, at his team's sideline, and worry about some young kid taking his job. At Forest Hill High School in West Palm Beach, he was among the finest running backs in the state of Florida. The University of Miami offered a scholarship to the eighteen-year-old raised an hour south of the Coral Gables campus. During Anderson's first preseason, head coach Carl Selmer promoted him to the varsity. By late September, the true freshman was carrying the ball during critical fourth-quarter snaps of the Hurricanes' near-upset of the top-ranked, reigning, and eventual repeat, national champion Oklahoma Sooners. Two months later, he totaled 148 rushing and receiving yards against Notre Dame.

As a sophomore for the floundering Hurricanes program, Anderson became the offense's centerpiece, as his 213 carries set a new school record. He finished just thirty-three yards shy of Miami's single-season rushing mark.

Given the prowess he had during the mid-1970s—and the powerful build with sprinter's speed—Ottis Jerome Anderson was appropriately dubbed "O.

J." And in the middle of his Miami career, the nickname became more than just homage to Orenthal James "O. J." Simpson, the Heisman Trophy–winning superstar. By his junior season, Anderson was running the same plays as the great Buffalo Bills rusher.

Consecutive 3-8 seasons prompted the Hurricanes' athletics department to dismiss Carl Selmer after the 1976 season and hire former Bills head coach Lou Saban. Apart from winning consecutive AFL titles, Saban presided over the team while Simpson rewrote professional football's record books. Simpson never rushed for one thousand yards under any other head coach.*

"I hope he runs the same things he did at Buffalo with O. J. Simpson," Anderson said upon Saban's hire.

Saban coaxed Simpson-like statistics during Anderson's senior season: 1,266 yards and a 5.7 yards-per-carry average. Despite a one-sided attack— the passing game was so dreadful that eighteen-year-old freshman Jim Kelly nearly won the quarterback job—Anderson became one of the nation's top runners and set the school's career yardage figure.

The historic résumé (he remains Miami's all-time leader in rushing yards and attempts) along with his size and speed enticed pro suitors. In the 1979 NFL draft, St. Louis chose Anderson with their first-round selection.

"He shows up to that first minicamp, and I think like all of my teammates, my first impression was, 'Wow, this guy is a lot bigger than I thought he was going to be,'" Cardinals Hall of Fame lineman Dan Dierdorf recalled. "The thing of it was that he just had such deceptive speed. . . . I can't begin to tell you how many yards he got by bouncing it to the outside and breaking containment on a defense because they thought they took the proper angle to tackle him. And he would beat them to the corner because he was just so much faster than he looked. He constantly made defensive guys look bad."

The Cardinals were fortunate that Anderson was still available when they selected eighth. Picking one spot earlier was the Giants, a team desperately needing a running back. New Yorkers responded with "booing, hissing, cursing and fist-waving" when newly hired general manager George Young shocked everyone by selecting a quarterback from Morehead State, Phil Simms.

---

*In 1976, Saban resigned as head coach of the Bills after five games; Jim Ringo replaced Saban and Simpson won his fourth rushing and final rushing title at the end of that season.

St. Louis fans, however, were delighted to have Anderson. As a rookie, he tallied nine one-hundred-yard games, including a dominant late-season performance in the team's 29-20 victory over the team that passed on him in May's draft.

"He's a great running back," Giants head coach Ray Perkins said after Anderson's twenty-nine carries, 140 yards, and two touchdowns. "He might go down as the greatest there's ever been."

Anderson finished 1979 with 1,605 yards rushing (a record for first-year backs), earned the Associated Press' Rookie of the Year Award, and first-team all-pro honors. Despite another disappointing team season for the 5-11 Cardinals, Anderson's presence energized his teammates.

"I'd like to thank O. J. Anderson for making football fun again," all-pro offensive lineman Bob Young said at a postseason banquet.

Fun continued over the next five years. He rushed for more than eleven hundred yards in all but one season (the strike-shortened 1982 campaign) and soon reached eleventh on the all-time leading-rusher list.

But 1985 was a disaster for both Anderson and the Cardinals. A 3-1 record to open the season inspired hope within the players, the organization, and dejected St. Louis fans. Foot and calf injuries to their star back contributed to a 2-10 finish. An aching Anderson played in only three games during the team's downward spiral.

Achieving only one playoff berth during the previous decade prompted a change in leadership, and management brought in Dallas Cowboys assistant Gene Stallings to redirect their fortunes. Toward the end of the 1985 season, Stump Mitchell performed well in Anderson's place. Stallings recognized the value of an offense featuring Mitchell, the smaller, quicker runner, and the powerful workhorse Anderson, and split the carries between both backs. Not pleased with a reduced role, Anderson lashed out toward the end of the 1986 season opener. Stallings used Mitchell exclusively at the end of a 16-10 loss to the Rams, sparking a heated sideline argument. Anderson demanded to be traded.

St. Louis shipped Anderson—the franchise's twenty-nine-year-old all-time leading rusher—to the New York Giants for a pair of draft picks. And although he went on to score a touchdown in Super Bowl XXI, 1986 was largely uneventful for Anderson: thirty-one carries for eighty-seven yards during his fourteen regular and postseason games.

He contributed even less (two rushing attempts despite not missing games due to injury) the next season before his role increased a bit in 1988. That December he helped to end the playoff hopes of his former team—now the Phoenix Cardinals—and old boss Gene Stallings, scoring three second-half touchdowns in a late-season game at the Meadowlands.

Still, the team's feature back, Joe Morris, carried the ball over three hundred times that season, far more than Anderson's sixty-five rushes. The Giants allowed Anderson's contract to expire the following spring and added two running backs—Lewis Tillman and Dave Meggett—in April's draft. New York eventually signed Anderson to a deal (a considerable pay cut) later that summer. He was a long shot to make the roster: thirty-two-year-old running backs don't usually survive training camps.

"Every year, people say you're 30-something and you've been in the league X amount of years. They start writing you off. I don't think I'm old. I think the media feels that if you've been in the league five years you're good and if you're under 30, good. Once you're over 30, they think you're over the hill. It's supposed to be a young man's game."

But Joe Morris broke his ankle in the team's final preseason game and Anderson set out to prove that he could carry the load. During his first start in three seasons, Anderson gained ninety-three yards on twenty-three carries and scored a critical fourth-quarter touchdown in the Giants' win. He remained healthy and a career-high fourteen touchdowns helped New York win the NFC East title. Another milestone meant more to Anderson than any previous achievement.

"This was my sweetest 1,000-yard season. It happened so late in my career. Nobody felt I had anything left. Nobody claimed me. Nobody thought I was worth the risk," he said. "Nobody believed that Ottis Anderson could help the Giants win."

Despite 120 yards and a touchdown, Anderson couldn't help the Giants defeat the Rams in the first round of the playoffs, and for a second straight off-season, New York did not protect Anderson from free agency. Again, the Giants drafted his replacement that April, this time with their first-round selection. Big, quick, and durable, Georgia Bulldog Rodney Hampton resembled Anderson in every way, except that he was twelve years younger.

"I don't think anybody is interested in me," Anderson said about his prospects of playing in 1990. "My financial planner called a few teams: Kansas

City, Seattle, Miami, Phoenix. They said, yeah, he had a good year. That's as far as they went."

The Giants extended a one-year deal, which he accepted. And while the Giants' trio of young backs (Hampton, Meggett, and Tillman) waited hungrily on the sidelines, week after week, Anderson managed to keep them there—until December.

During the comeback victory over Minnesota—the day that began with Parcells' dislodged kidney stones and ended with Lawrence Taylor's "one man show"—Anderson recorded both touchdowns in the 23-15 win. In addition to the go-ahead score, he even grabbed a piece of history in the fourth quarter, becoming just the eighth man in league history to surpass ten thousand career rushing yards.

But Anderson finished the game with twenty-six yards on fifteen carries, an increasingly typical stat line for him that season. Rodney Hampton, not Anderson, had served as the workhorse that day, carrying the ball nineteen times for seventy-eight yards. Trailing 20-15 midway through the fourth quarter, the Giants relied on their big rookie. Hampton ran the ball on five of eight plays (including an eleven-yard gain that netted a vital first down) during the go-ahead touchdown drive.

"The passing of the torch may have been consummated yesterday," a *Newsday* writer stated the next day. "While Anderson has shown some signs of weary legs in recent weeks, Hampton appears ready to assume the role as the Giants' feature back."

Hampton followed up that "breakout" game with another in the loss to Buffalo. (His forty-one-yard run in the game's opening minutes set up New York's only touchdown.) Still Hampton did little to mask the Giants' offensive deficiencies; deficiencies largely caused by their starting quarterback's absence. With Simms sidelined due to his foot injury, the Giants failed repeatedly on short-yardage situations. Twice the Bills stuffed Anderson on third and short, the most critical coming late in the third period as the Giants, trailing 14-10, were on Buffalo's three-yard line.

"Continued trust needs to be placed in rookie running back Rodney Hampton, who has taken the reins from a tired Anderson. Hampton is going to be the guy for the playoffs," a New York columnist insisted. "Use Hampton in short-yardage situations as a complement to Anderson. Hampton's speed often will mean the difference between a first down and a punt.

If Anderson can't push the pile any more, the Giants must try something else."

In Jeff Hostetler's debut the next week against the 5-9 Cardinals, the Giants began trying something else. Fullback Maurice Carthon led the team with sixty-seven yards rushing, while Rodney Hampton and Hostetler combined for an additional eighty. Anderson's contribution was minimal: four carries for sixteen yards.

That day, New York had its most productive rushing effort of the season, which allowed Hostetler to settle in at quarterback. The de facto starter scrambled for a touchdown and tossed for another to give the Giants a 24-14 fourth-quarter lead.

Although they surrendered three touchdown passes in the second half, New York hung on to defeat the lowly Cardinals 24-21, earning the NFC's second seed. Having locked up a first-round playoff bye, the Giants did not sit their stars in the Week Seventeen finale against New England. For a team that had lost three of the previous five games—and surrendered 381 passing yards to Phoenix, the NFL's worst passing offense—they needed to play, not rest. And heading into the postseason with an unproved quarterback, every game-time snap would be vital.

"The more time I have to do it, the better it will go," said Hostetler. "The timing is going to improve. I'm going to get better throwing to the right place at the right time. The more reps I get the better it's going to be."

"Two weeks from now," Parcells said, "Jeff will be better able to play than now. Hopefully by (playoff) time, things will change for the better from a physical, psychological and performance standpoint."

On a drizzling final Sunday of the regular season, the Giants defeated New England 13-10. A three-point win over the 1-14 Patriots—losers of thirteen consecutive games—failed to excite the demanding New York fans and media. But at 13-3, with a bye during Wild-Card Weekend and a home game to follow, the Giants had survived a horrible December. And once the postseason arrived, they showcased the excellence that fashioned a magnificent 10-0 start.

The Giants drew Chicago in the second round of the postseason. Similar to their opponent, the Bears had fallen fast and hard after a fantastic start to the

1990 season. Mike Ditka's team began 9-1, only to lose four of their remaining six games. And despite their 16-6 wild-card triumph over New Orleans in the next round of the playoffs, they were no match for the Giants.

Bill Parcells and offensive coordinator Ron Erhardt showed faith in Hostetler from the very beginning. New York's opening possession came with the Giants pinned deep inside their own territory. Rather than play it safe and run the ball on first down, the Giants threw.

"That was a real confidence booster," Hostetler said. "That's not the easiest place to throw from."

Hostetler passed on first down six times in the first quarter alone, a whopping number for the run-dedicated head coach. Ahead 3-0, Parcells even shunned a forty-three-yard field goal attempt to throw on fourth down and inches to go: Hostetler rolled right and completed a six-yard pass to tight end Bob Mrosko. On the next play, Stephen Baker hauled in a perfectly placed, over-the-shoulder pass at the back-left corner of the end zone to give the Giants a 10-0 lead.

"All day, the play-calling, I felt, showed confidence in me," Hostetler said.

Confidence in the defense also soared after a critical fourth down and short early in the second quarter.

The Bears finished the 1990 season averaging 152 rushing yards per game, second in the NFL. Neal Anderson—the heir-apparent to Walter Payton—spearheaded the attack, posting his third consecutive 1,000-yard season. To defend Chicago, assistant coach Bill Belichick made the bold switch from their standard 3-4 defense to a 4-3 approach.

"Hopefully, it would give the Bears the most trouble," said the team's thirty-year-old defensive coordinator. "It wasn't that big an adjustment for our guys. Nobody played a position they hadn't been at sometime during the year. But the combination was a different look for the offense with Lawrence Taylor and Carl Banks as true outside linebackers."

The change was brilliant. Spurred on by a momentous fourth-down goal-line stand at the one-yard line, the Giants suffocated Chicago's offense.

"They forced us to a passing game," Ditka lamented. "And I don't like to play that kind of game."

Ill-equipped to be one-dimensional, Chicago's offense attempted thirty-six passes, gaining just 205 yards. The new-look Giants defense forced three turnovers, did not allow a single rushing first down, and kept the Bears out of the end zone the entire afternoon.

Meanwhile, New York's offense was efficient, if not spectacular, against the aging Bears. With under a minute remaining in the second quarter, Hostetler sprinted out of the pocket and flicked a five-yard touchdown pass to tight end Howard Cross, extending the lead to 17-3. In the second half, touchdown runs by Hostetler and Maurice Carthon built an insurmountable 31-3 advantage.

New York rushed for 194 yards, controlled the ball for thirty-eight minutes and converted all four of their fourth-down attempts, all the while gradually restoring faith to the quarterback position.

"We're very predictable around here," Parcells facetiously remarked in the locker room. "Today, I think you would have to say we were a little less predictable. We were still very predictable but we were a little less predictable today."

The lone objective that the Giants did not achieve against Chicago was to stay healthy.

In the second quarter, New York ran another surprising first-down pass play. Defensive tackle Steve McMichael sacked Hostetler, who fumbled. Rodney Hampton recovered the ball and picked up three yards before two Bears defenders pounced on him, shattering his left fibula.

"My leg felt numb after the play," the rookie said. "I stayed in for the next play, but it still felt numb, and I couldn't run my pass pattern."

As Hampton hobbled off the Meadowlands field, Ottis Anderson jogged past him and into the Giants' huddle.

With his production reducing each week—simultaneous to Hampton's late-season surge—Anderson wasn't entirely dressed for the role of feature back. He mistakenly wore his practice pants instead of the team-issued game pair against Chicago. (Because the Giants won, Bill Parcells insisted Anderson wear practice pants on game day for the duration of the postseason.)

"Ottis thought he wouldn't play much right before the game," Maurice Carthon said. "I told him, 'You'll get a lot of work.' Now, he thinks I'm psychic."

In Hampton's place, Anderson totaled eighty yards on twenty-one attempts and added a six-yard reception. He touched the ball twenty-two times, nearly one-third of the Giants' total play count. And it was his goal-line block—of enormous William "The Refrigerator" Perry—that sprung Hostetler for New York's third touchdown.

Anderson became the second-oldest back in NFL history to post more than seventy-five yards rushing in a playoff game.

"I ain't throwing no Gatorade," Anderson told a teammate who asked for his help in a postgame showering of Bill Parcells. "I'm too tired to throw Gatorade."

The franchise's first playoff win since Super Bowl XXI set up an NFC Championship Game showdown with the 49ers. At 14-2, San Francisco owned the best record in the NFL and had earned the number-one seed in the NFC, a reward for defeating the Giants 7-3 in early December.

The Giants and 49ers were similar in many ways. Parcells and San Francisco's George Seifert had each earned exactly one Super Bowl ring as a head coach. And both men had worked their way up through the organization, from position coach, to defensive coordinator, and finally to head coach. Although Parcells' sideline and postgame press conference demeanor was the antithesis of the subdued Seifert, they both craved defensive excellence. As a result, Parcells' Giants and Seifert's 49ers were among the best in the league, two of the best units in the modern era. Twelve of the twenty-two starting Giants and 49ers defenders were once or future Pro Bowlers. The two teams even finished the 1990 season with unusually similar statistics: 4.6 yards allowed per play, and only five first downs and three turnovers separated that year's totals.

Offense—and specifically the decorations with which offensive personnel were adorned—made for the lone disparity between the two teams.

Forty-niners quarterback Joe Montana won his second consecutive MVP Award in 1990. In three of the four Super Bowl titles that San Francisco won during the decade, Montana was named the game's Most Valuable Player. Ironically, the one Super Bowl victory in which he did not receive the trophy was arguably the greatest performance of his career. He passed for a record 357 yards and two touchdowns, the second of which completed a 92-yard drive in the final minutes of a 20-16 victory over Cincinnati.

Instead of Montana, the MVP for that Super Bowl XXIII triumph went to wide receiver Jerry Rice. The finest pass catcher of his or, perhaps, any era, Rice set a new personal record in 1990 with one hundred receptions. After six seasons, the twenty-eight-year-old was already halfway past breaking every receiving record in league history.

Although the "Montana-to-Rice" mantra became etched in pro football history throughout the second half of the 1980s, San Francisco's run at an unprecedented three consecutive Super Bowl titles (the popularly labeled "three-peat") was fueled by a roster of all-stars. Versatile running back Roger Craig along with prototypical fullback Tom Rathman comprised a phenomenal backfield. John Taylor and Brent Jones, one of the league's premier tight ends, gave the 49er passing game several weapons to complement Rice. And with the same five players starting every game that season, the San Francisco offensive line was among the most consistent and productive in the NFL.

Even with a healthy Simms and a healthy Hampton, the Giants scored only a field goal in the regular-season loss to San Francisco. A month later, the 49ers still possessed the same talent, while the Giants offense now featured second-stringers at quarterback and running back. Few gave New York much of a chance.

"People talk about Hostetler; how he's a seven-year veteran. Yeah, but he's a seven-year backup quarterback," said John Madden, the Super Bowl winning coach who, along with Pat Summerall, would broadcast the NFC Championship Game for CBS.

> How will he respond on the road in a hostile environment? His sense of poise and running ability has to be of concern to (49ers coach) George Seifert. But can he have back-to-back great games? It will be tough. . . . He did well against Chicago because he was kind of an unknown. But after last week, the 49ers have more film. The 49ers will be practicing all week to prepare for him. For the Giants to win, Hostetler has to play the greatest game of his life. And it's going to be much, much more difficult this week.

By game day, San Francisco was an eight-point favorite. But the veteran Giants paid little attention to the prognosticators. They had already proven once in 1990 that they could match up well with their prolific opponent: holding Montana's unit to just one score during the December loss marked the lowest output from the famed 49er offense in thirty-five games. And in the only postseason showdown between the two franchises, during the 1986 playoffs, the Giants walloped San Francisco 49-3. (During the rout, a brutal hit by a Giants defensive lineman knocked Joe Montana out of the game.)

The mostly veteran Giants squad didn't need fiery confidence-boosting speeches by their head coach. Bill Parcells delivered one anyway.

"There was just a one-week interval before the Super Bowl," Parcells said in 2010. "I told our team before we went to San Francisco that I wanted them to pack for ten days because we weren't coming home. A lot of players have mentioned that to me over the years that that was a display of confidence that I really believed we could beat San Francisco—even though not many people did."

Forty-niners wide receiver John Taylor had a knack for the big play.

A league suspension sidelined Taylor for the opening four weeks of the 1988 NFL season. But in his first game back, the third-round draft pick out of Delaware State fielded a punt deep in his own territory and sprinted seventy-seven yards for a touchdown. That third-quarter score proved to be the difference in San Francisco's 20-13 victory over Detroit. In November, against the World Champion Washington Redskins, Taylor violated the cardinal rule that forbids fielding a punt inside the ten-yard line. He atoned for the sin, soaring ninety-five yards for an incredible touchdown.

Of course, the most famous moment in Taylor's career came the following January, when he caught Montana's game-winning touchdown pass with thirty-four seconds remaining in Super Bowl XXIII.

A year later, as the bookend receiver to Jerry Rice, he grabbed sixty receptions for 1,077 yards and ten touchdowns. That postseason, Taylor was on the receiving end of a Montana touchdown pass in each of the 49ers' three playoff victories against the Minnesota Vikings, Los Angeles Rams, and Denver Broncos.

But in 1990, no team felt the sting of Taylor's penchant for clutch catches and electrifying runs more than the New York Giants.

The only points allowed by the Giants defense during the Monday night loss to San Francisco in early December came on a twenty-three-yard touchdown strike from Montana to a sliding Taylor.

"I was supposed to be over in the middle area," defensive back Everson Walls said. "When Montana pumped, I got drawn in. He took me out of my area."

Montana had been fooling NFL defensive backs for twelve seasons. But to Everson Walls, Taylor's touchdown was eerily familiar.

Nine seasons earlier, in the same south end zone of Candlestick Park, Montana pump-faked, then hooked up with Dwight Clark for the most famous six-yard touchdown in NFL history: "The Catch" vaulted San Francisco to a win over Dallas in the 1981 NFC Championship Game and, two weeks later, the Super Bowl championship. The Cowboys rookie cornerback over whom Clark snagged that dynasty-forging pass was Everson Walls.

"Each time I play [the 49ers] I think about the play, no doubt about it," Walls said on the Tuesday before the 1990 NFC Championship Game. "Stepping in Candlestick gives me a feeling of intensity and alertness because I never want to be caught in that position again."

A decade after "The Catch," Walls found himself in that position—or, rather, out of position—at another critical moment of an NFC Championship Game played beside San Francisco Bay.

The Giants and 49ers played to a 6-6 tie through the first half of the 1990 NFC title game. Early in the third quarter, New York's Sean Landeta boomed a punt downfield where John Taylor dangerously fielded the kick at his own seven-yard line. Taylor took two steps right, noticed a wall of blockers aligning by the opposite sideline, reversed field, then turned up and gained thirty-two yards. Only Landeta—who forced him out-of-bounds—could prevent the tie-breaking score.

Landeta's "tackle" didn't really matter, however. He simply delayed a Taylor touchdown by one play. On first and ten from his own thirty-nine-yard line, Montana took a five-step drop, scanned the field, and spotted Taylor eighteen yards away, near the sideline. Everson Walls, locked in man-to-man coverage with Taylor, sprinted toward that spot.

"I went for the interception," said Walls. "I got a hand on it, but he got two on it. My break was good. My execution was bad."

Intercepting quarterbacks had made Walls a Pro Bowler. In 1981, the undrafted rookie from Grambling State posted a league-high eleven interceptions. And although he was "posterized" by Montana's pass to Dwight Clark, Walls had played tremendous defense prior to yielding "The Catch." He picked off Montana twice, recovered a fumble, and accounted for eight tackles.

"You can't blame Everson for just one play," Cowboys great Charlie Waters said. "We had double coverage on Clark. It had to be a perfect throw and a perfect catch . . . he just made a spectacular catch."

After nine seasons and forty-four interceptions, Dallas released the home-town veteran. The Giants signed him for the 1990 season. At age thirty, Walls started all sixteen games, scored his first career touchdown on a fumble recovery, and paced the team with six interceptions.

But Walls' attempt to nab Montana's toss in the third quarter of the NFC Championship Game came up short. Taylor caught the ball, spun around, and bolted for the end zone.

"Everson Walls is a gambler, always has been," John Madden said, breaking down the play during the CBS television broadcast. "He goes [for the interception] in front of Taylor, and now the bad thing is when you miss the interception and you go for it in front of him and there's no one behind ya, it's a touchdown."

Walls' heart sank: "I thought, 'Oh [shit.]' I knew he was gone."

Taylor's sixty-one-yard touchdown reception lifted San Francisco to a 13-6 advantage.

"It wasn't the first time that we had had our back against the wall that season," Everson Walls said. "No panic, no change. We had plenty of time left. So even though there was frustration, we were still very poised as a team."

That poise even extended to kicker Matt Bahr, another retread who the Giants scooped up that year when no one else wanted him.

Bahr's career as a professional athlete began in relative obscurity, as a defenseman for the Colorado Caribous of the North American Soccer League. Within eighteen months, however, Bahr was playing in the Super Bowl. He kicked a forty-one-yard field goal and four extra points as the 1979 Pittsburgh Steelers won a fourth championship in six seasons.

Pittsburgh surprisingly cut Bahr prior to the start of the 1981 season, so when San Francisco offered him a temp job (49er Ray Wersching was injured in the opener), he accepted. Within a month, Wersching returned and Bahr was shipped to Cleveland. Upon exiting San Francisco's locker room, he left a note on the bulletin board: "Good luck in the Super Bowl, I know you'll be there."

Not long after leaving that note, Bahr returned to Candlestick. In Week Eleven, the 5-6 Browns traveled to San Francisco, and with forty-three seconds remaining, Bahr nailed the game-winning field goal to defeat the 49ers.

"I can't say enough good things about the 49ers," he said after the win. "I made a lot of friends in my short (four-week) stay here. It's good to come back and say hello."

Bahr did not enjoy the rest of 1981 nearly as much as his former team-mates. The 15-12 victory was Cleveland's last of the season and they finished 5-11; San Francisco won their next eight games, including Super Bowl XVI.

He spent eight more seasons kicking for Cleveland, but by age thirty-four, Bahr was again out of a job. The Browns cut him during the 1990 preseason in favor of a Canadian Football League kicker. Only an injured right groin suffered by Giants kicker Raul Allegre kept Bahr from retirement. Beginning in Week Four, Bahr became an efficient replacement for New York in 1990. He converted seventeen of twenty-three field goal attempts, including one in the final seconds that completed Jeff Hostetler's unexpected comeback against Phoenix. Hostetler—who served as the Giants' holder—found plenty to talk about with the team's new kicker.

Bahr earned a degree in electrical engineering from Penn State: he too followed his older brother, all-American kicker Chris, to State College, Pennsylvania. Relying on consistent accuracy, Matt surpassed each of his brother's school records during three varsity seasons from 1976 through 1978. Among his many Nittany Lion teammates those years were Ron and Doug Hostetler.

"I held for a lot of kickers," Jeff Hostetler later said. "Matt Bahr had, without a doubt, the greatest disposition as far as a kicker, because, lots of them, you can do it a hundred times in a row and hold the ball the same way, but if they miss, it was always, 'you leaned [the ball] too far forward or you leaned it a little this, or you just missed the mark.' Matt Bahr was always 'just get it down.'"

On the chewed-up natural grass of Candlestick Park, Hostetler "got it down," enabling Bahr to convert his third field goal in three attempts during the 1990 NFC Championship Game. The successful forty-six-yarder—six minutes after John Taylor's touchdown—made the score 13-9.

Given the Giants' inability to score touchdowns in more than six quarters against San Francisco that season, to win the conference title, they would likely have to pitch a shutout the rest of the way.

The Giants forced a punt, and after Ottis Anderson gobbled up thirty-six yards to set up a first and ten inside the red zone, momentum had seemed to shift. But the offense failed to gain another yard, and when Bahr hooked a thirty-seven-yard field goal wide left early in the final period, all Bill Parcells could do was seethe in disgust.

Parcells' mood only worsened over the next few minutes. After the Giants made another defensive stop, Hostetler hit wide receiver Mark Ingram on a fourteen-yard square-in route. The first down, which pushed them into San Francisco territory, was costly, however.

To make the crisp throw, Hostetler stepped upfield, straightening his front leg. Just as the ball left his fingertips, 49ers defensive lineman Jim Burt—a former Giant—dove at Hostetler and locked ahold of his knee, twisting him to the ground.

Several members of the Giants' sideline, including Parcells, were outraged and shouted at both Burt and the referees. They thought the hit was both late and a cheap shot.

"That's the way Burt plays," said Lawrence Taylor. "He goes for the knees. So I yelled, 'If that's the way you want to play, somebody else is going to lose a quarterback.'"

Wincing and curled up on his side, Hostetler semi-coherently answered the questions of trainers and the team doctor. He eventually stood up and slowly limped off the field with a hyperextended knee.

For the second time in six weeks, Parcells had to send an unprepared quarterback with minimal game-time experience onto the field during a critical game. Under the Giants' first- and second-string quarterbacks, points had come sparingly that year against San Francisco; thirteen-year veteran Matt Cavanaugh couldn't move the ball either. Coming off the sidelines with only seconds to warm up, he fired one pass ten yards over his receiver's head, was sacked on the next play, and New York had to punt.

While doctors and coaches surrounded Hostetler on the bench, the defense took the field, hopeful they could keep the deficit at four points. Once again, they followed Lawrence Taylor's lead.

On third and ten from his own twenty-three-yard line, Montana dropped back to pass and looked left where he saw an opening in the defense. He cocked his arm, ready to throw a post-pattern to John Taylor. A more cautious Everson Walls sprung toward Taylor—not the football—and shut Montana's window.

Montana sensed the pocket was collapsing and rolled right, eyes glued downfield.

Deep along the near sideline, he spied Rice, two steps ahead of safety Myron Guyton. He also noticed Taylor bearing down on him. Montana slammed on the brakes, set his feet, and with Lawrence Taylor unable to pull up, reached back to heave the ball downfield and end the Giants' season. But setting his feet to throw bought defensive end Leonard Marshall an extra split-second of pass-rushing time.

Prior to the play, Marshall lined up outside of 49ers left tackle Bubba Paris. At the snap, Marshall gave Paris a head fake to the inside, forcing the 350-pounder off balance. Marshall swam around Paris, but was unable to keep his feet. Fullback Tom Rathman pushed him to the ground. As Montana veered to his right, Marshall staggered to his feet, lunged for the quarterback, then stumbled again. Showing uncanny persistence, Marshall crawled on his hands and knees until he could get upright. When Montana paused to avoid Lawrence Taylor, Marshall closed the gap and plowed right into the back of the unsuspecting league MVP. For a moment, Montana looked like he was wearing Marshall as a cape.

"It was a clean lick," Marshall told reporters following the game. "I wasn't trying to put him out of the game or end his career."

End over end the football floated up in the air before hitting the ground thirty-five feet from where the vicious blow had been delivered. Cornerback Mark Collins leapt toward the ball but could not cradle it. Offensive lineman Steve Wallace swooped in to make the recovery. The 49ers had retained possession but now had bigger problems: Montana was hurt.

Doubled over, Montana knelt motionless on the ground. Steve Young, the 49ers' backup, charged onto the field. Montana gently rolled over onto his back and lay there for several minutes. Trainers sat him up and "Joe Cool" soon got to his feet, only to spend the rest of the day huddled with doctors and paramedics. He had a broken bone in his hand, a bruised sternum, and struggled to breathe.

It had been a rough week for Montana. Thursday night, he was hit with a flu bug and missed practice on both Friday and Saturday. On the first play from scrimmage, Montana didn't look sharp, tossing a low, wobbly pass a few yards short of his receiver's feet: Lawrence Taylor clobbered him just as he released the ball.

"After the second series, when he left from under center, he was already passive, you could see it," said Giants safety Dave Duerson. "He was expecting to get hit. Even when he handed off he was flinching."

Early in the fourth quarter, Taylor accidently kicked Montana in the knee at the end of a pass play. He limped off the field. Half an hour later, Marshall clobbered Montana, knocking him out of the game. Although nobody knew it at the time, Joe Montana had taken his last snap as the 49ers' starting quarterback. Steve Young, the former Brigham Young University star and seldom-used professional, warmed up along the sideline.

Across the field, Jeff Hostetler—the Giants' backup who had waited years for an opportunity to play—was ready to return despite a throbbing knee.

"Coach Parcells asked me how the knee felt, if I could go several times," Hostetler said. "Finally I told him I was going. As long as it was stable, I was going back in. This was a huge game and I've waited a long time for the opportunity."

Hostetler's comeback went from improbable to incredible when, on second and seven he avoided a sack, scrambled left, and sprinted to within a yard of the first down. But on third and short, a pair of 49ers bottled up Ottis Anderson behind the line of scrimmage, and the Giants' drive stalled.

Sean Landeta and the special teams unit got into position near midfield. The "very predictable" Giants did not punt the ball.

"They were ready to get their wall going for Taylor, and I noticed an opening on the right," said linebacker Gary Reasons, who served as personal protector in the Giants punt team. "We had the play on all game, and I had the go-ahead to call it when I saw it."

The play Reasons called was a fake punt. Prior to Landeta receiving the ball from long-snapper Steve DeOssie, Reasons had the option of shouting out an audible. The call alerted DeOssie to snap the ball to Reasons and instructed the Giants on the line of scrimmage to block for him.

DeOssie snapped the ball directly to Reasons, who ran untouched for thirty yards, until a bewildered John Taylor cut him down.

"I'm just looking for a hole in the line," Reasons said. "You could have driven a Mack truck through that one."

Reasons' run gave New York life at the San Francisco twenty-four-yard line. But once again, the Giants could not get the ball in the end zone. Three plays produced three yards, and Bahr was sent in to attempt a fifth field goal, which he made.

Less than six minutes remained; New York trailed 13-12 and needed to get the ball back. That didn't appear likely during the 49ers' ensuing drive, which ate up thirty-seven yards and more than three minutes of game clock. The Giants looked buried.

"I remember Mark Ingram saying, 'Here's my chance to go to Tampa; my chance to play in the Super Bowl, and now it's going down the drain,'" recalled Ottis Anderson.

"And I said, 'Ingy, it's my destiny; we're gonna go to the Super Bowl.'

"'Come on, Juice,' he said. 'They got the ball. They're running out the clock.'

"I said, 'I'm telling you, Ingy; it's my destiny; it's gonna happen, something's gonna happen.'"

Ingram had good reason to be pessimistic. Roger Craig had helped the 49ers preserve dozens of victories during the past eight seasons. But the running back turned thirty that year, and a nagging knee injury forced him to miss five games; he had never missed a game prior to 1990.

Although Craig told John Madden before the NFC Championship Game that he "felt as good today as [I've] felt all year," the 49ers' ground game totaled just thirty-nine yards on eleven carries. Not until three-and-a-half minutes remained in the fourth quarter did San Francisco gain a single rushing first down. They would not get another.

Craig had already fumbled once on that possession, the first play of the drive; teammate Bubba Paris recovered it. With the clock approaching two-and-a-half minutes, Craig accepted a handoff (his third in three plays) and plunged into a blur of his own linemen and defenders. One member of that pile was Giants nose tackle Erik Howard, who got two hands on Craig and a helmet on the football, which squirted out. At the Giants' forty-three-yard line, Lawrence Taylor swallowed up the fumble.

"I knew we'd come up with something sooner or later," Howard said about the game's lone turnover. "We'd been fighting so hard the whole game."

Behind by only a single point, New York was now content—for the first time in eight quarters against the vaunted San Francisco defense—with a field goal attempt.

"To me, it was like being in the backyard with my two older brothers against my younger brother Todd and I. It didn't matter what age we were, it was us against them," Hostetler said years later. "And we would take a beating, and we'd get up and keep going. And for me, that's what I was going to do. I think that we were so focused, we were in a battle with these guys; we'd played them earlier and we'd lost the game and we knew we should have beat 'em. And it was the same [in the NFC Championship Game]. We knew we should beat 'em and that I could attack them on the edges and make some plays. And that's what we did."

The mid-December injury to Phil Simms—a Super Bowl MVP and the franchise's starter for virtually an entire decade—had been a terrible blow to the Giants. But there was one glimmer of silver lining in the unintended quarterback swap. Hostetler's athleticism and mobility added a new dimension to the Giants offense, a dimension never explored during Simms' long tenure.

"This might be just what the Giants need at this time," a league insider told *Newsday*'s Bob Glauber in late December of 1990. "Simms can't run, and Hostetler can buy time. Teams can't load up any more because they don't know what Hostetler is going to do."

Hostetler's agility produced more than just rushing yards or the occasional rushing touchdown. When he moved away from the pocket, defensive backs and linebackers were caught between two choices: remain tethered to the receiver, or attempt to tackle the quarterback before he gains positive yardage. In case of the latter, Hostetler's receivers knew to break off of their routes and improvise. As a result, defenders' coverage responsibilities—who covers who, who has which zone—became muddled, oftentimes enabling receivers to find an opening.

To start their last-minute, game-deciding drive, Hostetler faked a handoff to Ottis Anderson, escaped the grasp of two 49er linemen, then bolted to his right. Just a few steps from the sideline, he hurled the ball across his body toward Mark Bavaro for a nineteen-yard pickup.

"The pass to Bavaro was supposed to be a drop-back pass," Hostetler recalled. "But when the rush got heavy, I moved out to the right and the flow went with me. Mark made a great move against the grain to get open."

Passing on first down had been essential to New York's crushing playoff victory over the Bears. And against the 49ers, Bavaro's fifth catch of the day brought the Giants past midfield as the clock ticked to the two-minute warning. But when the action resumed, the Giants returned to the ground. A trademark off-tackle run didn't fool anyone in Candlestick Park, especially 49ers defensive end Kevin Fagan, who brought O. J. Anderson down for a four-yard loss.

With the line of scrimmage now pushed back to San Francisco's forty-three-yard line, the Giants needed at least one more first down to even consider attempting the game-winning field goal. And despite possessing all three of his time-outs, Parcells let the clock dwindle. Less than eighty seconds remained by the time New York ran their next play. It was worth the wait.

Faced with a second and fourteen, Hostetler took the snap, retreated into the pocket, then sprinted to his right. From an off-balance position, he fired the ball near the sideline, directly at the stomach of Stephen Baker.

"When they called the play, I said, 'you know what, this is it. This is gonna be the best route I'm gonna run in my life. This is what I worked all my life for, this one moment right here to get our team to the Super Bowl. I ran that route so hard," remembered Baker, the Giants' five-foot, eight-inch receiver. "Oddly enough, we call it a 'squirrel route' because they used to say I looked like a little squirrel running so fast down the field. It was a ten-yard out and then I bursted up field for eighteen yards, acting like I'm running deep and then stop on a dime, and Hostetler's rolling outside to my side and fires it right for the sticks."

Baker caught the ball and delicately touched both feet down in bounds.

Hostetler's college coach, Don Nehlen, had seen him make this play hundreds of times: during practices, in the "Backyard Brawl" rivalry matchup against Pitt, and in two bowl games. Still, even Nehlen was amazed as he watched, in person, his son-in-law perform.

"Jeff scrambled out of there and how in the hell he ever found the guy, to get him the ball, I'll never know," said Nehlen, who was in California to coach college's East-West All-Star Game later that month. "Jeff was absolutely unbelievable in that game."

Now it was third and one at the 49ers' twenty-seven-yard line. This was the play of the game, of the season. A conversion here would do much more than shorten the winning attempt for Matt Bahr. A fresh set of downs meant that the Giants could drain the clock and kick a field goal without having to give the ball back to San Francisco.

Hostetler handed the ball off to Ottis Anderson, who plowed toward a path cleared out by Jumbo Elliott and William Roberts.

"We let Ottis take it and hit it up in there, we felt we could always make a yard," Ron Erhardt recalled. "We had that mentality."

The Giants put the ball in Anderson's hands once more, then, on third down, with one time-out and twelve seconds remaining, Hostetler nudged into the line in order to position the ball in the center of the field. Out trotted Matt Bahr. The 49ers called a time-out to "ice" the kicker.

"It could be an eternity for Matt Bahr if he should miss, and he'd never know he got on the airplane if he makes it," Pat Summerall, ironically once a New York Giants kicker himself, told the CBS audience. "That is a lonely world, believe me."

Giants receiver Mark Ingram actually wanted to be alone at that moment. Hands locked together and with both knees touching the ground, he prayed silently, then crossed himself.

Bill Parcells and Bill Belichick paced up and down the Giants' sidelines, passing a large group of Giants all holding hands. Bavaro, Greg Jackson, Roger Brown, and the rest of the prayer circle refused to watch.

"Those last few minutes we were all praying. And I mean praying like we've never prayed before," Jackson remembered a few years later.

Everson Walls disturbed the silent benediction. He wanted to narrate the moment for his teammates.

"He's setting up for the kick," Walls informed the group.

"That's enough. We don't want to hear it," Pepper Johnson interrupted.

"He's ready for the snap," Walls added.

"Shut up, Walls!" Mark Collins screamed.

Matt Bahr was the calmest man in the stadium.

"I didn't notice the guys kneeling on the sidelines," Bahr said. "I guess you could say I was fighting the rush of adrenaline. Sure I knew the score and what this meant to the team. But I had to focus on my job. I try to take the same attitude to kicking an extra point in the first quarter as I do kicking a field goal in the last seconds with the game on the line."

Through his classic, single-bar helmet, Bahr locked eyes with Hostetler. The two emergency stand-ins—each once a Pennsylvania teenager whom Joe Paterno brought to Happy Valley during the 1970s—were now ready to deliver New York to the Super Bowl. Steve DeOssie crouched over the football and fired it back to Hostetler. A perfect snap and perfect placement allowed Bahr to smoothly swipe at the ball.

Into abnormally calm air along the San Francisco Bay, the ball soared downfield, veering slightly toward the left goalpost. Bahr leaned right as he watched, hoping the ball would follow his command. It did.

"I didn't want to look, I couldn't look," Mark Collins said. "I just closed my eyes and waited for the reaction from the crowd. When I heard that dull sound, I knew he made it."

In Candlestick Park, 65,750 patrons, minus a few transplanted New York fans, fell silent. The Giants' sidelines went wild. Belichick hugged Parcells, ruffled his boss' gray hair, and the two hopped around like Little Leaguers who just won the city championship.

"When I saw it was good, I didn't jump up and down. I just breathed a sigh of relief," Bahr said. "I may not have looked excited outside, but on the inside, I was excited."

Stephen Baker couldn't quite keep his emotions in check.

"I just remember turning around 'cause their stadium, the fans were right behind us, and I'll never forget they were berating us all day, talking about [Giants running back Dave] Meggett, calling him a midget, calling me a midget, calling Sean Landeta fat," said Baker. "When we won, I turned around and I gave them the old 'one-finger salute' and threw my helmet up as high as I could because I couldn't believe it."

Back on the field, Jeff Hostetler had to somersault out of the path of Giants teammates charging onto the field toward Matt Bahr. Despite a sore neck that nearly kept him sidelined that day (X-rays had to be taken after he tried to tackle a Chicago kick returner the week before), the five-foot, eight-inch, 174-pound Bahr didn't mind being bear-hugged by Lawrence Taylor.

"It was a good kick, but I'll tell you what, this victory is for [my teammates]. They worked so hard through training camp; they overcame so many obstacles. I'm just happy to be along for the ride."

In the visitors' locker room, reporters and writers surrounded Bahr and Hostetler, the game's two last-second stars. Both men had waited a long time for this moment. So had Everson Walls.

"I've been trying to negate ["The Catch"] all my career, and nobody ever let me," he said. "This is the only way to negate it. Go to the Super Bowl."

After praising his team behind closed doors and accepting the George Halas NFC Championship Trophy, Parcells addressed a throng of reporters.

"We had them all the way," he said with a smirk.

Moments later, Parcells noticed Mark Ingram, who, late in the final period, had not been quite as optimistic while talking to Ottis Anderson.

"It's better than Christmas morning, isn't it?" Parcells asked.

"This is better," replied Ingram.

"That's probably the greatest game I ever coached in. There were a lot of great players playing in that game. Some on our side and certainly quite a number on San Francisco," Bill Parcells said in 2010, four years after coaching the last of 505 NFL and collegiate games. "I think everyone who played in that game realized that that was a very special game. It certainly was for me."

"Jerry Markbreit was the referee of the game. He told me years later that he was the head referee for [437] games. He told me that was the greatest game he ever officiated."

Anyone not in Candlestick Park that afternoon nearly missed the sights and sounds of the Giants' miraculous win.

All afternoon, NFL Commissioner Paul Tagliabue remained on-call, ready to replace the national CBS television broadcast in favor of live coverage from the Persian Gulf.

"The decision was made as close to kickoff as he could make it," NFL Vice President of Communications Joe Browne said. "It was made after he saw there were no major events."

Still, on at least one occasion, television producers somehow relayed a message informing the referee to extend an on-the-field time-out. They did not want the viewers at home to miss a single play while CBS anchor Dan Rather's report on a missile attack in Saudi Arabia ran long.

Even at Candlestick, the war was not far from people's minds. San Francisco police on special duty and mounted officers guarded the field up until an hour before game time. Inside the Giants' locker room, the war couldn't be ignored. Ottis Anderson, Pepper Johnson, Gary Reasons, and Matt Cavanaugh each had a cousin in the military, as was Bob Mrosko's brother. And linebacker Johnie Cooks stayed up most of Wednesday night and Thursday morning with his sobbing wife as they watched the news: his uncle, cousin, and brother-in-law each served in the Gulf.

"Life has to go on," Cooks said. "It would be better to be playing and give people something else to think about for three hours. We're sad about what's going on, but it's something we've got to deal with."

On game day, Giants players wore yellow wristbands to honor the American sailors and soldiers. Giants owner Wellington Mara—a naval lieutenant commander during World War II—approved the wardrobe addition.

After his kick sailed through the goalposts, Bahr shouted, "This is for the troops," and waved the wristband in the air.

"The NFL didn't like it," Bahr said years later.

League officials probably also didn't like Mark Ingram's political statement. Ingram, the Giants' leading receiver that day, played the entire game with the word "PEACE" written in black marker across athletic tape covering his left wrist.

To the players, fans, and the television executives, this was largely uncharted territory.

"This game, of course, was played under heavy security," CBS' Greg Gumbel asked Lawrence Taylor during a postgame interview. "A great deal of discussion about whether or not football games should even be played. Did that enter into your thinking at all as you came out onto the field or as you played today?"

"When you see all the security," Taylor responded, "it makes you realize that the war is real, it's not a joke. And even though it's fought all the way over there in Saudi Arabia and Iraq, it's touching home right now. It's a little scary but as far as the guys over there, I'm proud of them, bring us back a victory. And I just wish the people over here would stop all the protesting and support those guys. Those guys are fighting for us."

A day before the city hosted its fourth NFC Championship Game in ten years, thirty-five thousand people marched from San Francisco's Mission Dolores Park to an antiwar rally at the Civic Center Plaza. Seventeen hundred demonstrators had already been arrested that week in San Francisco, and upwards of forty thousand protesters were expected to protest the next day outside Candlestick Park, prior to and during the NFC Championship Game.* That weekend, tens of thousands more demonstrated in Los Angeles, Boston, and Washington, D.C. And rallies—some pro-war, some antiwar,

---

*Only a handful of people actually demonstrated outside of Candlestick Park during the NFC Championship Game. According to the *Kansas City Star*, "Instead, the war protesters held placards in the park alongside one of the main roads into the stadium. A peace symbol made of red material was laid out on the ground—not clearly visible to passers-by but clearly seen from the Fuji blimp that circled the stadium during the game."

some both—cropped up across the rest of the nation, in places like Lawrence, Kansas, Charleston, West Virginia, and Fayetteville, Arkansas.

But for most of the enormous television audience (Neilson ratings estimated a 26.9 share of the market, 24.4 million homes), the Giants' engrossing victory served as a much-needed pause from a week's worth of frightful headlines and televised Pentagon briefings.

"Nobody forgot about the guys over there," said Barney Fitzpatrick, a bartender at an Upper West Side Manhattan sports bar, "but the country needs morale over here too. The American way is here, and football is part of the American way. Why let Saddam ruin our game?"

Americans didn't let Hussein ruin the game that Sunday; neither did the American servicemen and servicewomen who watched or listened to the NFC Championship Game on the Armed Forces Network.

"How many were able to see it, we don't know. We have no way of telling," said Air Force Colonel Richard L. Fuller. "We haven't had any mail yet and we don't get any phone calls from them. They're pretty busy, but they tell us to keep up the news and thanks for the sports."

5

Respect Week

Pan Am flight 8207 from Buffalo landed in west Florida early Monday evening, January 21. Crushing Los Angeles by forty-eight points in the AFC title game put Bills players in a good mood. While a few enjoyed the in-flight movie (*Dick Tracy*, starring Warren Beatty), others played cards or reminisced over the highlights of their great victory.

"It was a good plane ride," said defensive tackle Jeff Wright. "Everybody was laughing and joking and having a good time. There's no sense in being in a tense mood right now."

The excitement carried out of the plane and onto the tarmac at Tampa International Airport.

"Showtime . . . it's showtime!" Bruce Smith and Cornelius Bennett announced to writers and cameramen.

The Bills intended to savor their first brush with the Super Bowl stage.

"I want all the media I can get while I'm here," Bennett told the press that week. "I won't turn a reporter down while I'm here."

Bennett was not alone in basking beneath the spotlight. Jim Kelly drew the most media attention, and the Bills quarterback gave them plenty to report on. Hours after the Bills plane landed, Kelly and Lawrence Taylor—one of the Giants who would be chasing him on Sunday—served as judges for a "beauty contest" at Thee Dollhouse Lounge, a local Tampa strip club. Another compelling angle for reporters was the identity of one of Kelly's special guests to the Super Bowl: Sandi Korn, who reportedly once dated Kelly's former USFL boss, Donald Trump. (Under the pseudonym Sandra Taylor, Korn would be *Penthouse*'s Pet of the Month that March.)

"I'm going to enjoy myself like everyone else," said Kelly. "Hey, I'm single, I think you can enjoy yourself and stay focused. It remains a business trip."

Kelly openly mingling with beautiful, half-clad women would have been enough for the already-established Joe Namath comparisons to swell. But reporters weren't satisfied.

Surrounded that week by dozens of interviewers—including one who asked "Joe, Joe, what do you think of all these questions?"—Kelly spoke with trademark confidence.

"Our goal is not to be in Tampa. Our goal is to win in Tampa. If we execute as we should, we should have no problems."

Some reporters translated his comment into a guarantee. The *Newport News Daily Press* ran that quote beneath a headline "Report: Bills QB Almost Pulls a Namath." Too great was the temptation of sensationalizing another western Pennsylvania-born quarterback who guaranteed victory during Super Bowl week in Florida.

Kelly's cryptic "promise" of victory came on Tuesday, during the NFL's prearranged extensive press session. For every player and coach, Media Day, as it became known, was mandatory. At age sixty-two, head coach Marv Levy didn't bother attending. He had waited a long time to get to the Super Bowl and didn't want to waste precious time talking with reporters.

Two seasons of high-school coaching and two more as an assistant at his alma mater, Coe College, prepared Levy to take over as head coach at the University of New Mexico in 1958. Consecutive winning seasons for the Lobos gave way to a more prominent gig, rebuilding the University of California. But in four seasons at Berkeley, the Bears posted eight wins in forty games and he resigned "in the best interests of the university." Arguably, his finest accomplishment at Cal came away from the gridiron. In February 1960, he gave Fremont High School's head coach, Bill Walsh, his first collegiate job.

Following a five-year, mixed-results tenure at the College of William & Mary, in 1969 Levy joined the professional game. Brief stints in the NFL prepared him for a head-coaching job with the Montreal Alouettes of the Canadian Football League. There he won a pair of league titles until Lamar Hunt lured him away to coach the Kansas City Chiefs, where he failed to make the

playoffs in each of his five seasons. He was fired in 1982. And a season direct-
ing the Chicago franchise of the USFL didn't prove any better. Under Levy—
who learned a day after taking the job that his entire roster was swapped with
the Arizona Wranglers' roster—the Blitz finished 5-13.

Despite poor records at his most recent stops, Bill Polian knew that Levy
could coach.

"I felt beyond a shadow of a doubt that Marv Levy was the right guy," said
Polian, who worked under Levy in both Montreal and Kansas City. "I was
absolutely convinced he could do the job."

Within two seasons, the Bills were championship contenders. And when
the Bills earned their first Super Bowl berth, Levy spent Tuesday watching
film and crafting his game plan, instead of providing copy for reporters.

"I've been coaching for 40 years," Levy said. "This is the game I've been
preparing for all my life, and I'm not going to cut any corners for it."

League officials threatened Levy with a $5,000 fine if he did not apologize
(which he did) to the press. Without Levy, reporters found exciting, even
controversial, sound bites to run for their headlines or broadcasts. Bills players were hardly soft-spoken.

Beginning with the day he arrived in Tampa, Thurman Thomas complained to reporters about a lack of respect.

"When people talk about the great backs you hear Neal Anderson, Herschel Walker, Barry Sanders, and Eric Dickerson mentioned," he said. "All
those guys get big paragraphs and I get a little diddly one."

It was a curious statement considering that for the second straight season,
he had been selected to the Pro Bowl. And in that week's issue of *Sports Illustrated*, columnist Peter King succinctly summed up the Buffalo offense with
the metaphor, "Kelly draws the blueprint and Thomas erects the building."
But Thomas' feeling of slight was probably justified. Although he accounted
for more than one-third of the team's total yardage during the past two seasons, he still played for "Jim Kelly's Buffalo Bills."

Teammate Darryl Talley also felt slightly underappreciated. The eight-year
veteran enjoyed his best season in 1990, leading the team with 123 tackles,
chipping in four sacks, and scoring his first career touchdown. And his
twenty-seven-yard interception return for a touchdown against the Raiders
turned the AFC Championship Game into a rout. Talley, however, was again
denied a spot on the player-voted Pro Bowl team.

"Evidently I'm not popular enough with my peers," Talley said. "When you play on a star-studded defense, somebody is bound to get overlooked, and I just feel I'm that person."*

Even veteran James Lofton couldn't keep from hinting that many Bills felt like second-class citizens in Tampa.

"There's probably only one nice hotel in Tampa, and I guess the Giants have that."

Apparently, the Hilton wasn't nice enough for the Bills.

But in the weeklong disrespect diatribe, one Buffalo Bill, defensive end Bruce Smith, stole the spotlight.

Smith never lacked confidence.

"I hope we're going to have a winning season. No, we are going to have a winning season," Smith said during his first training camp in 1985. "It felt great to be the first player drafted. It's something I'd been hoping for. But I didn't feel any pressure because of where I was drafted. The only pressure I felt was to come here and do the things I'm capable of doing."

Eventually, Smith validated his hype, winning consecutive AFC Defensive Player of the Year Awards in 1987 and 1988. And despite not joining the league until 1985, he was named to the NFL's all-decade team for the 1980s.

After five years of cut blocks from offensive tackles, Smith needed knee surgery following the 1989 season and was forced to change his off-season preparation. A new conditioning program and a change in diet reduced his body-fat percentage to 6.1 (down from 15 percent just two years earlier). Shedding the weight added significant quickness.

"I just decided not to fail," he said. "I didn't want to end my career just being some former No. 1 draft-pick fat cat who looks back after it's over and regrets that he didn't push himself from a good to a great career."

In 1990, Smith continued to harass NFL quarterbacks, breaking his own franchise record with nineteen sacks. His contributions to Buffalo's run defense transformed him from an elite pass rusher into an elite defender.

Frequent double-, even triple-teams, could not slow Smith down and he accounted for 101 tackles. And the attention Smith drew from opposing

---

*A day after making that statement, Talley was added to the Pro Bowl roster: Art Shell, the head coach of the AFC squad, added Talley as a "need player," an appointment made at the coach's discretion.

coaches and players freed up his teammates to make plays when he couldn't. At the end of the regular season, Smith was named NFL Defensive Player of the Year.

As a single-season honor, the award wasn't enough for Smith. He wanted to be recognized unequivocally as the best defensive player in the league. With Lawrence Taylor still around, that had not yet happened.

"Over the last 10 years, he's probably been the most dominant player in the league. . . I just think right now, I've taken it up a notch above that. I can't take anything away from Lawrence. I've admired him for so many years," Smith told reporters the week of Buffalo's regular-season matchup with the Giants. "He's a friend of mine and I respect him. But right now, I think it's time to give credit to the person that really deserves it."

In Tampa, Smith reiterated his earnest belief that he was the league's best: "I still think I'm the best defensive player right now, is there any reason not to?"

Smith made even more noise when reporters asked him to comment on the Bills' Super Bowl opponent.

"I'd rather have played the 49ers," Smith told reporters. "The 49ers are famous and everybody says they are this and that. It makes me sick. I wanted the 49ers."

Teammate Carwell Garnered agreed.

"I wish we could have played the 49ers too, and I mean it like Bruce does, with no disrespect to the Giants," the rookie fullback said. "The 49ers were the team of the 80's, and we wanted to show against them that we're going to be the team of the 90's."

That week a handful of Bills expressed a desire to be appreciated outside of the comparatively small market just a few hundred miles from Times Square and the World Trade Center. Sharing the Super Bowl stage with a team from the country's largest and most prominent metropolis revealed a subtle resentment within the Bills.

"My reason for making the statement I made was to get the credit I deserve," Smith said. "I really didn't think I was getting it and probably one of the reasons is that Buffalo has only one newspaper. It's been frustrating at times," he said Wednesday. "It would be nice for endorsements and things like that. You have to play extremely well to get noticed in Buffalo. If I played like that for the New York Jets or somebody, I would be a legend."

Lawrence Taylor was already a legend, and he would have been one wherever or whenever he played.

The Giants selected Taylor with the second overall pick in the 1981 NFL draft, and he immediately became one of the game's best players. He won back-to-back NFL Defensive Player of the Year awards during his first two seasons in the league. In 1986, as the Giants charged to a Super Bowl victory, Taylor became just the second defensive player in league history to win the regular season's Most Valuable Player Award.

Despite scandalous behavior over the years—habitual drug use, arrests, a league suspension a few years earlier, and a casual relationship with prostitutes—Taylor's play always bailed him out with the coaching staff and the fans.

But Taylor was set to turn thirty-two-years old the week after Super Bowl XXV, and with an influx of younger linebackers emulating his model, he no longer symbolized state-of-the-art. A Week Three hamstring injury literally slowed Taylor down, and by the middle of the season he admitted to feeling "heavy" when he chased after mobile quarterbacks like Randall Cunningham. An heir apparent even surfaced that season. In his second season, Kansas City Chiefs outside linebacker Derrick Thomas recorded twenty sacks, including a record-setting seven-sack performance in Week Ten against Seattle.

Taylor said little to protest his skeptics. In response to Bruce Smith declaring himself the league's premier defender—prior to the Bills-Giants Week Fifteen matchup—Taylor said, "It doesn't bother me. It doesn't concern me. Everybody's time passes."

And on Media Day, he was content to acknowledge, "Right now, Bruce Smith is the best."

Accepting another pass-rusher's superiority wasn't quite as absurd or blasphemous as the New York media portrayed. Smith did have an incredible season in 1990: he garnered thirty-nine of the forty-two votes for the NFL Defensive Player of the Year Award.

It was the self-effacing tone with which he spoke during the week of Super Bowl XXV that seemed entirely out of Taylor's character.

"Can I jump over buildings in a single bound? No, and I'm not trying to," said Taylor. "At this point in my career, I'm not trying to be Superman. I'm

happy with being Clark Kent. Clark Kent can get the job done if he has to.
. . . You come to the realization that no man is invincible."

Super Bowl XXV shaped up as a battle of the old guard versus the new guard. No player on Buffalo's roster ever suited up for a Super Bowl before; twenty-two Giants had. The Bills were younger, louder, and with their frenetic, high-scoring offense, more exciting: a new team for a new decade. Compared to their opponent, the Giants were relics. Like Taylor, the Giants starter at right cornerback, Everson Walls, was finishing his tenth season. The league's oldest kicker accounted for all New York's scoring in their NFC Championship Game victory. And the NFL's oldest running back spearheaded the team's snail's-paced offensive attack. The Giants appeared very 1980s, very passé.

"They're cocky," New York's cornerback Mark Collins replied. "They're supposed to be. I didn't fly here to lose. But we're not talking a good game. We want to play it."

Perhaps the rest of the Giants were too tired to engage the Bills in a war of words: their trip to Tampa wasn't quite as swift as their opponent's. After the brutally physical win in San Francisco, the Giants had to travel cross-country to reach the Super Bowl site. With the time change, they didn't arrive until early Monday morning.

Many aboard were too excited by the victory to sleep, dancing the conga through the aisle to the music on Pepper Johnson's portable sound system.

"I think for anybody that was on the plane, it's one of the most memorable times in our sporting lives because it was very euphoric," Parcells said. "Have a couple beers, relax, enjoy the fruits of victory."

Even after the team settled, players and coaches chose their words carefully when speaking to reporters. During New York's Media Day session, no Giant would announce, "I'd rather have played the Raiders."

Instead, offensive tackle Jumbo Elliott called Bruce Smith the "best player I've ever gone against," a fact that was not overlooked by the head coach.

"Obviously, Bruce Smith was going to be a key," former *New York Post* beat-writer Hank Gola recalled. "And Jumbo was kind of a laid-back guy. And Parcells loved to push buttons and motivate individually.

Jumbo was a little tougher nut to crack in that way because he was so laid back, nothing bothered him, he was very even-keeled. But [Parcells] knew that Jumbo faced this tremendous challenge in Bruce Smith. So he instructed [Lawrence Taylor] during practice that week to just harass, get in his face, and irritate him and get him so angry that he would take it out on Bruce Smith in the game.

[Parcells] knew that was a key matchup and he didn't want to have to give Jumbo a lot of help: double teams, sliding protection, or anything. He knew that if Jumbo could take Bruce Smith one-on-one, then the rest of the game plan had a chance of working.

The overwhelming public praise for Buffalo—both through the press and on the Giants' practice field—wasn't only directed toward Bruce Smith.

Talking about the Bills and their back-to-back offensive explosions, Parcells admitted to reporters that the combination of Thomas, Kelly, James Lofton, and Andre Reed would be a major concern for the Giants.

"The Bills have everything going for them," Carl Banks added. "And that makes us nervous."

While several Bills repeatedly complained to reporters about having gone unacknowledged, the Giants could make the same claim. But they didn't, at least not publicly—not even when they checked into their hotel, the Hyatt Regency Westshore.

"We get there and they didn't even have the ability to change who was staying in our room," Giants left tackle Doug Riesenberg said years later. "I was [49ers left tackle] 'Mr. Harris Barton' for four or five days. They didn't even have the ability to take off the 'Congratulations San Francisco' signs."

The Hyatt staff and Tampa's Super Bowl Planning Committee must have read the *San Francisco Chronicle* article that reported that the 49ers sent staffers to Tampa to rent and install $30,000 worth of office equipment (fax machines, filing cabinets, computers, sixty-eight desks, and 112 telephone lines) at the hotel. The team also ordered Super Bowl buttons and tickets to a postgame party in Tampa.

"I remember one of the guys working in the hotel," said fullback Maurice Carthon.

He says to me and O. J. when we were walking to our room, "you guys cost us a lot of money." And we were like, "what do you mean?" He said, "'cause as soon as you guys won the game, we had to take all this 49ers stuff out of here. The 49ers were gonna have all these big parties, and they were gonna spend like two or three million dollars at our hotel."

And I remember that morning, O. J. and I got up and we were still excited about being at the Super Bowl at seven in the morning, so we started driving around town. And Nike had these two big bulletin boards. At one part of the city of Tampa Bay, they had Joe Montana on it and the other part of the city they had Jerry Rice catching the ball. And that kinda fueled our fire for the whole week for the Super Bowl and into the game, because nobody gave us a chance.

Still, no member of the media hauled in quotes from a New York player citing a lack of respect.

"That's a testament to Parcells. The more you say, the more you gotta take back," Riesenberg said.

There did, however, come a breaking point for the media-savvy, veteran group and they could no longer dish out a wealth of flowery words. The Bills often embarrassed their opponents, especially in the postseason. But the Giants defense yielded the fewest points in the NFL and managed, in two San Francisco road trips that season, to limit one of the greatest offenses in history to just ten points per game.

"We would have to have seven guys break their legs and everybody come out there not prepared in order for a team to score 40 points on us," Pepper Johnson said. "I don't see anybody marching the ball up and down the field on us."

Giants players and staff never feared Buffalo's offense. They simply immersed themselves in film and preparations.

Although the press had reported that the 49ers sent staff members to Tampa, before the NFC Championship Game, to ready hotel rooms and offices, the Giants had (more covertly) done the same. Parcells' personal secretary, Kim Kolbe, and George Young's personal secretary, Janice Gavazzi, also flew to Tampa that week with simple, yet specific instructions from Parcells: "Get it like I want it."

"I'll be darned," Parcells recalled, "[Kim] met us at the plane at about 3:30 in the morning, all the [hotel room] keys were out, the players knew where to go, our offices were set up. And we were up and ready and working by 7:30 that morning."

Giants players had Monday off. Gary Reasons (nine-over-par 81) and Lawrence Taylor (four-over-par 76) played golf at the North Course of Largo's Bardmoor Country Club. That week, Taylor remarked, "I'd rather go to the

Super Bowl than shoot 70. [But] I'd rather shoot 65 than play in the Super Bowl." Golf had become a huge part of Taylor's life: In his 1987 autobiography, *LT: Living on the Edge*, he claimed that the "golf course was my detox tank" for his cocaine habit.

While Taylor and Reasons hit the links, Jeff Hostetler and Raul Allegre, along with Bart Oates, John Washington, Eric Dorsey, and Mike Fox—a combined eleven hundred pounds crammed together—rode the roller coasters at nearby Busch Gardens. And although each was given twenty-five Super Bowl tickets, more than a handful of players spent their day off trying to find more for friends and family members.

Meanwhile, Bill Parcells and his staff were hard at work.

"There's a way to do it . . . a way to win. You just have to find it. That's the mentality that coaching is really about. Nobody else understands," Parcells told famed sportswriter Jerry Izenberg during the writing of *No Medals for Trying*, a behind-the-scenes look at one week of the Giants' 1989 season. "Mickey [Corcoran, his old high school basketball coach] taught me that. He always said there was a way to win every game. Finding it is what separates some people from others."

By the time the Bills plane landed in Tampa, they had already put in a full day's work, the first of seven that week. For the coaches, in between practice, game planning, and meetings with players, film study consumed the rest of their days and nights.

"Did you ever eat a meal in the dark? We've gotten good at it," said Bill Belichick.

Belichick's unit had already strung together a pair of exemplary defensive performances in two playoff games. Parcells expected another one on Super Bowl Sunday. Still, he knew that might not be enough to defeat the Bills.

For the Giants offense, touchdowns were usually the result of a carefully executed, meticulously crafted, lengthy drive. In a close game, Buffalo's quick-strike ability could pose a real problem.

"I don't think we can win a shootout game with Buffalo," Parcells said. "I don't think our team has proven it can win any kind of shootout game this year. But I think it has proven it can win a lot of methodical games. So if we can play our style, and keep them from playing theirs, then we have a better chance of making it."

While his defensive staff and players burned their eyes out watching film, Parcells and Ron Erhardt devised a supplementary strategy for curtailing Buffalo's potent scoring: keep Jim Kelly, Thurman Thomas, and the rest of the exceptional Bills skill players off the field.

"Our whole plan was to shorten the game for Buffalo," Parcells said. "We wanted the ball and we didn't want them to have it."

In addition to stifling the K-Gun, that approach would have a two-pronged effect. Each first down New York gained would further wear down the Bills, both physically and emotionally. Allowing the opponent to convert on third down—when the defense is just one stop away from ending a drive and giving the ball back to their offense—can demoralize a team. Every successive play meant linebackers and 275-pound defensive linemen would have to chase ball carriers across the field, and do so with little recovery time in between snaps. With Buffalo's defense tired, the Giants hoped to collect points, and piece together a lead.

Meanwhile, on the sidelines, Giants defenders could catch their breath and prepare for their next bout with the fast-paced, intricate no-huddle.

"There were stretches this season when we were able to control the ball between 36 and 40 minutes per game," tackle Jumbo Elliott said that week. "This gives our defense the opportunity to rest. So when they do go onto the field, they can really sell out, go out there for three downs then get off."

Parcells' vision of how to defeat Buffalo made sense. "Power football," as he called it, had been a reliable victory formula for decades. "It's always been vindicated. It's the new stuff that had something to prove," he said by week's end.

Still, no matter how well designed the Giants' symbiotic game plan was, it was up to his players to execute. Especially in one phase of the game: the quintessential element of "power football."

"You've got to feel that we have to run the ball," Ottis Anderson said on Thursday. "The only way you can keep Jim Kelly off the field is to run the ball, and that's what we're going to try to do."

Sixty nations would broadcast the Bills and Giants battle for the NFL title. For the first time, curious sports fans in Argentina, Portugal, and Switzerland would be able to see the Super Bowl live. But, to virtually every country outside the United States, football's world champion had been crowned: not in Tampa that winter evening, but in Italy the previous summer.

In July 1990, Andreas Brehme, Lothar Matthäus, Jürgen Klinsmann, and Rudi Völler of the West German soccer team—benefiting from the post–Berlin Wall reunification just a few months earlier—defeated Argentina 1-0 to win a third FIFA World Cup title.

The U.S. men's team did not fare well in Italy. Because they failed to qualify each time, Team USA did not even compete in the elimination bracket of the World Cup from 1954 to 1986. So when the United States finally did reach round one in the 1990 World Cup, their 0-0-3 record was not surprising. Following a 2-1 loss to Austria, the team returned home.

Forty years had now passed since the U.S. team won a single World Cup match and American soccer fans had to be discouraged—especially sixty-three-year-old Walter Bahr.

Back in 1950, Bahr was earning $50 a week as a physical education teacher at a Philadelphia high school. He pulled down an extra $100 as a midfielder playing for the U.S. team that traveled to Brazil in June to compete in the World Cup.

Bahr and his teammates lost their opening match to Spain, then drew England, the world's foremost soccer powerhouse. But great goaltending from goalie Frank Borghi—who made his living as an undertaker—kept the United States in contention against the Brits, a team comprised of full-time professionals. Late in the first half, Bahr laced a kick from twenty-five feet away and watched his teammate Joe Gaetjens head the ball in for the go-ahead goal. England played a relentless second half, but the United States held on to win 1-0 in what is considered one of the greatest upsets in soccer history.

"It would be like a high school team almost beating the New York Yankees," Bahr said in 2010. "A Division III basketball team beating the Lakers."

Despite the forty years of World Cup failure that followed the U.S. improbable triumph over England, Walter Bahr was not starved for victories. His playing career ended in 1957, and he became a coach, first for Philadelphia's franchise in the American Soccer League, then at the collegiate level, with the Temple Owls and Penn State University Nittany Lions.

During that time, Bahr, and his wife, Davies Ann, raised three sons—daughter Davies Ann Bahr became an all-American collegiate gymnast—and taught soccer to each of them. Aside from passing, trapping, and other fundamentals, Walter Bahr instilled in his boys a simple lesson about sports competition, one learned during that June victory over England in 1950: "If the better team always won the game, they wouldn't play it."

Although neither would completely follow in his father's footsteps, the two youngest boys eventually discovered the same thrill of historic victory felt by Walter Bahr in June 1950.

"[Growing up] we actually pretended we were in the World Cup," Matt Bahr said. "Soccer gave us everything we have in football."

Within a few years of leaving Penn State, each Bahr had earned Super Bowl rings, not a grip of the FIFA World Cup Trophy. Chris kicked two field goals and three extra points in the Oakland Raiders' 27-10 victory over Philadelphia in Super Bowl XV. Three years later, his eight points (five PATs and a field goal) contributed to the Raiders' 38-9 blowout of Washington in Super Bowl XVIII.

A poor 1989 campaign prompted the San Diego Chargers to release Chris. The following August, his younger brother Matt—the seven-year incumbent kicker for the Cleveland Browns—tried to find him a job kicking for the New York Giants.

"I can remember it like it was yesterday," later said Giants Director of Personnel Tim Rooney. "Basically, the gist of what he said was, 'Tim, if you're looking for a kicker anytime this year, how about considering my brother Chris, please?' I'll be the first to admit that I didn't pay that much attention to him. I remember I nodded, because I didn't want the kid to think I was being ignorant or anything. [But] I didn't really figure we'd need another kicker this season."

A month later, *both* Bahrs were unemployed until the Giants signed Matt in September 1990. And because the mid-season replacement had accounted for every point in the Giants' NFC Championship Game victory over San Francisco—including the last-second forty-two-yarder—Bahr drew a lot of attention during the week of Super Bowl XXV.

"Because it was a game-winning field goal, both kickers were asked invariably, 'Do you want the Super Bowl to come down to a field goal?'" Bahr recalled years later. "And my answer always was, 'Hell No! I want to win by two touchdowns. It's much more fun winning by a bunch, then you can enjoy the game. Things get pretty tense when it's last second.'"

Bahr's counterpart on Super Bowl Sunday, Scott Norwood, also grew up in a professional sports family. Del Norwood pitched for San Jose of the California League in the early 1950s. The Boston Red Sox invited "Red" to spring training in March 1954, and he allowed just one single in three innings during an exhibition game against the reigning World Series Champion New York Yankees. After ending his playing career in 1959 as part of the Washington Senators farm team in Charlotte, Del Norwood managed for the Minnesota Twins Appalachian Rookie League team in Wytheville, Virginia. One of his first players was future all-star Tony Oliva. In the mid-1960s, Norwood left the pros to teach and coach baseball at Washington-Lee High School in Arlington.

Del's eldest son, Steve, went on to pitch for the University of Virginia and, in 1978, was drafted by the Milwaukee Brewers organization, with whom he spent the next four seasons, pitching for the Newark Co-Pilots and Burlington Bees. Daughter Sandra was also a fine basketball, soccer, and field-hockey player at Thomas Jefferson High in Alexandria.

Although Scott, the middle child, was also talented at baseball, soccer was his true passion.

"[Football] wasn't a dream as I was growing up," he said years later. "I was dreaming about playing in the World Cup."

Twice Norwood earned all-metropolitan honors as a sweeper for the Colonials. But as a senior, Jefferson High's football coach approached him about becoming a placekicker. Hoping to contribute where needed, he became a two-sport athlete during the fall season.

Father and son worked together to turn Scott into a reliable soccer-style kicker, and beginning in 1978, Norwood was a two-sport athlete for Division I-AA James Madison University. As a freshman, he kicked the game-winning field goal against Mars Hill on a Saturday, drove to Baltimore with his parents, then scored the winning goal in a match with St. Peter's College. That winter, Norwood quit soccer to focus on placekicking.

"I gave up soccer because I thought I had leveled off," said Norwood, whose five goals as a freshman ranked third on the Dukes soccer team. "I didn't think I'd get much better. I had watched football and enjoyed it."

During his first year, Norwood shared the kicking duties with Joe Showker, then took over full time for the 1979 season.

"He's capable of hitting anything from 55 yards and in," Dukes head coach Challace McMillin said about the five-foot, eight-inch sophomore, "and he's got excellent accuracy from 40 yards in."

Norwood was a preseason all-American prior to his senior year. Applying visualization and relaxation methods to his pre-kick routine helped immensely.

"I really began to feel settled at the end of last season. I've just gotten a lot of practice, that's the main thing. I not only have practiced physically, but I've also practiced mentally. A lot depends on your mental attitude," Norwood said as a junior. "I feel I can be successful consistently from the 40-yard line and in when I'm kicking well and coming through the ball. When you get out farther, you think about kicking the ball hard and that takes away from other things."

On November 22, 1981, the Dukes took on the host East Tennessee State Buccaneers at the "mini dome" of Memorial Center Field. In his final college game, Norwood's twenty-yarder with nine seconds left broke a 14-14 tie and gave James Madison its first victory over a Division I school since switching to I-AA in 1980.

That kick was not the last game-winner for the future professional. Although the Atlanta Falcons signed Norwood out of college, he was cut prior to the 1982 season. He caught on with the Birmingham Stallions of the USFL and, as a rookie, set a league record with five goals against Herschel Walker's New Jersey Generals. In Week Three of the 1984 season, however, a roughing-the-kicker penalty by a Pittsburgh Maulers defender injured his knee, and he missed the remainder of the schedule.

Rehab and diligent practice back home in Virginia with his father rejuvenated his kicking stroke, and the Bills invited him to their training camp in the summer of 1985. There, he beat out nine others to gain the starting job.

His teammates immediately liked their shy, soft-spoken kicker; and not just because he accounted for every point the Bills scored in the opening two weeks (four total field goals in losses to San Diego and the New York Jets) of the 1985 Season.

"Scott was just a guy who showed up every day, worked his butt off, did everything he was told, didn't cause any problems, was a nice guy, and did his thing," said John Kidd, Buffalo's punter and holder for placekickers from

1984 to 1989. "And he was really good at it. He worked really hard at being the best kickoff guy that he could be, and really trying to do everything field position–wise to help the team win. And he was an accurate field-goal kicker with a really good leg and handled the conditions in Buffalo really well."

As the Bills began to mold a championship-caliber team in the later part of the decade, Norwood was a key contributor to the success. An overtime field goal in Week Six of the 1987 season snapped a six-game losing streak against division-rival Miami. An exuberant Norwood jumped into the arms of teammate Steve Tasker.

The next season—the precise time that the Bills morphed into a contender—Norwood was the conference's best kicker. A pair of overtime winners—a last-second forty-one-yarder to defeat New England, and two field goals in the final quarter of Buffalo's 9-6 comeback over Miami—helped produce four of their franchise-record twelve victories. In late November against the Jets, his thirty-yard kick in overtime clinched the AFC East title.

"In 1988, we finished 12-4 and New England finished 10-6," Bills special teams coach Bruce DeHaven recalled. "If he doesn't hit those field goals, New England finishes 12-4 and we're 10-6, and they go into the playoffs."

That string of clutch performances, along with an NFL-best thirty-two field goals and 129 points, earned Norwood a spot on the all-pro team and a trip to Honolulu for the Pro Bowl. The following season, Buffalo repeated as division champions, and again, Norwood finished among the league's best in points and field goals. That year, he surpassed O. J. Simpson as the team's all-time leading scorer.

But punter John Kidd's off-season departure meant a new holder for Norwood: backup quarterback Frank Reich. For a meticulous and nuanced person like Norwood, the drastic change had a tremendous effect. He missed six field goals and two extra points in the first six games of the 1990 season.

With the help of his father, who attended all his games to observe his son's technique from the stands with a pair of binoculars, Norwood recognized and corrected a flaw in his approach.

"You set yourself up for failure if your angle is too shallow, if you're not out far enough," he said. "If you start out straight, your hips have only one way to go, and it sets you up for a hook, whereas if I'm over more, the hips can't go through that far. It takes a few misses like that to come up with such an evaluation."

It was no wonder that he had such an elaborate explanation for his struggles: Norwood was a perfectionist. Teammates playfully teased him for a few of his habits. He brushed his teeth religiously, three, four times, at the stadium on game day. He also shaved and combed his hair before each practice and carried a detailed appointment book everywhere he went.

"He's always right on time for team meetings, and he's so organized and clean," Steve Tasker said. "I roped his locker off one day with tape and put a sign on it that said, 'A clean locker is a sign of a sick man.' I'm all over him about that. You look at him and think 'Now that's a guy my mom would really be proud of.' His mom has to look at him and just beam."

And his exactness translated onto the field.

"He's very picky about things," Frank Reich said, "especially the way I hold for him. It's like if you put the ball down and you miss the spot by an eighth of an inch, it's like 'Frank, you missed the spot by an eighth of an inch.' But that's good. You shoot for perfection and then your margin for error, I think, becomes less if you really focus on those things."

Despite the inconsistencies, his teammates and the coaching staff showed endless confidence in their kicker.

"If I had to have someone in the NFL kick a field goal to get us into the play-offs tomorrow," DeHaven said in October 1990, "Scott Norwood is the guy I'd want kicking it, regardless of what's happened in recent weeks. There isn't a kicker in the league who hasn't had a time when he's struggled a bit."

DeHaven knew that a few misses wouldn't affect his veteran placekicker.

"He had the perfect personality for a kicker," DeHaven said in 2010.

He just never gets very high or very low. I remember him telling me one time, we'd been someplace and he noticed how the other kicker was setting his tee up on kickoffs, that he was somehow managing to get just a little bit extra height out of placing the ball there. [Scott] said, "I can't tell you how excited I am about that." I said, "Well I'm glad you told me that," 'cause I couldn't have told. When Scott was really excited, you wouldn't have noticed. And I think that always helped him as a kicker—that he had such a level emotional state about him.

Having analyzed and resolved his early season kicking woes, Norwood returned to his reliable form. Beginning in Week Eight, he made thirty-four consecutive extra points and ten field goals in thirteen attempts. He didn't miss a single kick in the Bills' last three regular-season games and the playoff victory over Miami—all but one of those was played outside in cold, wintery Buffalo.

"I was in a little slump. I missed some early in the season, and the fans got on me. When I started making my kicks again, the fans got behind me. They know I can do the job. Things like that just happen in this game," Norwood said. "It was never anything mental. It was just mechanics. With a new holder, it takes a little while to gel, to get to know each other and to communicate. It's not something that happens overnight."

When the Bills arrived in Tampa, Norwood had solid kicking workouts on the natural grass at the Buccaneers' practice facility. And in sharp contrast to Matt Bahr, his Super Bowl counterpart, Scott Norwood approached the greatest challenge a kicker could possibly face, with his customary confidence.

"Now that I'm in the Super Bowl, I've had a mental picture of winning the game. It could happen," Norwood said during Super Bowl week. "It would be an exciting opportunity. I'm confident in any situation. I'm prepared to take advantage of any opportunity I'm given. I look forward to a chance to win the game, but I don't want to make it too nerve-wracking for my teammates."

6

Super Sunday

Two late-night pieces of key lime pie probably were not responsible for keeping Stephen Baker awake past midnight on Sunday morning January 27, 1991. He had eaten the Hyatt's room-service dessert every evening since arriving in Tampa as a reward for sharp practices each day. Rather than sweets, butterflies in his stomach (like many of his teammates) prevented the Giants' four-year veteran from falling asleep.

Waiting to digest the traditional family vice—"My name is Baker, so I like baked goods"—he found ways to keep occupied. For the long road trip, the twenty-five-year-old had packed his Sega Genesis and a popular video game, the original John Madden Football.

"That video game is big now, and it was big back then. Graphics weren't as good, but I used to take my video game on the road with me," Baker said two decades later. "I played Giants versus the Bills on there. Of course we won."

Baker eventually caught some sleep the next morning: with kickoff not until 6:18 p.m., he could afford to. He awoke several hours before the team bus left for Tampa Stadium and phoned his Alexander Hamilton (Los Angeles) high school football coach and his West Los Angeles junior college track coach, each a major influence in his career.

"It just makes you reminisce, like what it took to get to that point," he said. "You thank a lot of people for getting you there."

While Baker took advantage of the hotel's complementary long-distance calls, the rest of New York's roster and coaching staff tried to fill the morning as well. The team bus didn't leave the Hyatt until roughly noon.

"I hate waiting," Bill Parcells told a reporter, while sipping coffee in the lobby with his high school basketball coach Mickey Corcoran and Giants veteran Matt Cavanaugh. "Every game should be at 1 o'clock in the afternoon."

Three miles down the road at the Hilton, Bills players attended chapel services, mingled with friends and family, or just killed time before eating their pregame meal of "spaghetti, baked potatoes, and other foods high in carbohydrates." Late in the morning, their team bus left.

"The ride to the stadium was unbelievably moving," Bill Polian remembered. "We took that same route and had a police escort, obviously, and we were moving slowly. And both sides of Dale Mabry Boulevard were lined with Bills fans who, it was obvious after a little bit, had come out to watch the buses go by. Now they weren't tailgating; they weren't in the parking lot; they were out there to watch the buses go by. And they had signs, and they were waving and cheering; it was just incredibly emotional."

Giants (several wearing white tee shirts that read "Show No Mercy") and Bills players got off their respective buses and headed into the locker rooms to relax, tape up, and suit up. Others walked across the grass at Tampa Stadium, in an attempt to burn off nervous energy.

As players dressed, members of both teams' coaching staffs—such as Bill Belichick and linebackers coach Al Groh—surveyed the field and discussed last-minute details.

"I told Charlie and Rac that we'll get together and go in there and go over it," Belichick said to Groh.

"I talked to Banks and Lawrence, and I'm gonna talk to Pepper here in a minute that we're probably gonna open in the dime," said Groh. "What I want to make sure of is that those two inside guys have the proper pad fit, 'cause they have the gap all by themselves this week."

"Right, okay," Belichick acknowledged.

While Belichick, Groh, Rac (defensive line coach Romeo Crennel), Charlie (special assistant Charlie Weis), and the rest of the defensive staff met in the locker room, a few Giants and Bills exited the players' tunnel: kickers and other specialists at 4:45, the full team ten minutes later.

Their forty-five-minute warm-up and run-through finished, all players and coaches were ordered off the field at 5:35 so the pregame entertainment could begin: Up with People, and members of The Temptations and Three Dog Night, performed for ten minutes.

For the millions at home that tuned in to ABC to see football, not a concert, the next segment of the pregame show was for them.

Long before the Bills and Giants earned the right to play for the world championship, one team had already been invited to appear that day at Tampa Stadium.

The twenty-fifth installment of the Super Bowl was a ready-made milestone. To celebrate the first quarter century of the championship, an all-time Super Bowl team was selected, beginning in the summer of 1990. A group of media members and league officials who had witnessed every Super Bowl named 105 of the game's greatest players and coaches for the honorary squad. Over one million fans voted on the nominees throughout the NFL season and in the end, 25 players were chosen.

"First of all, this was very surprising to me," said Willie Wood, the Packers great safety. "I didn't think we old-timers had a chance to be on a team like this. I figured people kind of forgot about us."

On the day before Super Bowl XXV, the team was honored during Tampa's annual Bamboleo Festival, an African-Cuban themed celebration featuring floats, bands, and dancing. Roughly 150,000 people stood in cold weather and light rain to watch the two-and-a-half-mile parade down Bayshore Boulevard. Canceled appearances by Miss USA, Chuck Norris, and Chita Rivera went unnoticed by football fans thrilled to see Larry Csonka and Mike Singletary pass by in Buick convertibles.

Less than an hour before Sunday's kickoff, the team was introduced, one by one, to the crowd during the pregame festivities. Video of each player's individual Super Bowl highlights appeared on the Sony JumboTron at Tampa Stadium.

"I was moved by my selection to this Silver Anniversary team because of the way we got here—through the fans," Steelers defensive tackle "Mean" Joe Greene said. "This is probably the most special recognition I've ever gotten for my football skills because fans took the time to go out and vote."

Several of Greene's former Pittsburgh teammates stood with him during the ceremony, including five from the fabled "Steel Curtain" defense: L. C.

Greenwood, Jack Lambert, Jack Ham, Mel Blount, and Donnie Shell. In total, eight members of the 1970s Steelers dynasty (far more than any other franchise) were chosen for the silver-anniversary team. But only one of them actually came to Tampa Stadium that day to work.

Two wide receivers had been named to the all-time team. Although San Francisco's Jerry Rice had played in just two Super Bowls, he owned both the single-game and career record for receiving yardage and touchdown catches. The MVP of Super Bowl XXIII was an easy choice for the all-time team. So was the other wide receiver selection, the Steelers' Lynn Swann.

In Super Bowl IX, Pittsburgh faced the Minnesota Vikings at a chilly Tulane Stadium in New Orleans. A rookie from the University of Southern California, Swann did not catch a pass in the Steelers' 16-6 victory. Neither did most of his teammates. Quarterback Terry Bradshaw completed just nine attempts, as running back Franco Harris and the Steel Curtain defense claimed their first-ever NFL championship.

The following season (1975), Swann emerged as one of the league's premier receivers and a focal point of the Pittsburgh offense, leading the team in touchdowns, receiving yardage, and receptions. But when Pittsburgh repeated as conference champions the following January, it seemed likely—even before kickoff—that again Swann would go without a reception in the Super Bowl. He left the AFC Championship Game two weeks earlier on a stretcher: a concussion resulting from a defensive back's crushing hit.

"I did not think I was gonna be able to play," Swann told NFL Films in 2007. "I was certainly unsure. I had never sustained a concussion of that level. I was in the hospital for two or three days—wasn't catching the ball extremely well at practice. Frankly, my confidence was a little bit low. And the doctors essentially left it up to me as to whether or not I felt that I could play the game."

On game day, he elected to play, and in the Super Bowl's tenth anniversary showdown, Swann stole the show. He caught four passes for 161 yards, and it was his fourth-quarter touchdown that proved the difference in Pittsburgh's 21-17 victory over the Dallas Cowboys.

Swann's statistics, impact on the victory, and return from injury earned him the Most Valuable Player Award. But it was *how* he caught those passes that forged an indelible place in American sports history. Each reception was a mesmerizing display of concentration and grace.

The first came adjacent to the sidelines, where he twisted high in the air and inconceivably brought both feet down in bounds. Next was the most famous: leaping over a defensive back, juggling the ball midair, and sprawling out to make the grab. But the pièce de résistance was a sixty-four-yard bomb down the middle that Swann settled under and made an over-the-shoulder grab with three minutes remaining in the game.

"I never had a day when I felt as loose as this in my life," he told the press in the locker room afterward.

The Steelers returned to win another pair of Super Bowls at the end of the 1978 and 1979 seasons. In those two victories, he combined for twelve catches, 203 yards, and two touchdowns. Until Jerry Rice came along, Swann owned or shared the Super Bowl record for career catches, receiving yards, and touchdowns.

But Swann would have been on the field at Tampa Stadium for Super Bowl XXV even if he had not been selected to the silver-anniversary team. He was also chosen to fill a key position on another celebrated roster: ABC's Super Bowl broadcast team.

During his playing career, Swann participated in ABC's *Wide World of Sports* and *The Superstars* challenges, and delivered sideline commentary during one of the network's Pro Bowl broadcasts. Upon retirement, the thirty-year-old joined ABC full-time in January 1983.

Throughout the decade, he served as an on-site reporter for the Olympics, United States Football League games, Triple Crown horse races, as well as the network's weekly college football games. And as the sideline and halftime commentator for Monday Night Football, Swann appeared on prime-time television each week of the NFL season.

Not long before hustling over to midfield to be introduced as part of the silver-anniversary team, Swann delivered a live report for the Brent Musburger–hosted pregame show.

But ABC's broadcast on Sunday would feature the voices of more than just one of the sport's legends. Two more NFL greats—along with an iconic broadcaster—occupied the broadcast booth.

A twelve-year playing career with the Giants—highlighted by five appearances in the NFL title game and the league MVP during New York's 1956 world championship season—earned halfback Frank Gifford a place in the Pro Football Hall of Fame. Gifford retired from football after the 1964 season, three years before the advent of the Super Bowl. Still, when the Packers and Chiefs met for the inaugural AFL-NFL title game (aka, Super Bowl I), Gifford was there as a play-by-play voice for CBS' telecast. In 1971, he switched to ABC and became one-third of the famous Monday Night Football gang that featured Howard Cosell and Don Meredith.

Fifteen years after Gifford joined Monday Night Football, ABC revamped a lineup that had undergone several changes in recent seasons. Joe Namath and O. J. Simpson were replaced, and Gifford was paired with forty-two-year-old Al Michaels. Best known for coining the phrase "Do you believe in miracles?" to punctuate the U.S. Ice Hockey team's victory over Russia in the 1980 Winter Olympics, Michaels was a versatile broadcaster who eventually became the only man to deliver play-by-play for the World Series, Super Bowl, NBA finals, and Stanley Cup finals. Beginning with the 1986 NFL season, he brought his customary enthusiasm to Monday Night Football.

A year later, ABC returned to the familiar three-man format. Dan Dierdorf, the perennial Pro Bowl lineman for the St. Louis Cardinals (and a Hall of Fame selection in 1996) joined Gifford and Michaels in the booth.

The three very different personalities eventually gelled, boosting television ratings.

"I think it took a little while for the three-announcer booth to come together," the show's producer, Ken Wolfe, said prior to Super Bowl XXV. "The three guys really enjoy each other now, and it comes across on the air. We've all grown."

The trio passed their first Super Bowl test in January 1988: they kept viewers awake during the unwatchable second half of Washington's 42-10 rout of Denver. Three years later, they eagerly awaited the next Super Bowl broadcast and hoped the game would be more competitive.

But when they arrived in Tampa to prepare for the Giants-Bills matchup, ABC's star-studded broadcast team—just like everyone else that week—faced an extraordinary landscape.

"I'm having a hard time going to sleep every night," Gifford said. "You're holding your breath. I think that's the feeling here. It is the Super Bowl. It is important. It's important to play it and go on with our lives. But there will be a cloud hanging over the game. I feel a little peculiar, more than any game I've ever done."

Almost immediately, once Super Bowl week began, whispers spread that—because of the Gulf War—perhaps the game should not be played.

On Monday, the annual commissioner's party, two days before the game—which by 1991 cost more than $1 million—was canceled. So was Anheuser-Busch's "Bud Bowl" party. Instead of chauffeuring celebrities and executives around town, limousines in Tampa Bay sat on lots. Postponing the game seemed to be the next logical step.

"[The] game ought to be canceled as a grand and grave gesture of concern, of a spreading war in an age of nuclear weapons," *St. Petersburg Times* columnist Mary Jo Melone wrote. "Maybe if we halted this thing America loves so, just once, the world could stop and ponder what it was doing to itself."

Virtually anyone asked, at least by the press, whole-heartedly disagreed. Especially the principles: fans, players, coaches, league officials, even the president of the United States.

"Somebody asked me a while back about the Super Bowl. You think we ought to cancel the Super Bowl because of this situation?" President George H. W. Bush said at a White House press briefing four days before the game.

> One, the war is a serious business and the nation is focused on it. But two, life goes on.
>
> [The] boys and men and women in the gulf, they want to see this game go on . . . and this is priority: getting this war concluded properly. But we are not going to screech everything to a halt in terms of our domestic agenda. We're not going to screech everything to a halt in terms of the recreational activities, and I cite the Super Bowl and I am not going to screech my life to a halt out of some fear about Saddam Hussein.

American soldiers and sailors serving in the Gulf wanted the game to continue as well.

"I don't think at all that it was inappropriate to play the game," said Air Force Master Sergeant Rick Fuller, who watched the kickoff from a military base at Dhahran International Airport in Saudi Arabia's Eastern Province. "A lot of people over there saw it as a real morale booster because it was something they could identify with—something that they were very familiar with and they were used to doing at that particular time of year."

Many vowed to watch the game. And those few thousand soldiers and sailors would be doing so—as ABC News' Judd Rose noted—into early morning, January 28, 1991: in the Arabia standard time zone (several hours ahead of eastern standard time), Super Bowl XXV kicked off Monday at 2:18 a.m. local time.

"Saddam has a history of hitting us right in the middle of something good," one solider told Judd Rose at Camp Jack, an air base in Saudi Arabia.

"What happens if that happens?" Rose asked during a taped segment aired during halftime.

"Oh, put on our [gas] masks and hopefully just keep watching if it's not too bad."

By the time soldiers at Camp Jack or troops on patrol throughout the desert tuned in to the Armed Forces Radio and Television Network to hear the game, such threats had become commonplace. On Tuesday, one of Iraq's Scud missiles slipped past the American Patriot missile system and hit an apartment building in Tel Aviv. Three Israelis died from heart attacks. American fighter jets shot down Iraqi planes and knocked out several bridges in Iraq, cutting off supplies. A few days later, Patriots intercepted seven Scuds launched at Tel Aviv and Haifa. It was the fifth attack in eight days.

Hussein's strategy expanded beyond random, isolated Scud launchings. In the Kuwaiti city of Mina Ahmadi, Iraqi soldiers began pumping oil into the Persian Gulf. By game day, more than one hundred million gallons of oil filled the Gulf: the goal was to shut down Saudi Arabian desalinization plants and thereby ruin the American ally's drinking water. The ten-mile-wide, thirty-five-mile-long oil-covered water also hindered U.S. naval operations in the region. During a conflict between the Iraqi patrol boats and U.S. vessels, the oil caught on fire. On Friday, American F-111s bombed the supply pipes in order to cut off the flow.

A ground war was not expected to commence for weeks, but U.S. Marines and Iraqi soldiers fired at one another along the Saudi Arabian–Kuwait border. Given that Hussein's military owned more land mines than any other military in history—roughly five hundred thousand had already been laid according to U.S intelligence—soldiers on patrol lived in constant danger.

Respect for Americans risking their lives was a major part of the concern in the Super Bowl postponement debate—but not the only reason.

Across the country, citizens worried about the danger reaching the United States. Chemical warfare was a significant threat to the troops in Saudi Arabia and Kuwait: Iraqi Scud missiles might include warheads filled with biological hazards. But the Scuds could not reach across the Atlantic Ocean to hit the United States. Instead, Hussein extended the conflict beyond conventional boundaries.

Terrorist groups (it remains unclear if they were working in conjunction with Hussein) set off explosions at American and British banks in Greece. On January 19, a plot to bomb an American cultural center in Manila was thwarted. And although he spoke of a low-level threat within the United States, Assistant Director of the FBI William Baker acknowledged that "various terrorist groups have infrastructures in the United States" and that "all of these organizations have the capability of having contact from abroad and could carry out activity in our country."

"At the time it was a very considerable fear," said David Isby, a Washington-based defense and foreign-policy consultant.

It became much more so after the World Trade Center bombings some years later, even more so after 9/11. But there was a very real concern. The most important thing was that Saddam Hussein had some months before put out a public announcement, a call for acts of terrorism worldwide. And that's not an inconsequential thing. . . . Saddam basically put his credibility at stake. To be a third-world dictator, if you call for worldwide terrorism in solidarity and the terrorists of the world blow you off, that doesn't add to your credibility. So, the fact that he had gone up and done this, there was a great deal of expectation.

Many Americans were hesitant to attend churches and synagogues, open Federal Express packages, or go to public places like malls and shopping centers. On Beverly Hills' Rodeo Drive, in front of the Louis Vuitton store, a bomb squad swooped in to defuse a suspicious-looking bag. (They were relieved to discover that the package contained a pillow.)

Mitchell Airport in Milwaukee, Wisconsin, prohibited both curbside check-ins and unattended vehicles. Only people with boarding passes were allowed access to the gates. At O'Hare and Midway in Chicago, all mailboxes, coin-operated newspaper racks, trashcans, and even ashtrays were removed. International travel fell drastically.

Non-metropolises also feared the worst. In North Carolina, some people flocked to G.I. Joe's Army Surplus and the Quartermaster Company, as did many in Brentwood, Pennsylvania's Bonn's Outdoor Army and Navy Surplus Inc. There, they stocked up supplies; gas masks were the most popular item.

"Probably not since the Cuban missile crisis of October 1962 have Americans felt a keener threat of calamity on American soil, a fear reinforced by televised images of Federal agents in gas masks practicing how they would combat terrorists at the Super Bowl in Tampa, Fla., this Sunday, of armed guards closing off public access to the Birmingham Water Works in Alabama, and of new security rules at airports," the *New York Times* reported that week.

According to a CBS/*New York Times* poll, 63 percent of Americans were "very concerned" about an impending terrorist attack.

The NFL and those in charge of preparations for Super Bowl Sunday could not ignore the growing concerns. Extreme security precautions were implemented throughout the week. A six-foot-high fence and concrete barriers surrounded the stadium to keep any truck or car loaded with explosives from crashing into the stadium.

"We really didn't hear any threats until about the third day before the game," recalled Jim Steeg, the NFL's executive director of special events for twenty-six Super Bowls. "Then we heard through one of the intelligence security sources that somebody was going to steal a police car and load it with bombs and drive it into the side of the stadium. Everybody was kinda skeptical. And then on Saturday afternoon, a St. Petersburg police car was stolen. . . . You didn't hear a lot, but the people were concerned."

The Federal Bureau of Investigation's antiterrorist SWAT team—armed with machine guns—patrolled around and atop the stadium. In total, more than twenty-five hundred police and private-security personnel also stalked the area. Tampa Police, U.S. Army, and U.S. Coast Guard helicopters waited near the stadium in case unauthorized aircraft flew by the area. So did a U.S. Customs Blackhawk helicopter, the same model that soared across deserts in the Middle East. Even the Goodyear Blimp was denied access to all airspace within five miles of the game.

"A black helicopter came out of the north sometime in the second or first quarter," recalled Steeg. "Everybody was worried about what it was and they couldn't get ahold of the pilot to identify what it was. The story that I was told is that the SWAT guys zeroed and were ready to shoot the guy and all of a sudden the door opens up and they realize it was a guy with a camera. Or else they would have shot the guy down. They were deadly serious to say the least."

Inside Tampa Stadium, as the broadcast team of Al Michaels, Frank Gifford, and Dan Dierdorf learned after a relaxing Saturday evening dinner together with their wives, the safety measures in place bordered on morbid.

"The three of us go into this room, and there's some representative from the Tampa Police there," Dierdorf recalled. "There's also representatives of the FBI and one of the people there was from the Tampa SWAT team."

The joint security team informed Gifford, Michaels, and Dierdorf of the FBI's plan should terrorists attempt to take them hostage and hijack ABC's live coverage. Throughout the entire game, atop the luxury boxes at Tampa Stadium, snipers were in position, aimed directly at the broadcast booth.

"They proceed to give us a little mini-lesson on how to be a hostage," Dierdorf said.

> On how to let all the air out of your lungs, collapse your shoulders, and shrink and try to make yourself as small as possible. It was during the middle of that that I'm looking at Al, and I'm looking at Frank and well aware that I am noticeably bigger. You can give me all the lectures in the world about how to make yourself smaller, there's a limit there.
>
> So I'm thinking to myself, I can just hear them at the press conference: "That Dan was a hell of a guy. It's a shame that he just happened to be so much bigger than the two of us." I'm not gonna lie . . . that was sobering.

Another contingency plan affected far more people than those three celebrities in the broadcast booth. The Super Bowl, the quintessentially decadent American extravaganza, seemed a likely target should Hussein's public call inspire terrorism.

"It was pretty hard not to get the sense that we were going to have something happen," said Dr. Ricardo Martinez, the NFL's senior medical advisor. "Not necessarily inside the stadium, but I couldn't believe that somebody was going to let that [game] go by without making their point. My belief was that it would be something outside the stadium."

In addition to patrolling the sidelines during Super Bowl XXV in order to direct any emergency responses among fire, police, medical, FBI, and the like,

Dr. Martinez had another daunting task that week in Tampa. It was his job to acquire the antidote should a terrorist attack involve sarin (or nerve) gas.

> That area of Florida was known for drug trafficking: planes coming in and out all the time underneath the radar. You got an airport one hundred yards, two hundred yards away [from Tampa Stadium]. All they have to do is put some stuff in the back of a plane, fly up, and fly in. That's a very real threat. When you talk about sarin, this is not a nuclear weapon. You can make this chemical; you can buy versions of it most anywhere. We use this type of chemical to kill roaches. . . . It's not like this is a really hard chemical to get. You just have to have a lot of it.

In case of such an attack—and the organophosphate poisoning that would befall victims—an atropine injection was needed to combat the poison. The NFL purchased all the available atropine not reserved for the military. Those thousands of injection pens were stored inside Tampa Stadium, or in the pockets of medical staff, security supervisors, and usher captains.

"We tend to forget but it was a seminal moment in mass care and mass events. It transformed it," said Martinez, an emergency room physician at Stanford University in 1991. "I thought we were going to get hit. I would have never considered a rocket coming in or anything like that. But having seen threat reports occur every day and seeing how low the threshold was to be a player . . . we were sitting ducks. With all respect to the Blackhawk [helicopter], they weren't taking anybody down. They have a hard time taking down the guys flying [planes] with banners. To me, it was a perfect way for someone to do great damage."

Martinez and the other health and safety personnel were just as concerned with the chaos that would inevitably follow that type of attack. A stampede during the hysteric exodus might be just as life threatening as the chemical warfare. Evacuation plans inside and around the Super Bowl site were paramount to the safety precautions. But before the crowd of more than seventy thousand people could even get into the stadium, they had to pass through security.

"That Super Bowl was a bit of a stand-alone situation, because the Gulf War came up, we went to war, we had to secure the stadium," said Jerry Anderson, the NFL's architectural advisor for the Super Bowl since 1983. "We did not go back to that level until 9/11. What it did, though, was start the thinking: what does it take to secure and then respond to a mass threat? And there were things we never contemplated before in a serious manner."

X-ray machines, metal detectors, and security personnel patting people down guarded each of the sixty-eight gates. Cameras, camcorders, televisions, radios, beepers, and cell phones were all prohibited. Any bags or purses brought in by spectators were searched twice: first when they entered a bag-check area, and again when presenting tickets to the game. Even upon exiting their respective buses and approaching the locker rooms, all players and their equipment bags were subject to inspection by bomb-sniffing dogs.

"We've always had some presence for rapid response, but the degree of this was greatly enhanced," said Anderson, who has also served as an advisor for several Olympics and World Cup events.

It was a pivotal moment because I think it changed how people were thinking about a mass-event situation with the new threat of terrorism as opposed to cults, criminal activity that we'd seen in the past. . . . I found it real interesting how we had to respond after 9/11 because, fortunately, we were already plugged in with the federal government because of the Salt Lake Olympics, and what happened with the NFL came so fast and furious and it was a brilliant plan. But it was a good thing that [Super Bowl XXV] had already paved the way for that.

The extra screening may have been a hassle and a reminder of the danger— "Usually, Americans don't take to being searched or stopped," Tampa policeman Brian Seely said on game day—but it was also a comfort.

"I'm real glad to see all the security," said Harold Arlen of Bridgewater, New Jersey. "The more the better. I was kind of worried about coming to the game in the beginning. This may be the safest place in the world today."

Eventually, the lines became extremely long, and the men and women in bright yellow jackets reading "Security" hurried their pace.

"It's just taking too long," a Tampa officer said an hour into working the gate. "They'd never get the crowd in on time, so they just stopped being as thorough with the metal detectors."

Roughly an hour before kickoff, most of the spectators who paid $150 face value for their tickets had entered the stadium. And for their patience (few incidents between irritable fans and security personnel were reported), each spectator was given a small reward upon passing the turnstile: a four-inch-by-six-inch American flag.

As the tens of thousands began to settle into their seats, at precisely 6 p.m., the Bills players and coaching staff vacated their locker room—presumably, Jim Kelly had already thrown up— then stopped at the base of the opening adjacent to the field.

Introduced by Al Michaels, a cluster of Bills sprinted onto the field to an equal chorus of boos and cheers. They were followed by the team's starting defensive lineup and head coach Marv Levy. One by one, they jogged through a channel formed by the Bills' cheerleaders (the Buffalo "Jills"). Next, the Giants' eleven offensive starters and head coach Bill Parcells were announced.

"Running out of that tunnel [sic], fellas, I can't explain it," said Parcells, "but it's euphoria."

Kickoff was now only minutes away. But for Parcells and his Giants, Levy and his Bills, the 73,618 people in their seats, and the millions more watching at home, the euphoria of Super Bowl Sunday was momentarily preempted.

"And now to honor America," Frank Gifford called into the public address system, "especially the brave men and women serving our nation in the Persian Gulf and throughout the world, please join in the singing of our national anthem."

Along both sides of the field's twenty-five-yard lines, American soldiers and sailors stood, either holding giant flags of foreign allies or, at attention, saluting their Stars and Stripes. At midfield, a group of children and teenagers waited to unfold umbrellas that, once opened, would form an enormous American flag. And in front of the umbrella-toting flag bearers, the Florida Orchestra, under the direction of Maestro Jahja Ling, held basses, cellos, violins, and other instruments.

There were hundreds of people down on the football field, including more than two hundred players, coaches, trainers, and executives, aligned across their respective sidelines. But the eyes of everyone were locked on the woman at midfield.

"It was the most electric moment that I've ever seen in sports," Frank Gifford later said. "We come together like no other country in the history of civilization. We've proven that over and over."

Dressed in a white sweatsuit with a touch of red and blue fabric, Grammy Award–winning singer Whitney Houston stood atop a small wooden platform. And over the next one minute and fifty-five seconds, Houston delivered the most graceful, inspiring, goose bump–inducing rendition of the "Star-Spangled Banner" of all time.

"I keep pride inside when I think about the day that I saw Whitney Houston singing the national anthem when our son was so far away," remembered Martha Weaver, the mother of a navy man at sea. "Pride that he was part of what she was singing about: freedom for our nation, and not only for our nation, but for our nation helping other people who are in need."

Just as Houston belted out the final note of the performance, four F-16 jets—out of the Fifty-sixth Tactical Training Wing at MacDill Air Force Base—soared above the crowd.

"We were in white with blue numbers and red helmets. The Giants had blue jerseys and with white pants and red piping on their helmet so everything was red, white, and blue," Steve Tasker recalled. "She hit the last note of that anthem, then I turn around and the official I'm standing next to is in tears. Marv is wiping tears, and Jim [Kelly]. I look around and everybody in the stadium has got a flag in one hand, is wiping tears out of their eyes with the other."

All week long, stark contrasts between the Bills and Giants consumed the media's attention. Buffalo's offense was quick, explosive, and fast; New York's was traditional, methodical, and patient. Kelly, Thomas, Bruce Smith were all new Super Bowl faces; the Giants had been here before.

Off the field, the franchises projected very different personas: seven-point favorites, the Bills emitted a brash, even cocky, attitude; the Giants relished the role of the underdog lying in the weeds. Despite residing in the same state, even the cities represented by the franchises seemed to be polar opposites.

But for all the differences, in the final moments leading up to the kickoff of Super Bowl XXV, nothing separated the two teams.

"Here we are big football players," Stephen Baker remembered, "I had to look around and see if it was OK to cry. And I saw [Giants guard] William Roberts—one of the biggest guys on the team—he was crying. Now, I was like, 'It's OK to cry.'"

"It just made you proud to be an American, knowing that here we are, playing this big game, and our troops are over there fighting for us. When those F-16s flew over, it just made you feel good. Everybody shed a tear. And then after that, it was time to play."

The First Thirty Minutes

The surreal, patriotic scene of Whitney Houston and the jet flyover having disappeared in a matter of minutes, football returned to Tampa Stadium. Just after 6:15 p.m., Lawrence Taylor and Carl Banks stood on one side of the freshly painted Super Bowl XXV logo at midfield. Buffalo captains Mark Kelso, Kent Hull, Steve Tasker, Andre Reed, and Darryl Talley waited opposite them.

Walking out to join the group of Pro Bowlers and future Hall of Famers was a sharply dressed elderly gentleman. His hands crossed, resting at his waist, the sixty-four-year-old looked modest, even uncomfortable, standing center stage with the eyes of the world upon him. But the opening moments to the Super Bowl's quarter-century celebration deserved the presence of Alvin Ray "Pete" Rozelle.

From the game's bold moniker to the grand and occasionally gaudy half-time performances, Rozelle invented the Super Bowl. As commissioner for twenty-nine years, he expanded the NFL financially and geographically far beyond anyone's imagination. With the proclamation of the annual late-January holiday, the Super Bowl became the most important event on the annual sporting calendar.

In November 1989, Rozelle stepped down as league commissioner, a post he had held since 1960. So when San Francisco crushed Denver in Super Bowl XXIV, for the first time ever, Rozelle was not inside the winning locker room to present the Lombardi Trophy. Fittingly, for the silver anniversary, he returned to participate in another ceremonial moment: the pregame coin toss. Later that evening, the game's Most Valuable Player would receive the recently renamed Pete Rozelle Trophy. Super Bowl XXV would begin and end with a nod to the sport's greatest visionary.

"No name is more synonymous with the Super Bowl than Pete Rozelle," Commissioner Tagliabue said that week. "It was Pete's imagination and foresight that made this great event a reality."

Nurturing the Super Bowl from a matchup between two football teams into a worldwide event was Rozelle's crowning achievement as NFL commissioner. But all week long in Tampa, Rozelle was reminded of his greatest regret.

On the day after President Kennedy was assassinated in November 1963, Rozelle spoke with a former classmate at the University of San Francisco: Pierre Salinger, the White House press secretary. Salinger urged the commissioner to continue on with Week Eleven of the 1963 NFL season. As Rozelle stated, "It has been traditional in sports for athletes to perform in times of great personal tragedy. Football was Mr. Kennedy's game. He thrived on competition."

The NFL played its full slate of Sunday games.

In an interview around the time he announced his retirement, Rozelle was asked what his biggest mistake was as league commissioner: "Playing the game on Kennedy Sunday," he answered.

Three decades after being soundly criticized for the decision to play on "Kennedy Sunday," Rozelle still believed sports possessed some sort of healing power.

"President Roosevelt urged sports to continue [during World War II]," Rozelle told the *New York Times* when the Gulf War broke out. "And they did. He felt that people needed diversion because if they brooded about war, all their waking hours, they would be very depressed people."

After a week of watching Commissioner Tagliabue address unprecedented security measures and speculation about postponing the game, both Rozelle and his successor reaffirmed their belief that the game should go on.

Asked why, during stressful times, Americans found comfort in professional football, Tagliabue replied that "the Super Bowl is the winter version of the Fourth of July, an event without parallel."

Clearly, the new commissioner intended to link a distinctly American game with the chief American holiday: the Fourth of July is an annual celebration, when Americans come together, eat way too much food, and cheer and shout over explosive violence. So is the Super Bowl.

"It'd be like cancelling the Fourth of July to cancel [the Super Bowl]," fan Bill Urseth said. His wife, Cathy, agreed: "And if you did, Saddam wins."

With the flick of his right thumb, Pete Rozelle officially began Super Bowl XXV.

"Commissioner Rozelle, will you please toss the coin," head referee Jerry Seeman asked.

Standing in the eye of the hurricane that he brought to America, Rozelle flipped the specially minted commemorative coin into the air.

"Heads," called out Reed, a member of the so-called visiting team.

The coin landed heads up. Buffalo elected to receive; the Giants chose to defend the north end zone. The pregame pageantry now over, both teams' special teams units readied to take the field.

"Don't be offsides, let's start it off right!" one member of the Giants' kickoff team shouted in the sideline huddle with special teams coach Mike Sweatman. "Hit somebody!"

The Giants' kickoff team dispersed across their own thirty-yard line. Kicker Matt Bahr teed up the ball from his own thirty-five-yard line, then sent a booming end-over-end kick into the seventy-one-degree night air. Returner Don Smith accepted it at the fourteen-yard line and charged upfield before Bahr, the smallest, slowest, and oldest man on the field, wrapped two arms around Smith and wrestled him to the ground. Curiously, a kicker starred on the first play of Super Bowl XXV.

Sans huddle, ten Bills assembled along the thirty-four-yard line. All alone in the backfield (Thurman Thomas split out as a receiver), Jim Kelly stood in the shotgun, four yards behind his center, Kent Hull. To no one's surprise, the Bills would come out throwing.

On the opposite side of the line of scrimmage, there *was* a surprise. As Kelly peered past his offensive line, he saw a bizarre defensive alignment: only two Giants down-linemen.

Years later, in his acclaimed biography, *The Education of a Coach*, the brilliant author David Halberstam summed up Belichick's Super Bowl XXV game plan.

"He did not want Jim Kelly throwing on every down. The Bills were less dangerous, he thought, given the superb abilities of the New York defense, if they went to their running game, which also had the advantage of taking more time off the clock. He thought the Giants could stop Thurman Thomas, even though he was an exceptional back, if and when they needed to, because they were so good against the run," Halberstam wrote. "What Belichick really hoped was, in effect, to tease Kelly, to offer him the running game in the second half and then at critical moments take it away from him."

Though counterintuitive, Belichick openly welcomed a Thurman Thomas–led offensive attack and used a peculiar two-man defensive line (most teams have four or, at least, three) to encourage Buffalo's running game. By using more speed-oriented defenses—variations on the dime and nickel packages—Belichick believed the Giants would be in a better position both to saturate Kelly's passing lanes and bring down Thomas in the running game.

The "Big Nickel" package featured only two defensive linemen; linebackers Lawrence Taylor and Pepper Johnson rushed the passer as stand-up defensive ends. Along with Carl Banks, six defensive backs patrolled the passing lanes. In the "Little Nickel," a defensive back was swapped out for one linebacker. In short, the Giants were rushing four men, dropping seven.

"We went into the game thinking we gotta stop the passing game. We felt like they would have a lot of respect for our run defense. So we put our best pass defense out there," Belichick said in 2011. "They wouldn't expect us to play a small group to start the game so what we tried to do was get our best pass rushers out there and get our best pass defenders out there and really try and take away the middle of the field."

The fresh game plan was also intended to catch the Bills off guard.

"They were used to rolling in that no-huddle offense," nose tackle Erik Howard said. "At that time, I think the Bills had to be saying 'what is this, a completely different look?' and they were going to have to adjust to it. There was no way they could prepare for that.

"That was a major deal: sitting us all down and saying 'We're putting in a completely new defense.' We hadn't played that all season. I think that action alone inspired a whole lot of confidence."

As the game wore on, the Giants stuck to their game plan and even (occasionally) pulled defensive end Leonard Marshall off the field: only one defensive lineman was on the field for New York. To combat the unorthodox offense of the Buffalo Bills, Belichick crafted an equally quirky defense.

On that first-and-ten, opening play from scrimmage, Kelly surveyed the field as three Giants neared his right side. Just as Marshall—nearing another gruesome championship game tackle of a Pro Bowl quarterback—leapt at him, Kelly unloaded the ball downfield, far beyond his intended receiver, Andre Reed.

Kelly looking for number "83" was nothing new. Not only had Reed been Buffalo's most dangerous receiver all season, he was by far the quarterback's favorite target.

Reed, who turned twenty-seven two days after the Super Bowl, starred for Kutztown University, a Division II football program roughly eighty miles northwest of Philadelphia. Team scout Elbert Dubenion—a small school (Bluffton College) product himself—saw potential in Reed, and the Bills chose him in the fourth round of the 1985 draft.

"Supposedly, I was a diamond in the rough," Reed said. "And [Dubenion] was one of the guys who got me up here. He just told me I had as much of a chance as anyone else of making the team."

As Buffalo's offense improved, Reed blossomed into the best wide receiver in the AFC, leading his conference in receptions and yardage in 1989. A year later, he earned a second consecutive spot on the all-pro team. From the moment Kelly joined the Bills in 1986, Reed led the team in catches each season. And by the time their careers were complete, the Kelly-Reed duo would produce more touchdowns than even the celebrated Joe Montana–to–Jerry Rice combination.

"Everybody talks about Jerry Rice, but I'll stick with Andre," Kelly said that week in Tampa. "The guy is unbelievable."

Having missed Reed on the game's first snap, Kelly returned to him on the next two plays, and this time both passes were completions. But on each reception, the Giants defense and its wall of bodies in the middle of the field—in place of pass-rushing linemen—swallowed Reed up as soon as he made the catch. Buffalo did not gain a first down and was forced to punt.

Dave Meggett's twenty-yard return of a Rick Tuten punt provided the Giants with a good starting point, the Buffalo forty-three-yard line, for their first offensive series. While the Bills had opened the game in the shotgun with an empty backfield and five receivers, New York's offense formation was, predictably, the complete opposite.

From a three–tight end, single-back set, Hostetler handed the ball off to Ottis Anderson for a short loss. Because Darryl Talley had been offsides at the time of the snap, the play was nullified, and New York was awarded five free yards. Benefiting from the game's first penalty, the Giants strung together a pair of first downs by way of a play-action pass from Hostetler to tight end Howard Cross and a run from Meggett.

But after crossing their opponents thirty-five, an incompletion and a short run brought up a third and seven. Forced into a passing situation, the Giants replaced the three-tight-end running alignment with their own four-receiver shotgun set. Hostetler completed a short pass to the slot receiver, Mark Ingram, who broke a tackle and eluded two others, to pick up sixteen yards. New York's fourth first down in six offensive snaps set the Giants up at the Buffalo fifteen.

Just a few minutes into Super Bowl XXV, the Giants, not the Bills, looked like the team with the offensive edge.

Buffalo's defense promptly stiffened, and the Giants could only gain a few yards over the next three plays. Well within Matt Bahr's range, New York attempted a twenty-eight-yard field goal that split the uprights. With a little more than seven minutes remaining in the first quarter, the Giants led 3-0.

FLASHBACK: SUPER BOWL I

"I don't think any of us knew what to expect," Bill Curry said years later. "But we certainly didn't expect thirty thousand empty seats at the biggest game in the history of the world."

Prior to the 1966 NFL season, Curry, a second-year center from Georgia Tech, earned the starting job for the Green Bay Packers. The dual duty of snapping to and blocking for the great Bart Starr, combined with the eye of head coach Vince Lombardi scrutinizing his every move, prepared him for just about any pressure situation. By the end of that season, he was more than ready to play before a fully packed stadium for the Packers' NFL title game against Dallas.

Seventy-five thousand, five hundred four people filled the seats at the Cotton Bowl that day, witnesses to Green Bay's 34-27 defeat of the Cowboys. So when the Packers and Kansas City Chiefs met two weeks later to play in the first ever AFL-NFL Championship Game before a one-third empty Los Angeles Coliseum, Curry and most of his teammates were stunned.

"There were a few writers, there was a sparse crowd, and we played a game, and it just didn't feel big time."

The fourteen-point underdog Chiefs of the allegedly inferior American Football League met the Packers on January 15, 1967, and even caught a break on the third play from scrimmage. While blocking to help spring fullback Jim Taylor for a first down, Packer tight end Boyd Dowler separated his shoulder and left the game.

During the previous four seasons, Dowler caught more passes than did any other Green Bay player. Against Kansas City's defense—led by future Hall of Famers Buck Buchanan and Bobby Bell, as well as boastful, yet talented all-star Fred "the Hammer" Williamson—the loss of Dowler threatened to severely handicap the passing game.

Fortunately, the Packers had a suitable replacement on their sidelines: former Pro Bowler Max McGee. But the thirty-four-year-old McGee only caught four passes during the 1966 season, despite suiting up for every game. Even more troublesome to the Packer cause, was McGee's physical and mental status when Vince Lombardi called for the eleven-year veteran.

"He didn't come in the huddle bright eyed and bushy tailed," Packer guard Jerry Kramer remembered. "He was like he was half-way hungover or something, or half-way asleep. He wasn't what you'd like to see coming into the huddle at that particular point in time."

McGee wasn't half-way hungover; he was full-blown hungover.

"I was rooming with Paul Hornung, my buddy, and we're both single and here we are, last night in Hollywood, and boy I tell you, we went out and hit a few of the hot spots, the normal places and we ran into a group of stewardesses who were having a little fun," McGee told NFL Films years later. "Well all at once: curfew. So we head back to make curfew and we jumped into bed. And for some reason, Hawg Hanner was checking curfew, not Vince. Well, I played with Hawg, he was my good buddy. . . . He opened the door and said, 'Ok, if you two guys are in, everybody's in.' Well, when he went back out, we almost ran over him, I did, getting out of there."

A stern warning had been delivered to the entire Packers team earlier that day:

"Men, if you bust curfew tonight, not only will I fine you $2,500," Lombardi told his players, "But I will see to it that you never play another game in the National Football League."

McGee, who informed reporters all week that he was retiring after the AFL-NFL championship, didn't care. He didn't return to the team hotel until the next morning, just as quarterback Bart Starr walked through the lobby to pick up a newspaper.

"They had these little dressing cubicles in the Los Angeles Coliseum," Dowler recalled. "Max was right next door. . . . I sat down with Max and he gave a big sigh of [exhaustion]—like 'Oh my gosh.'"

"What's the matter with you?" Dowler asked.

"Don't go down today," McGee told Dowler.

"Tell me about it," Dowler replied.

"So he told me about it. So I knew what was going on," Dowler said, four decades later. "I hear there were two young ladies involved. He referred to them as 'fiancés.'"

Not expecting to play, still hungover, and operating without sleep, McGee was ill-prepared when Dowler was injured.

"Here's McGee on the sidelines," teammate Bob Long recalled years later, "he's looking around, scurrying around, he starts yelling 'Where's my helmet, where's my helmet?' Someone shouts out 'Max, you left it in the locker room.' Can you imagine that! He didn't have a helmet. So I kinda felt sorry for him at that moment, I said, 'Here Max, take my helmet.' Max took my helmet."

A series after he wobbled into the huddle, the Packers faced a third down at the Kansas City thirty-seven. The Chiefs had already rebuffed Green Bay on a third down the previous drive: their front four penetrated Green Bay's offensive line and sacked quarterback Bart Starr, forcing a punt.

Rather than (predictably) running the ball on third and three, the Packers went to the air. Again, the Chiefs formidable defensive line collapsed the pocket. Because no one blocked him, blitzing linebacker Chuck Hurston crashed into Starr, slightly altering the release. The pass soared downfield to the twenty-two-yard line, intended for McGee, who was running a post-pattern near the middle of the field.

"A lot of guys on the team would tell you that Max was the best athlete on that team," said Bill Curry. "He could just do anything, including get drunk all night and come play and then say 'Being drunk one night is not gonna destroy twenty-five years of conditioning.' That was the most hilarious line in the whole thing: Getting drunk one night can destroy anything."

McGee beat defensive back Willie Mitchell to the inside and was wide open. Starr's rhythm disrupted, the ball ended up several feet behind his target. With sharp reflexes that defied the effects of his nighttime adventures, McGee stuck out his right hand—continuing to run at full speed—nabbed the football with his fingertips, pulled it into his chest, and sprinted into the end zone.

"Max took my helmet, and he caught the first pass ever for a touchdown in a Super Bowl, so I get to tell my kids, 'I didn't catch the pass but my helmet helped Max McGee catch the first touchdown ever.' That was my helmet, it was Max McGee's body," Bob Long said. "As Max would tell it, the story, I heard him tell this all the time. Everybody up here [in Green Bay] says 'Hey Max, you caught that ball one-hand, behind your back.' Max says 'Yea, my eyes were so bloodshot I looked back for the pass from Bart Starr I saw two footballs coming. I really didn't know what to do but I thought quickly, I'll put my arm right in the middle between them. And that's where the ball stuck.'"

For a sports spectacle that would produce countless unforgettable moments over the decades, McGee's miraculous thirty-seven-yard catch was the first touchdown in Super Bowl history.

In his dubiously self-declared "final game" (he would return to the team next season), McGee was not content with the one catch. Starr and McGee hooked up on six more receptions.

"[Willie] Mitchell was out there trying to cover Max McGee by himself," Bill Curry said. "And Max was running in the huddle saying, 'God Almighty, throw me the ball, that guy can't cover me.' Which, of course, was exactly right."

McGee and the passing game stretched Kansas City's defense. The increasingly over-aggressive front line of the Chiefs, eager to bring down Starr, left holes at the line of scrimmage and Packers running backs found room to run. In the second half, Green Bay overwhelmed their AFL counterpart.

With the score 21-10 late in the third quarter and the Packers inside the red zone, McGee ran another post-pattern. He swam around the underneath safety, cut in front of Mitchell, and again found an open spot in the secondary. Right at the goal line, Starr targeted McGee. Although it was a perfectly placed, over-the-shoulder pass, McGee made another dazzling circus catch for a Packer touchdown. The ball hit his hands, bounded into the air, and the juggling McGee pulled it down for a thirteen-yard score. He finished the game with seven receptions for 138 yards and two touchdowns.

"He thought he should have been the MVP," Curry said about McGee, who passed away in 2007. "Bart [the MVP Award winner of Super Bowl I] tried to give it to him!"

At 28-10 with just a quarter to play, McGee's second touchdown put the game out of reach. Early in the final period, running back Elijah Pitts' rushing touchdown pushed the lead to 35-10, sealing the game.

Not much happened after that. Green Bay tried to kill time off the clock, and the Chiefs essentially surrendered, replacing perennial AFL all-star quarterback Len Dawson with backup Pete Beathard. Now a blowout, many spectators began to lose interest, including a ten-year-old boy whose home stood just a few miles from the Los Angeles Coliseum.

"I was just a kid and I wanted to know when I was going to get the popcorn and the hot dog and the soda," he remembered. "And probably, after I finished that, I was ready to go."

Mike Lofton, an army sergeant major and single parent, surprised his son, James, with tickets (albeit, not very good tickets) to the big game. With so many vacant seats in the stadium, Mike and James snuck closer and closer to the field. By halftime, the father and son watched from a wonderful viewing point near the thirty-yard line.

"I really didn't know much about the teams that were playing, but I was always grateful for his taking me to that game," James Lofton said about his father, who passed away in October 1990. "It was a real special memory."

Lofton soon learned to make his own spectacular touchdown catches, first at George Washington High in Los Angeles, then at Stanford University. Over the years, the memories of what took place on the field during Super Bowl I faded for Lofton. But at the start of his own NFL career, he would become thoroughly reacquainted with the tale of Max McGee and the first touchdown in Super Bowl history: The sixth overall selection in the 1978 NFL draft, he was selected by the Green Bay Packers. Lofton's rookie season would be Mc-Gee's fourth as a folksy, colorful contributor to the Packer radio broadcasts.

"I talked to those guys a little bit about what it was like playing in that game," said Lofton. "[I came] to know Max over the years, [and saw] that play countless times."

While McGee broadcast games well into the 1990s, Lofton left Green Bay and joined his hometown Los Angeles Raiders in 1987. After nine seasons (including six under head coach Bart Starr) as a member of the Packer franchise that won the first two Super Bowls, Lofton yearned for a chance to play in "the biggest game in the history of the world." Even if a spectacular circus catch wasn't one of his goals.

"[Playing the Super Bowl is] a fantasy, sure," he said a few days before his Buffalo Bills faced the Giants. "There's the one-handed, reverse catch that you always want to make. But, you know, I usually tell guys, when you go out trying for the spectacular, something for the blooper film usually results."

Seeing Matt Bahr's field goal provide the underdog Giants an early lead left Buffalo's high-powered offense eager to make a big play. After all, when the Giants forced a three-and-out at the outset of Super Bowl XXV, it marked the first time the Bills were kept without an opening-drive touchdown in that postseason.

On second and eight from their own thirty-one-yard line, the no-huddle hurried to the line, following a short Thurman Thomas run. From the shotgun, Kelly looked right—momentarily freezing Giants defensive back Everson Walls—then heaved a deep ball down the left sideline. At the New York twenty-seven-yard line, James Lofton was one step past nickel cornerback Perry Williams.

"The ball was really hanging up there," Lofton remembered. "Had Jim been able to throw it three or four yards further, 'cause I had beaten him easily, and the ball was kinda underthrown a little bit . . . it would have been an easy score."

Williams leapt, sprawling out in midair, then deflected the ball with the fingertips on his right hand. The tipped pass spun end over end, high above the ground. The extra hang time allowed Lofton to adjust and locate the ball.

"He got a lot of the ball, so it wasn't a bad deflection. He was coming down when the ball was coming down. He really wasn't out of position," Lofton noted. "Those are the kind of plays you can't predict. You certainly don't practice them."

Displaying remarkable concentration, Lofton pulled in the wobbly ball. He danced along the sideline, trying to stay in bounds to reach the end zone. Lofton's tiptoeing—and the additional split-second in which the tipped ball floated in the air—gave Everson Walls time to swoop in and knock Lofton out-of-bounds at the eight-yard line.

"I played safety like I played cornerback," said Walls, a cornerback who played safety in the Giants' nickel and dime packages. "I could still sit back and read an offense extremely well, and I was good at anticipating. And I knew that's where [Kelly] was going with the pass. That's what allowed me to get a jump on it and stop Lofton from scoring a touchdown."

In the previous twenty-four Super Bowls, only nine plays from scrimmage netted more yards, and each of those produced a touchdown. Although Walls prevented Lofton from scoring, the sixty-one-yard catch-and-run seemed destined to yield a touchdown and, perhaps, spark Buffalo's great offense into a scoring frenzy. But two incompletions from Kelly, sandwiched between a short Thomas rush up the middle, stalled the drive, and kicker Scott Norwood converted on a short field goal to even the score at three.

At the start of their next drive, the Giants offense picked up where they had left off. From their standard, multiple tight-end set, consecutive rushes by Anderson and Hostetler gave New York a first down.

Hostetler then fired a pass downfield to Stephen Baker and saw tight end Howard Cross—who thought the ball was intended for him—stick his hand up and deflect the ball. The ball slowed down and fluttered through the air, but stayed on target: Baker pulled the ball into his stomach. The second fluke, tipped-pass reception of the quarter garnered a sizable chunk of yardage and moved the Giants to midfield.

Buffalo's defense had now surrendered eighty-eight yards and six first downs. A week earlier in the AFC Championship Game against Los Angeles, at the three-minute mark of the opening period, Darryl Talley was returning an interception for a touchdown to boost their lead to 21-3. Seven days later, at the exact same three-minute mark, the Bills were embroiled in a much different contest.

"I've never been so tired in a football game in my life," said Shane Conlan. "I was even tired in the first quarter. They kept pounding with guys like Anderson, and that wears you out. . . . I broke my face mask on Anderson in the first half. It just snapped and turned all the way around to the right side of my helmet. I mean, jeez, it's the first time I ever broke a face mask."

"They were sagging," said tight end Bob Mrosko, who needed postgame stitches on his forehead following a collision with Darryl Talley. "They weren't pursuing as hard. In practice we had told ourselves that no matter what happened, we'd play our style of football."

While Anderson was vital to the offensive game plan, the Giants needed to mix passes into the ground-heavy attack. And after Anderson pounded out four yards on a first and ten from midfield, miscues in the passing game—a far-too-high Hostetler pass and a drop by Meggett—led to a Sean Landeta punt.

At the twenty-yard line, Buffalo began their third attempt at cracking the league's top-ranked defense. This time the renowned K-Gun finally appeared. Three quick completions from Kelly to Reed (in the span of just four plays) gained thirty-five yards and surged Buffalo across midfield. The opening quarter came to a close, and the teams paused to switch sides and catch a breath while another sequence of $800,000-per-thirty-second advertisements entertained ABC's viewing audience.

The momentary break in action did not interrupt the Bills' rhythm. Healthy gains followed, via a catch by Thomas for thirteen yards and Kelly's sixth completion to Andre Reed, which picked up another nine. Kelly then connected with tight end Keith McKeller; a penalty—Leonard Marshall blindsided Kelly and shoved him to the ground well after the quarterback released the ball—added four yards to McKeller's catch and Buffalo advanced to the four-yard line.

On the previous drive, Buffalo had squandered an opportunity deep inside Giants territory. Following Lofton's sixty-one-yard grab and the subsequent first and goal, the Bills stayed in their familiar no-huddle, shotgun offense: only a field goal resulted.

For their second chance so close to the Giants goal line, the Bills switched to a more conventional short-yardage offense: three tight ends, two backs, no shotgun. A sneaky run up the middle to seldom-used fullback Jamie Mueller came up just inches shy: only a crushing hit by Lawrence Taylor kept him from scoring. Instant replay was even used to determine if Mueller broke the plane of the goal line.

Again, from their unfamiliar formation, the Bills lined up, center Kent Hull gripping a football that flirted with the end zone's white line. At the snap, a powerful surge by Hull and guard Jim Ritcher opened up a spot in the Giants defensive front. Reserve running back Don Smith aimed for the hole and, behind Mueller's piercing block of Gary Reasons, squeezed into the end zone for the first Super Bowl touchdown in Buffalo Bills history.

"It was really great coming back here, especially scoring a touchdown here," said Smith, a former Mississippi State quarterback who played the previous three seasons with the Buccaneers before joining Buffalo as a free agent. "I had never scored a touchdown in this stadium before. The fact that it was the Super Bowl made it even better."

The 10-3 lead gave Buffalo slight command of the scoreboard. Over the next few minutes, they seized command of the game.

Consecutive marginal gains at the start of the ensuing drive left the Giants with a third and six from their own thirty-six: not ideal positioning for an offense designed to leave minimal distances on third down.

From the shotgun with four wide receivers, Hostetler surveyed the field and fired an incomplete pass, far off-line from his target, rookie Troy Kyles. The quick three-and-out (New York ran only a minute and a half off the clock) troubled Parcells and the entire New York sideline. But there was a much more damaging result of the third-down incompletion.

Giants left tackle Doug Riesenberg, concerned by the inside rush of NFL Defensive Player of the Year Bruce Smith, unknowingly allowed Buffalo's Leon Seals a clear path into the backfield. (This defensive line stunt is known as an "outside twist.") Seals, the man initially responsible for Phil Simms' injured foot back in Week Fifteen, clobbered Hostetler just as the ball was thrown.

"Seals is a big, powerful man, and he got what a defensive lineman would call a great hit," remembered Hostetler, "because he came down on top of me with his whole body weight and nothing stopping it."

Hostetler stumbled to the bench and sat there for several minutes with smelling salts pinned to his nose: "I couldn't even smell the ammonia, I was so woozy. My vision was fuzzy. I thought I might have to come out."

Meanwhile, Buffalo's offense, fresh off their twelve-play, eighty-yard touchdown drive, sprang into action. Consecutive Thurman Thomas rushes, against the two-down-linemen Giants front, netted eighteen yards. But patience and confidence in Belichick's unusual defensive approach promptly paid off.

No matter how good Thurman Thomas was, the Bills were not going to run him on every down. And by flooding the field with quick defenders very capable in pass coverage, the Giants could limit Jim Kelly's options when the Bills did try and stay balanced by throwing the football.

Following a pair of rushes, Kelly returned to the air. On the run to avoid pressure, he tossed the ball to Reed who was unable to hang on after being decked midair by Myron Guyton. Punishing Buffalo receivers was another part of the Giants' strategy in defending the pass game. The strategy had a prolonged impact. On the next play, a third and one near midfield, Kelly again targeted Reed on a short pass over the middle. No defender was within three yards of him, and Kelly's pass was precise. Still, Reed dropped the ball: he must have noticed Pepper Johnson, the Giant linebacker in position to pound Reed had he hauled in the football.

"In the tapes of other games," said Carl Banks, "they had guys catch the ball and run through the defense for large gains. We backed up in our zones, changed the coverages and rushes, and when receivers caught the ball, we wanted to punish them. They have the kind of offense that is going to make some plays. We knew that, but we wanted them to understand that we were going to hammer them when they caught it."

The Giants defense had held, but the Bills were about to add to their lead.

A good punt by Rick Tuten pinned the Giants back at their own six-yard line. Despite the noticeable wear and tear on their quarterback, Parcells and his offensive staff remained confident in Hostetler. Play-action on first down (Hostetler was actually standing three yards deep in his own end zone as he scanned the field) gained seven yards, which was lost on second down, the result of a holding penalty.

On the next snap, Hostetler again receded into the backfield with the intention of putting the ball in the air.

"I remember the play, it was '258,' it was a straight drop back and rollout to the right and what Ottis [Anderson] saw was that they had a blitz coming. And Ottis was trying to step up quick underneath me to pick up his guy," Hostetler said years later. "Well, in doing that, he stepped in and caught my foot as I'm dropping back."

Hostetler stumbled toward the ground, then regained balance and began to straighten up, hoping to either escape his own end zone or simply throw the ball away.

"[All] of a sudden I felt this big paw in my ear trying to strip the ball," he said.

That paw belonged to Bruce Smith, who locked hold of Hostetler's right wrist, then swiped at the ball with the other hand. Knowing that the difference between a safety and a touchdown would be his ability to maintain possession—by now there was no chance of escaping the swarm of Bills—Hostetler pulled the football into his stomach, smothering it like a grease fire.

"If I lost the ball there and they recover, we're probably finished, because that puts them up [17-3] at that point in the game, and I don't think we can recover from that. But holding on to it, and just giving them the safety, it turned out to be a huge, huge play for us. For me it was like in the backyard with my two older brothers again: getting beat up and trying to hold on to the football."

"That was a huge play, and it could have been an even bigger play," Smith said years later. "But he just had a strong grip, a strong hold on the ball, and was able to hold onto it, and we ended up getting a safety and two points out of it but the ultimate would have been to get the strip and get the touchdown."

Smith—who was flagged for an excessive celebration penalty—and the Bills' sideline showed little angst. In addition to two points, the Bills also received possession of the football by way of a free kick from New York.

"[Parcells] said it multiple times that week," recalled Bob Mrosko, the Giants tight end from Penn State,

> that we had to be patient. He said it as plain as day, there are going to be a couple of times in this game when things are going to start going bad for us. And no matter what we do, we have to stick with our game plan and we can't try and get in a shoot-out with this team.
>
> I remember Bill Parcells calling the whole defense over [after the safety], and he talked to them. I imagine he must have told them "stop 'em." Then he called the whole offense. Basically, he said, "I just talked to the defense: they're stopping [Buffalo] after we do the free kick. We're gonna get the ball back. We're gonna drive it down the field, and score, we're gonna get back in this game and take control of this game. . . . The way Bill Parcells coached—I've been around some great football coaches, college with Joe Paterno—but that guy was absolutely a prophet in how he designed a football game.

From there, the fast-paced first half momentarily slowed. A trio of incompletions—including another drop by Andre Reed, the result of another tough hit delivered from a Giants defender—forced the Bills to punt. A similarly uneventful Giants' three-and-out returned possession to Buffalo.

Five straight incompletions on five straight offensive snaps convinced Kelly to put the ball in the hands of their most elusive and reliable player. Thurman Thomas gashed the Giants for an eighteen-yard run on first down following the Giants' punt. The five-foot, ten-inch back punctuated his big gain by pounding safety Myron Guyton, just before three Giants brought him down.

"He runs so big, doesn't he, Dan," Frank Gifford wondered aloud, on camera to Dan Dierdorf, "198 pounds and he runs liked a 220-pound back. He's so quick, so shifty. . . . He just looks for guys, then hammers Guyton."

Thomas carried the ball on the next three plays—a run for four yards and back-to-back passes out of the backfield that yielded eighteen more—before taking a much-deserved rest on the sidelines.

"It's up to Thomas," Gifford said. "They're not going to change the offense much because he gets more work than any of the receivers, anyone else in that offensive unit. He's in the pass pattern, he runs the ball, he runs the draw, he runs on the screen. When he finally had it, he points his finger to himself, 'get me outta here,' and they bring in help."

Gifford, the Giants' all-time leader in total yardage, could appreciate a multitalented back who served as the cornerstone of a championship-caliber team.

But while Thomas stood on the sidelines catching his breath, the Buffalo offense screeched to a halt: an incompletion, a false-start penalty, and a short pass reception that failed to convert on third and seven. Buffalo punted.

"Thurman was an outstanding player; he could run and catch and could do a lot with the ball. I think he was really their ultimate weapon. He provided the balance for that team," Parcells said in 2010. "They were in the no-huddle, kinda a one-back offense and three wide receivers, the NFL hadn't seen a lot of that. And it was the offense of the '90s. The [Indianapolis] Colts still use, basically, the same thing. It's had a long lifespan, and almost every team uses some aspects of it."

Less than four minutes remained in the first half when Hostetler and the Giants offense took the field for a first and ten from their own thirteen. Despite the two-score deficit and being backed up near their own end zone late in the first half, the Giants didn't flinch.

"I had seen so much of the Giants," Eagles beat-writer Ray Didinger said,

I knew how mentally tough a team they were. And I knew how well coached they were. I never got the feeling they were gonna let that game get away from them. . . . That's usually how Super Bowls get out of hand: one team falls behind and the coaching staff would totally get away from what they've done all year and what they do well, and they get into sort of a panic mode, and they start try-ing to force the issue, and they start throwing the ball a lot and taking chances. And then all of a sudden, they start making mistakes, and a couple mistakes lead to more points, and the next thing you know, the roof has fallen in. The Giants, with Parcells and that coaching staff, they just weren't going to do that. That was not a group that was prone to panic.

Although there was no panic on the Giants' sideline, in the huddle, Jeff Hostetler alerted his teammates of the urgency.

"I told them it was time to stop screwing around," he said. "I told them that we were about to blow this thing for ourselves."

The Giants responded to their leader. After a nice gain on first down, Ot-tis Anderson burst through a crease in the Buffalo front to pick up eighteen. Then Hostetler slung a dart downfield along the right sideline, over a leaping cornerback, into the hands of Mark Ingram, who touched both feet down before falling out-of-bounds. An outside run by Meggett picked up seventeen yards. On three consecutive snaps, the Giants had gained more yards (fifty-seven) than they had on their previous four series combined.

Meggett's burst brought about the two-minute warning. Nearing Buffalo's red zone, the Giants could now think about putting points on the board. But no receivers opened up downfield on first or second down, and in order to keep the drive alive, the Giants would need to convert a third and seven from the twenty-one.

With the clock reading 1:13, Parcells signaled for a time-out: he wanted to discuss the play options with his quarterback and offensive coordinator. Mo-ments later, Hostetler returned to the field, broke the huddle, took the snap, and surveyed the field. After all that discussion, the second-string tight end was not the man Parcells, Hostetler, or Ron Erhardt were hoping to get the ball too. Nevertheless, Howard Cross came up with a huge play. On his knees, the second-year University of Alabama product caught the ball in the flats, a yard shy of the flagstick, then rolled sideways for an additional yard to gain the critical first down.

Cornelius Bennett batted down Hostetler's next pass, leaving the Giants with thirty-six seconds to gain the fourteen yards needed for a touchdown.

Throughout the first half, both quarterbacks struggled to make accurate passes. In addition to badly overthrowing Reed on the game's opening play from scrimmage, Kelly had already twice underthrown Lofton on deep passes, including the sixty-one-yard tipped ball completion early in the game. Hostetler—still in a haze from several crushing blows—accumulated his share of subpar tosses as well. During the Giants' lone scoring drive, he too had underthrown his receiver on a critical play: not leading Mark Ingram enough on a third-down throw into the end zone meant New York had to settle for a Matt Bahr field-goal attempt. Earlier in that drive, he also overthrew Mark Bavaro by several feet as the veteran tight end was wide open near the goal line.

On this drive late in the second period, he remained inconsistent. The twenty-two-yard strike to Ingram along the sideline hummed and was placed brilliantly. But his next throw was far out of reach for Maurice Carton. Even the critical third-down completion to Howard Cross had been errant.

"Hostetler has just been off in throwing the ball," Dan Dierdorf remarked to the ABC viewing audience. "That might have been a touchdown if he threw it and led Cross."

Despite several regrettable throws, the Giants kept turning to Hostetler. Even after another, seemingly devastating misfire.

From the fourteen-yard line, Hostetler took the snap and stood tall in the pocket. Leon Seals bearing down on him, Hostetler tossed the ball toward the center of the end zone. There, Stephen Baker had cut underneath safety Mark Kelso. A throw anywhere near the sure-handed receiver would result in six points. The ball hit the ground two feet in front of Baker, who dove forward to try and snag the pass.

"I was mad at myself because I knew I had underthrown him," Hostetler wrote. "I lost him momentarily behind the line and threw where I thought he would be. I was wrong."

"When he threw that first one in the dirt, I said, 'that's it, I'm not gonna get another chance to score,'" Baker remembered.

Rather than trying to avoid another miscue between quarterback and receiver, the Giants offensive staff turned right back to Hostetler and Baker via a familiar approach.

Back in October, the post-corner route—a receiver running toward the center of the field ("the post"), then breaking sharply downfield to the sidelines ("the corner" of the end zone)—had produced a thirty-eight-yard touchdown in Hostetler's fourth-quarter comeback against Phoenix. Three months later, Baker ran the post-corner in the divisional round and hauled in a Hostetler pass for the Giants' first touchdown against Chicago.

"When we got back in the huddle, the coaches called the same play we used to beat the Cardinals and also in the playoff game against the Bears. So he called my number."

Prior to the start of the play—called "back green X flag"—Hostetler read a blitz in the Buffalo formation: from the shotgun, he could see an expanded view of the field. At the snap, six members of the Bills front seven charged toward him. Although linebacker Ray Bentley breached the offensive line, Hostetler found enough time to float the ball toward the left corner before being touched.

"The line blocked well, and Hostetler made one of the best throws I think he's ever made because I didn't give him a lot of room to lead me," Baker said. "So he had to throw it on the line, and he put it there like a dart, and I ended up getting both feet down. I was so happy, I took the ball and spiked it like I did a reverse slam dunk on a basketball hoop."

Baker's clutch catch—in a narrow space between cornerback Nate Odomes and the sideline of the end zone—brought the Giants back into the game. Bahr nailed the extra point, and the Giants trailed just 12-10 with only twenty-five seconds showing on the clock.

"That was a very special moment," Baker remembered. "It got us back into the game; that was the most important thing."

The Bills, content to go into halftime ahead by two points, did not run another play. From his own thirteen-yard line, Jim Kelly took a knee, and the first-half clock expired. As both teams jogged into the locker room, one fact was clear: Buffalo had the lead, but the Giants had momentum.

"They're not used to going into halftime in a tough game," Giants Safety Mark Collins said. "They're used to being 21 or 35 points up on people and coasting."

8

Whipping Boys

During halftime, the Super Bowl crowd—those not waiting in lines at the concession stands or restrooms—watched the now globally renowned Super Bowl halftime show. Boy band and teen sensation The New Kids on the Block performed their popular songs "Step By Step" and "This One's For the Children." Michael Jackson made a cameo.

But for months, an intricate salute to Super Bowl history was also planned for the annual performance: a "Small World Salute to Twenty-five Years of the Super Bowl."

Houston Oilers quarterback and 1989 NFL Man of the Year Warren Moon, along with two thousand children—boys dressed in helmets, shoulder pads, and full football uniforms; girls wearing cheerleader outfits and holding pom-poms—participated in a choreographed routine. Because Disney was producing the show, Donald Duck, Tigger, and "coach" Roger Rabbit also appeared wearing football garb; Minnie Mouse was dressed as a cheerleader.

But given the serious nature of the Gulf War, the end of the show was tweaked to be more patriotic. With American flags throughout the stadium, and "America the Beautiful" playing in the background, fifty young children of American military personnel stationed in the Gulf took the field.

A brief address from President Bush and the First Lady followed.

"Today we should recognize the men and women in our armed forces far away from home. They protect freedom in the Persian Gulf and around the world. And just as we salute these brave Americans, let's remember their families on the field with you today in Tampa," Bush said. "To the children of these men and women, let me say that as this and every day draws to a close, it's your mothers and fathers, brothers and sisters, who are the true champions, the true heroes in our country."

For the viewers at home, an extended ABC News update followed. Anchored by Peter Jennings, segments included a report on the happenings in the Gulf, a clip from Commander of U.S. Central Command General Norman Schwarzkopf's most recent press briefing, and Judd Rose's piece on the troops watching Super Bowl XXV live from Camp Jack in Saudi Arabia.

The $26,667-per-second Bud Bowl III and Reebok sneakers commercials yielded a few minutes for more important matters.

While the television audience absorbed serious information, the New York Giants coaches assembled in a corner of the locker room. There they discussed the adjustments needed to overcome the 12-10 deficit against Buffalo.

Bill Parcells had been here before. At halftime of Super Bowl XXI, New York's players and staff sat in the Rose Bowl Stadium locker room, trailing Denver 10-9. On that day in late January 1987, Parcells gave his players no fiery, inspiring speeches, unveiled no secret plays. He simply instructed them to not panic and stick to their game plan. And as soon as the third quarter began, a crowd of over one hundred thousand people saw the Giants completely dominate John Elway's Broncos. The offense and quarterback Phil Simms took the second half's opening kickoff and marched sixty-three yards during a nine-play touchdown drive to take the lead. Simms completed all ten of his second half passes, produced five scores in all, and won Most Valuable Player honors in the 39-20 victory.

The triumph gave New York their first world championship since 1956. That Giants dynasty of the 1950s, headlined by Hall of Famers Frank Gifford and Sam Huff, made five successive appearances in the NFL title game and were defeated in each one. Of course, it was the first—the overtime loss to the Baltimore Colts in 1958—that became legendary.

That Colts' 23-17 victory at Yankee Stadium forever changed the destiny of the National Football League. NBC broadcast the drama of that late-December game, with forty-five million Americans watching. The game is often labeled the birth of the modern NFL, the moment when football overtook baseball as "America's Game."

Ottis Jerome (O. J.) Anderson stares at the camera during Super Bowl XXV. The New York Giants running back would finish the game with twenty-one carries, 102 yards rushing, one touchdown, and be named the Most Valuable Player. Michael P. Malarkey / Getty Images Sport

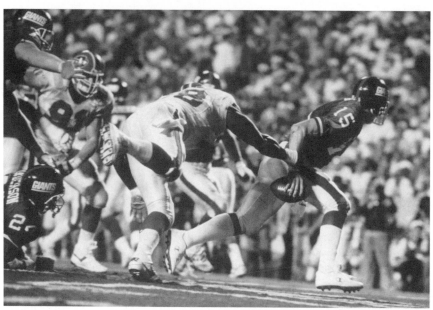

Buffalo's Bruce Smith tackles Giants quarterback Jeff Hostetler (#15) in the end zone midway through the second period. The safety increased the Bills' lead to 12-3, but Hostetler's ability to protect the ball and prevent a Buffalo touchdown proved to be a critical moment in Super Bowl XXV. Al Messerschmidt / Getty Images Sport

In the final minute of the first half, New York's Stephen Baker catches a fourteen-yard touchdown pass beside Bills cornerback Nate Odomes (#37). The reception capped a ten-play, eighty-seven-yard drive that cut Buffalo's lead to 12-10. Bill Waugh / Associated Press

With the Persian Gulf War just ten days old and a significant fear of stateside terrorism, Tampa Stadium featured unprecedented measures for Super Bowl XXV. A Black-hawk helicopter—the same craft used by the military in the Gulf region—patrolled the area day and night of the Bills-Giants game. George Rose / Getty Images Sport

After Buffalo's first drive of the third quarter ended with a punt, Bills quarterback Jim Kelly shouts instructions and encouragement to his offensive linemen. Mark Duncan / Associated Press

Thurman Thomas (#34) outruns Giants linebacker Lawrence Taylor (#56) to score on the first play of the fourth quarter. The thirty-one-yard touchdown regained the lead for Buffalo, 19-17. Al Messerschmidt / Getty Images Sport

Buffalo head coach Marv Levy, James Lofton (#80), Jamie Mueller (#41), Gary Baldinger (#99), Jim Kelly (#12), and Al Edwards (#85) watch the last-second field goal attempt from the sidelines. Craig Fujii / Associated Press

American soldiers at a base in eastern Saudi Arabia watch Super Bowl XXV via the Armed Forces Television Network, just before 3 a.m. on Monday morning (Arabia standard time), January 28, 1991. Bob Daugherty / Associated Press

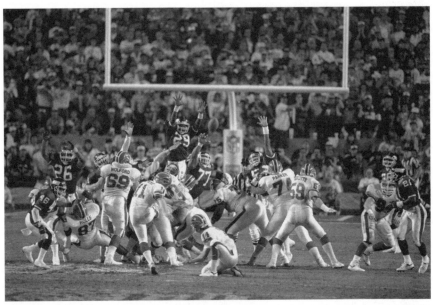

Behind 20-19, with eight seconds remaining in Super Bowl XXV, Buffalo Bills kicker Scott Norwood swipes at the potentially game-winning, forty-seven-yard field goal attempt. Phil Sandlin / Associated Press

Lifted up by Lawrence Taylor (#56) and Carl Banks (#58), Bill Parcells salutes the crowd seconds after the Giants victory. Super Bowl XXV would be his final game as the New York Giants head coach. Mike Powell / Getty Images Sport

Giants quarterback Jeff Hostetler holds his sons, Justin (left) and Jason (right), in the Tampa Stadium locker room following New York's 20-19 victory. Mike Powell / Getty Images Sport

Eighteen hours after the Bills lost Super Bowl XXV in Tampa, Florida, thirty thousand Buffalo fans greeted the team with cheers and applause at a rally in Niagara Square. Despite the Giants victory, neither New York City nor the state of New Jersey held a rally for the winning team.
Buffalo News

For one seventeen-year-old sitting in the stands at Yankee Stadium, that game was just as transformative.

The son of an FBI agent, Duane Charles Parcells grew up in New Jersey's Hasbrouck Heights, roughly four miles from where Giants Stadium would later be erected. He was a Giants fan, but football was not his passion.

"Baseball was my best sport. I thought I was gonna be a baseball player. I had an opportunity to play [professional] baseball coming out of high school, my dad wouldn't let me do it," Parcells said in 2010.

Although he continued to pursue a career as a major league catcher, witnessing the 1958 NFL title brought football to the forefront of his life.

"At that game, I decided [coaching the Giants was] what I wanted."

Parcells—who as a child preferred to be called "Bill" rather than his given name—was a standout quarterback, running back, tight end, and linebacker for River Dell Regional High in Oradell. He also excelled as a center and forward for head coach Mickey Corcoran's basketball team.

As a sophomore, Parcells scored three touchdowns—one rushing, two on defense—and tossed another during the Golden Hawks' 26-13 win over Fair Lawn. (Once he reached college, he was placed with the linemen "10 minutes after I stepped on the field and they saw me throw.")

In 1959, he graduated from River Dell and played football and baseball for Colgate University. But, yearning for a more competitive brand of athletics, he left the Chenango Valley for Kansas, enrolling at University of Wichita in the fall of 1961.

For a program that played games against top-notch teams like Tulsa, Louisville, and Arizona State, Parcells became a starter by his junior campaign. The next year, he was one of the top linemen in the Missouri Valley Conference and was named (Honorable Mention) to the all-conference team in 1963.

"We won the conference that year, and we had seven kids off that team that were either drafted or went as a free agent to the pros. We had some real talent on that team," said Bob Long, who attended Wichita (now called "Wichita State") on a basketball scholarship but joined the football team as a senior. "Our quarterback Hank Schichtle was drafted by the New York Giants; he played on the taxi squad behind Y. A. Tittle. We had a kid named Miller Farr, who was a great halfback. But in those days, guys played both ways; they played both ways in the pros too. So Parcells played both ways; he was a great linebacker and offensive tackle. I remember he made a lot of tackles [20] against Tulsa [in 1963]."

Off the field, Parcells kept busy. He was a dedicated student and earned a few dollars on the side, as a comanager at a budding nearby pizza franchise.

"It's called 'Pizza Hut.' It was founded by some Wichita ex-football players," said Parcells. "Several of the guys who were on the current team worked for them. And I did work for them. And when I graduated from college, they offered me a job in their organization. Had I not gone into coaching—which I was adamant about wanting to do—I probably would have wound up being a franchisee."

Parcells' Wichita teammate and comanager at the Pizza Hut, Bob Long, was selected by Green Bay in the fourth round of the 1964 draft. He played seven seasons in the NFL, won two Super Bowl rings as a wide receiver for Vince Lombardi, and supplied Max McGee with a helmet at the beginning of Super Bowl I. A car accident during the 1968 season devastated his career—he remarkably overcame numerous broken bones to play two more years. He soon retired, then returned to the Pizza Hut family.

"He wound up taking Pizza Hut to the state of Wisconsin and built fifty-six of them up there," Parcells said.

Three rounds after the Packers selected his Wichita teammate, the Detroit Lions selected Parcells in the 1964 NFL draft. By August, the six-foot, three-inch, 242-pound tackle began training camp at the team's Bloomfield Hills practice facility.

"I didn't think I was going to make the Packer team and I figured for sure—Bill was a pretty good player—he was going to make the Detroit Lion team. We both went to training camp in '64 and somehow I made the Packer team," Bob Long said. "I kept asking people, coaches, and scouts, 'How's Bill Parcells doing at Detroit?' They said, 'He's doing great over there, he's going to make the team, for sure.' And then about two weeks before training camp ended, someone came in and said, 'You won't believe it, but Bill Parcells walked out of the Detroit Lions camp.' I said, 'Really? Why'd he do that?' They said, 'He wants to go into coaching.'"

Within two days, he had a coaching job at Hastings College. Wife Judy and daughter Suzy moved with him to the Nebraska school. That fall, Parcells began a nomadic coaching odyssey that would last for more than a decade and a half.

From Hastings, he moved back to Wichita for a season, then spent four years at West Point, where he struck up a friendship with the academy's assistant basketball coach, Bob Knight.

"We are the same age," Parcells once said. "The other football coaches were older. We spent a lot of time together. I used to scout for him and go on trips with him."

Stints at Florida State, Vanderbilt, and Texas Tech readied Parcells for his first head-coaching job. In December 1977, the Air Force Academy hired him to resurrect a program that won just ten games during the previous four seasons.

"If you understand the game, and respect the game, and don't fear the game, then your players become the variables," he said following athletic director Col. John Clune's introduction to the press. "You have to strive to get 100 percent out of your players. You have to prepare them to play to their fullest potential and not settle for anything else."

But Parcells disliked fawning over high-school seniors, a must to be a good recruiter. In 1979, he forever left college football to join the pro ranks. The "rah-rah" approach that filled the college game wasn't Parcells' style.

"He's a typical guy from New Jersey," Everson Walls later said. "Tough acting. Loud talking. Wants to be the boss all the time. Into this power thing."

Well-paid, professional *men* received Parcells better than did still-maturing college kids. At the beginning of each year, he told his players: "If you're sensitive you're not going to last too long here." Parcells demanded toughness, intelligence, and hard work from his players. And although he could be a brutal dictator, players respected him. Others loved him.

The 1980 NFL season was his first coaching professionals. In charge of the linebackers for New England Patriots head coach Ron Erhardt, Parcells' players affectionately nicknamed him "Tuna."

"His personality is that he's going to rag on you when it's time, he's going to yell at you" said Lawrence McGrew, who started for Parcells' 1980 linebacker unit in New England, and reunited with Parcells ten years later for his final season. "He can make jokes about you. He can be derogatory. But it's to make a point, and I have no problem with it. This game takes a toll on everybody. He works hard. You can see that. He cares about his team. He cares about his players. I've had some coaches where I couldn't always say that was true."

After a season with the Patriots, Parcells returned home to join the New York Giants, where both he and head coach Ray Perkins hoped his second stint with the club would be longer and more fruitful than his first. In March 1979, Parcells resigned as head coach of Air Force to take the linebackers coach job with New York. Prior to training camp, he quit: reportedly, his wife and children did not want to uproot from their home in Colorado Springs. Parcells went back to Colorado to take a job outside of football, but returned to the NFL the following season, joining the Patriots staff under Ron Erhardt.

Good fortune would be with him during his next go-round with the team he grew up worshipping.

The 1981 NFL draft brought Lawrence Taylor to the Giants. Under Parcells' tutelage, he became the first-ever rookie to win NFL Defensive Player of the Year, an honor awarded him the next season as well.

Taylor's athleticism and instincts redefined his position. Before the advent of the nimble, six-foot, two-inch, 245-pound Virginia native, outside linebackers rarely attacked the line of scrimmage in passing situations.

"He really wasn't a linebacker in college; he was more like a defensive end, and so we made him a linebacker," said Bill Parcells. "But it was simple. He responded to competition very well. You just had to show him where the competition was. . . . He was one of the first of his kind: a combination linebacker–pass rusher. He really altered the game in a lot of ways."

Taylor possessed many athletic gifts, but it was Parcells' coaching style that transformed the raw linebacker into a first-team all-pro every season from 1981 to 1989.

"A lot of people over the last forty-two years, a lot of people have asked me, "Hey, Long, you played for Vince Lombardi, you knew Bill Parcells, how do you compare them?" Bob Long said.

Well, Lombardi probably was one of the greatest motivators of all time as coaches go; he could really motivate. He'd yell and scream. You could do that as a coach in the '60s because there wasn't free agency, you had to take it or leave, or he would get rid of you. But Bill Parcells, in my opinion, one of his greatest attributes as a coach—he has many, he's a great judge of talent, etc.—he is the greatest coaching psychologist I ever met. He is like a doctor of psychology out there.

I went back in the '80s to see [the Giants] play the Detroit Lions. He was walking around during pregame warm-ups; everybody's warming up and so forth on the field. He was walking around; I was following him. He came up to Lawrence Taylor—he tried to get in these guys' heads. Phil Simms—he would always be on him about something. Lawrence Taylor was warming up, and he walks around him and says, "L. T., you're not near as good as Dick Butkus or Ray Nitschke." And Lawrence Taylor is real emotional, and you could see him swelling up, getting upset. Finally, he spouted off and L. T. said, "I am too better than Dick Butkus and Ray Nitschke. I'm better than they are. . . . Watch, I'm gonna show you today." That's exactly what Parcells wanted to do; he got him all riled up. And that game was one of the greatest games I ever saw an outside linebacker play. He was all over the field, sacking the quarterback, making tackles. That is exactly what Parcells wanted to do, he got in his head, which he did with a lot of players.

Near the end of Taylor's second year (the strike-shortened season), the 3-3 Giants still had a shot at the postseason. But head coach Ray Perkins stunned the team and the New York media with an announcement. Iconic University of Alabama head coach Bear Bryant retired on December 15, 1982, and the next day, Perkins—the leading receiver on Bryant's national championship teams of 1964 and 1965—took his place.

Giants General Manager George Young tapped Parcells as the replacement.

"Very few people in the world get to do what they hoped to do," Parcells said at his introductory press conference. "I think the New York Giants for Bill Parcells are what the University of Alabama is to Ray Perkins. My first reaction when I got the job was that I was a very lucky guy. I would have done this for free. It's the job I always wanted."

"I think he'll make a great coach," Taylor said after he learned of the hiring. "When he want to be, he's tough. You know when Bill's in a bad mood that you'd better get in gear."

Eight years later, Taylor was the last remaining player (Phil Simms was inactive) from the roster Parcells inherited in December 1982. For most head coaches, the presence of Taylor—arguably the finest defensive player in NFL history—would have been enough of a good luck charm; not for Bill Parcells.

He carried a "lucky towel" in his bag. Prior to Super Bowl XXI, New Milford (N.J.) High School head coach Rich Conti sent Parcells a red towel, with a note reading, "Dear coach, this towel has never lost. It won two state championships in New Jersey; you take it to Pasadena with you."

Parcells' wife even participated in the superstition. At the urging of Giants fan Dan Paulino, who sat behind the coaches' wives' section at home games, Judy Parcells wore the same white Giants hat during the team's last twelve games of the 1986 season. New York won each game, including Super Bowl XXI. But because the Giants began the next year 0-5, Judy permanently stuffed the hat in a drawer.

After the Super Bowl victory over Denver, Parcells returned the lucky towel to coach Conti, who won the state title again in 1988. Conti mailed it back to Parcells before the NFC Championship Game, and the towel was present for Super Bowl XXV.

The rituals continued even before the team landed in Tampa. For the trip from California, he demanded that United Airlines pilot Augie Stasio fly them. "Augie from the Bronx," as Parcells called him, had flown the team plane to Pasadena the week of the Super Bowl XXI victory; he also flew the team to San Francisco for the NFC Championship Game.

And, of course, for Super Bowl Sunday, Ottis Anderson was again ordered to wear the same set of practice pants he wore during both playoff victories.

"We had a lot of superstitious guys: myself and Ottis and Lawrence," said Parcells. "We weren't tempting fate in those days."

Those superstitions comforted Parcells while he was standing in the visitors' locker room at Tampa Stadium during the halftime of Super Bowl XXV. So did the collection of football minds he counseled with.

After he took the Giants head-coaching gig, Parcells pursued continuity within his staff. He retained his former boss, offensive coordinator Ron Erhardt, and promoted the team's special assignments coach, Romeo Crennel, to special teams coach. Crennel and Parcells previously coached together for three seasons at Texas Tech.

Parcells also promoted the youngest member of the Giants staff. Thirty-year-old Bill Belichick moved from special teams to coaching the linebackers. That 1982 season was Belichick's fourth with the Giants and his seventh as a full-time coach. And he brought much more experience to the job than the lines on his résumé indicated.

Belichick's father, Steve Belichick, played fullback for Struthers High School and Western Reserve Academy, both in eastern Ohio. Like his son's future boss, he too dabbled briefly with a playing career for the Detroit Lions. During the 1941 season, Lions head coach Bill Edwards—the former coach at

Western Reserve—promoted Belichick from "towel boy" (more accurately, equipment manager) to play fullback. He scored three touchdowns—including a seventy-seven-yard punt return against Green Bay in the season finale—during his only year as a professional player.

Following service in the navy during World War II, Steve took the head coaching job at Hiram College, then moved on to assistant positions with Vanderbilt and North Carolina.

"He was a lot like Bill in his younger years," said Don Gleisner, a defensive back and team captain at Vanderbilt. "Steve was the kind of a guy who was loyal to his family, he was loyal to his wife, he was loyal to his employer, he was loyal to his players, and loyalty, integrity and trust were his reputation."

Steve and his wife, Jeannette—the Vanderbilt team's Spanish tutor—welcomed William Stephen to the family in 1952. By 1956, the Belichicks moved to Annapolis, where Steve found a permanent home, coaching and scouting for Navy. Growing up a part of the Midshipmen football program—a perennial football powerhouse until the late 1960s—Bill came to share in his father's passion.

Each year, as a young child, Bill spent the annual Army-Navy game on the sidelines. At age seven, he saw Joe Bellino, the Heisman Trophy winner that season, score three touchdowns in Navy's 43-12 win at Philadelphia Stadium. A few years later, the boy started surreptitiously scouting for the Midshipmen.

"There was a real close game," Belichick said years later. "There was a lot of confusion. I was walking by one of the Army coaches when something dropped out of his pocket. It was the game plan. At that point my father knew the system, and now he had all the terminology. The next year, he'd say, 'I see you ran the Jones special last week,' and they'd say, 'How did he know that?'"

Bill developed into a capable football player and fantastic lacrosse player at Annapolis High School, Phillips Academy, and Wesleyan College. But even at an early age, he showed a tremendous aptitude for diagramming football plays and understanding and interpreting game film.

"This guy decided he wanted to be a head coach when he was about seven," remembered Ernie Accorsi, the NFL general manager who later hired Belichick for his first head-coaching job. "I remember when [John F.] Kennedy was running for president. . . . When he first started talking early in his campaign, I said, 'This guy's been preparing to be president.' He knew exactly what he wanted to do if he ever became president. That's kind of the feeling

I had with Belichick. He knew he wanted to be a head coach. There was no question in his mind. That's what he geared his whole life for."

Belichick left Wesleyan in the spring of 1975 and went looking for a job in the NFL. Baltimore Colts head coach Ted Marchibroda planned on hiring General Manager Joe Thomas' cousin as a defensive assistant. Thomas' cousin became unavailable, and George Boutselis recommended Belichick for the job that mainly included breaking down film.

"That's when I hired Billy," Marchibroda said thirty-five years later. "I knew to begin with that he would be a hardworking fella, and also his father was working with the Naval Academy in the football department as a coach. And I thought that once I hired Billy and interviewed Billy, I thought, well gee, if Billy couldn't do the job, he could always go to his father. But that really wasn't necessary. Bill was the kind of guy, once you gave him an assignment, you didn't see him until it was completed."

Coaching assignments with Detroit, then Denver, impressed Ray Perkins, who brought in Belichick to assist with the New York Giants defense and handle the special teams for the 1979 season. On the plane from Denver to New York, he saw Bill Parcells, who had just left the Air Force Academy to take the linebackers job with the Giants.

Surrounded by tough, hard-nosed military coaches during his childhood, and a coach himself by age twenty-three, Belichick had several mentors. Among others, he patterned his style on the model set by coaches Len Fontes, Dan Sekanovich, and Pete McCulley, as well as his father's former Navy colleagues, Wayne Hardin and Rick Forzano.

"A lot of my philosophy and background comes from them," Belichick said during his second year with the Giants. "I apply it to special teams, mainly to be aggressive. Wayne Hardin and Rick Forzano were both a pretty wide-open type of coach. They weren't coaching to sit back. I've copied a lot of their ideas."

That aggressive approach occasionally frustrated his head coaches.

During the 1981 season (from the press-box level coaches' booth), he instructed Giants kicker Joe Danelo to "squib kick" after New York scored a go-ahead touchdown with under a minute remaining against the Redskins. Belichick wanted to keep the ball away from Mike Nelms, one of the league's top returners. The squib did not produce the results Belichick hoped for: a Redskin scooped up the kick and reached near midfield. Washington tied the game, then defeated the Giants in overtime. Head coach Ray Perkins was infuriated with Belichick's move.

"In the rain," Belichick said afterward, "when you put the ball on the ground, it's tough to handle. It skids. This time, it just didn't work out. But if the same situation came up again, I'd make the same recommendation."

That proactive, original, even stubborn, thinking would serve Belichick well once Bill Parcells promoted him to defensive coordinator for the 1985 season. That year, the pass-rushing trio of Lawrence Taylor (13 sacks), Leonard Marshall (15.5 sacks) and George Martin (10 sacks) each had career years. During Belichick's first two seasons of stewardship, the Giants defense yielded just 16.2 points and topped the NFC in sacks. And in the second half of Super Bowl XXI, Belichick's defense thoroughly shut down John Elway, one of the key factors in New York's victory.

That outstanding unit lost several of its stars after the 1988 season, however. George Martin and Hall of Famer Harry Carson retired. Former Pro Bowl defensive end Jim Burt was let go, as was starting safety Kenny Hill. Although Taylor, Marshall, Pepper Johnson, and Carl Banks remained, the defense needed to be rebuilt for 1989. Parcells trusted Belichick with the task, and he rewarded the head coach. The Giants surrendered the fewest points in the NFC.

"He's always given me the job to do and let me do it," Belichick said near the end of that season. "He's let me instill my personality in the defense, as opposed to being his clone and relaying everything he would want done."

On the surface, Parcells and Belichick were two very different men. Parcells' size and gruff demeanor instantly projected confidence and command. Physically, he diminished the five-foot, ten-inch, 190-pound Belichick. And Belichick's aloof, often quiet, nature didn't often inspire his players. Early on, according to George Martin, Belichick had "a terrible bedside manner." Several of his players referred to him as "Doom."

"They talked about him as being gruff, about having no personality; they talked about him as being coldhearted. None of that's true," Don Gleisner remembered. "I believe for some reason, he wanted to keep that gruff image, whether that would help him or not."

"Bill puts a great emphasis—as did his father, as I did, and I think I learned it from Steve Belichick—on the same principles that apply in business, apply in football. You've got to have discipline; you've got to have integrity. You've got to have loyalty. You've got to work hard. And those were all things that were ground into Bill, and ground into me. And I think we got them from Steve."

Bill Parcells shared those same principles. Both coaches also desperately wanted to win, and they knew that superb defense would achieve that. But differences in personality suggested they did not get along.

"Parcells would challenge Belichick to make a decision on anything from strategy to how to handle an injury with the media," the Newark Star-Ledger's Jerry Izenberg later said.

> The catch was, if Belichick's decision didn't work out, Parcells would say, "You're fired." He put him under a lot of pressure and fired him about four or five times during that period.
>
> I recall one game in Dallas when Belichick came out with some fancy blitz package on first down, and Parcells said, "What the hell are you doing?" And Belichick said, "I'm giving them a different look." And Parcells said, "No you're not, you're showing these 76,000 people how smart you are. You're being a circus act." Parcells then muttered, "You need those X's and O's guys during the week, but on the sidelines, they're not worth a damn."

Later, as opposing head coaches, Parcells and Belichick faced one another five times. Fittingly, each was a defensive battle, with Belichick winning three games, Parcells two: the average score was 15-11. They would also return to the coach–assistant coach relationship in the late 1990s, first with the New England Patriots, then the New York Jets. And the bizarre circumstances in 2000, surrounding the Jets head-coaching job, furthered the public's perception of acrimony.

On January 3, Jets head coach Bill Parcells announced his retirement and took on an advisory role with the team: "I'm not going to coach any more football games," he said. "This is definitely the end of my career." Belichick, the team's defensive coordinator, was named the head coach. The next day, he resigned, and he eventually took the head-coaching gig with the Jets' divisional rival, the New England Patriots.

"Most of the perceived conflict came when Bill left the Jets. He was doing what he thought was right, and I had a responsibility to run the business the way I thought was right, so there was a difference of opinion there," Parcells said ten years later. "Bill and I have a fine relationship now. . . . We did spend a lot of good years together, and both of us realize that."

Harmonious relationship or not, the Parcells-Belichick union flourished. "We're just two different people," Belichick said in 2011. "Maybe our strengths played off one another. . . . Bill is very good at big picture things. . . . I'm more detail oriented, sometimes maybe I get caught up in some details and I might miss something that's bigger picture. I think there's definitely a good balance there."

Throughout the 1980s, the Giants coaching staff remained uncommonly consistent, especially for a perennial playoff team. Parcells, Erhardt, and Belichick each kept the same job from 1985 to 1990. No other NFL team could boast that type of continuity at the head coach and coordinator positions.

Some Giants assistants inevitably left to take promotions elsewhere, but Parcells' fire and palpable hatred for losing attracted eager, talented replacements. By the later part of the decade, Parcells built a staff in his own image: young, hungry, no-nonsense. In 1988, he hired a passionate disciplinarian, Tom Coughlin, to coach his wide receivers. Al Groh, who served as defensive coordinator during Parcells' lone season at the Air Force—he also helped recruit Lawrence Taylor to the University of North Carolina—joined the Giants as a defensive assistant in 1989.

And before the 1990 season, Parcells hired Charlie Weis, who, in just one year as head coach at Somerset Franklin High School, defeated Watchung Hills and Ocean Township to win New Jersey's central group three sectional championship the previous November. Designated a "special assistant," Weis worked as the Giants' jack-of-all-trades, cutting film and completing other tasks for the rest of the staff.

"Charlie was the whipping boy," Parcells remembered years later. "I was the whipping boy once. Belichick was the whipping boy once. Everybody gets to be the whipping boy."

Parcells' assistants didn't remain whipping boys forever. As of 2010, that staff would, collectively, own thirty-one Super Bowl rings. Soon, several of them would be the ones giving the orders, rather than taking them. On that 1990 Giants staff, five of the assistants would go on to be NFL head coaches; Weis later became head coach at Notre Dame.

Parcells mentored his young staff and encouraged them to advance. And his "coaching tree" would ultimately become one of the most abundant in the modern era.

"I always laugh when people say 'oh well, this coach couldn't win without that coach.' We had a lot of that with Belichick and myself. I've always felt it was the job of the head coach to hire good coaches; I think I was fortunate enough to be able to do that," Parcells said years after his coaching career ended in 2007. "It was a unique group. I'm proud of them. I was very fortunate to have them. But I think collectively, we all learned from one another."

9

Grinding Out a Championship

"The first drive of the third quarter is the most important of the game," Parcells told his team just before taking the field for the second half. "We have to do something with it."

Behind 12-10, Hostetler and the New York offense opened the second half at their own twenty-four-yard line. From the outset, they did not seem to heed their head coach's advice. An incompletion, a false-start penalty, and a short screen play left the Giants with a difficult third and eight, deep inside their own territory. But an elusive catch-and-run by Dave Meggett—he caught the pass several yards shy of the first-down marker, then ran through the tackles of two Buffalo defenders—kept the drive alive. Within a few minutes, the man who Meggett often relieved did the same.

Ottis Anderson carried the ball just seven times in the first half: not nearly as many carries as he would have expected given the orders Bill Parcells issued that week.

"Parcells said, 'We just gonna pound [you] to death,'" Anderson remembered. "And we wanna know what plays you're comfortable with because we gonna run those fifteen to thirty times a game until we wear 'em down. . . . How you feel about that?' I said 'Bill, I'm ready to play; whatever you do is fine by me, and I look forward to the challenge.'"

Falling behind by nine points, coupled with the necessary pass-heavy approach on the drive late in the second quarter, limited Anderson's touches.

Still, he had been extremely efficient on those seven runs, gaining just under six yards per carry.

As the second half unfolded, the Giants would lean on their thirty-four-year-old veteran. Two plays after Meggett's pickup, the offense faced another big play: third down and one near midfield. From a two–tight end, single-back formation, Hostetler gave the ball to Anderson. With such a short distance needed for the Giants to gain the first down, the Bills looked to condense the center of the field. They expected Anderson to pound the ball up the middle. But the Giants gambled, running the ball to the outside. With left guard William Roberts leading, Anderson moved patiently, parallel to the line of scrimmage, then turned upfield, bursting through the hole for a huge gain. And much like his counterpart, Thurman Thomas, who had accentuated several runs with forearm shivers to approaching defenders, Anderson pounded safety Mark Kelso with an uppercut just before being dragged to the ground. The twenty-four-yard pickup advanced New York into field-goal range.

Watching the hard-nosed third-down efforts from Meggett and Anderson pleased Parcells, who expected nothing less. His "power football" philosophy did not just apply to the running backs, who made up such an integral part of the Giants offense.

Amassing 121 catches, twelve touchdowns, and more than eighteen hundred yards earned tight end Mark Bavaro first-team all-pro honors in 1986 and 1987. But his primary objective was to block. The same was true for Howard Cross and Bob Mrosko, New York's other tight ends, who combined for just eleven catches that season.

"I understood we were a running team more than a passing team," Bavaro said years later. "I loved Ron Erhardt's offense. I enjoyed blocking, and I enjoyed catching passes. Ron required both from his tight ends. I liked the fact that tight end on the Giants was a multidimensional position. As far as stats went, I knew my receiving production in 1990 was less than in 1986. But stats didn't mean much to us overall. What meant everything was winning or losing."

That unselfish attitude filled the entire Giants' offensive huddle.

Throughout the 1980s, individual passing and receiving records were continually broken, rewritten, and broken again. As the pro game morphed into a pass-first, run-second league, the obdurate Bill Parcells remained wedded to *his* style. Fortunately, his receivers bought into it.

"We went 13-3 this season," Stephen Baker said, "so I can't complain. Hey, I'd rather win 13 games and not get so many catches than make a lot of catches and have a losing season. Winning is really what counts the most."

Both Baker (third round) and wide receiver teammate Mark Ingram (first round) had been with the squad since their selections in the 1987 NFL draft. Each developed into capable blockers for the running game. The tandem also contributed several significant catches throughout the Giants' postseason run. Both Ingram and Baker made vital catches at the end of the NFC Championship Game.

Still, while high-profile, Pro-Bowl caliber receiving duos filled the rosters of several NFL teams—Jerry Rice and John Taylor in San Francisco, Mark Clayton and Mark Duper in Miami, Gary Clark and Art Monk in Washington, and, of course, Andre Reed and James Lofton for the Bills—New York's receiving corps was widely overlooked.

"It's always frustrating, because I would like to catch more balls," Ingram said during the 1991 playoffs. "Any receiver would. But as long as we're winning, I'm not going to complain. I know I can do more than I've shown. When they've thrown the ball to me I've produced. I'd like them to throw it to me more, but Bill doesn't like to mess with a winning formula."

They occasionally experimented with the formula midway through Super Bowl XXV.

Stephen Baker's beautiful over-the-shoulder touchdown grab in the final seconds of the first half provided a considerable swing in momentum. More important, it cut the Bills' lead to just two points. Only six minutes wore off the second-half game clock before Mark Ingram matched his teammate's tremendous and unforgettable reception.

Twice on their first possession of the second half, the Giants kept the drive alive by converting clutch third downs: Meggett's catch out of the backfield, paired with O. J. Anderson's charging run into the Buffalo secondary. New York's next third-down conversion was the most spectacular—not just of the drive or the game but, arguably, in Super Bowl history.

Anderson's big gainer set the Giants up at Buffalo's twenty-nine. Relying on the input from his players—"Our offensive linemen were saying that

Buffalo was getting a little tired, especially in the third quarter," Parcells said—the coaches wisely stuck to the power football game plan. After a hard-hitting Carthon run netted five yards, it was Dave Meggett's turn to carry the ball. The five-foot, nine-inch multipurpose back sidestepped two Bills defenders and bounced to the outside, picking up fifteen yards. But Meggett was only able to reach the edge because Mark Bavaro had illegally wrestled Buffalo linebacker Cornelius Bennett to the ground. Not only was Meggett's huge play nullified, but also, the holding penalty against Bavaro pushed the Giants back an additional ten yards.

On second and fifteen at the thirty-four (instead of first and ten at the fourteen), Hostetler dropped back to pass. Unable to find an open man and with the pocket collapsing, he scrambled upfield before being brought down just two yards past the line of scrimmage. From a fresh set of downs inside Buffalo's red zone to a third and thirteen at the thirty-two in the matter of a few snaps, the Giants now faced the very real possibility of scoring no points on the drive.

The play came in from the sidelines: "half-right–huddle-62-comeback-dig." Hostetler broke the huddle and the other ten men spread out to their pre-snap positions.

"Here we go! Big play!" wide receiver Mark Ingram told himself. "Here's our chance! So many times they've said we can't do it. Let's show 'em!"

From the shotgun, Hostetler flicked a pass across the middle of the field, seven yards short of the first down. Ingram pulled in the ball and wiggled out of a tackle.

Still six yards shy of where he needed to get to, Ingram pivoted upfield.

"All I saw was white jerseys coming at me," Ingram said afterwards. "I looked at the chains before the play started and I knew I had a long way to run to get the first down."

The first white jersey he saw read "56," that of Pro-Bowler Darryl Talley. In great position to make the tackle, Talley lunged at the ball carrier. But Ingram—once a track star at Michigan State—stopped instantaneously, spun back to the inside of the field, and avoided Talley.

Slowing down to spin out of Talley's tackle allowed the defense to advance on him. Six Bills now surrounded Ingram, who was still four yards behind the first down marker. Safety Mark Kelso swooped in to make the play, only to be frozen by a juke move from Ingram.

"We played a 'Cover Three' that time and I think we had one guy drop to the wrong zone," Kelso remembered two decades later. "They found the opening, and there was just a lot of room when he caught the football to move. And I was coming up from the deep middle. It looked like he was gonna be tackled; I don't know if I hesitated a second or not, but then he kinda jumped off to the side, and I just missed him cleanly."

The next man up with a chance to bring down Ingram was cornerback James Williams, the Bills first-round draft choice that year. He too failed. Once more, Ingram employed the spin move and avoided the Bills defender. Williams did manage to grab ahold of the receiver's foot, but Ingram was now within reach of his goal, the nineteen-yard line. Hounded by Williams and Talley—who relentlessly pursued the tackle for a second time—Ingram dove forward into a pile of players. The football landed a yard beyond the first-down mark.

"When I fell, I just looked over at the chains, and I saw that I was ahead of the stick. It was a good feeling."

"Every now and then," Dan Dierdorf announced to the ABC viewers, "in a football game you can look back to a play and it might set the tone for everything that happens after that. If the Giants win this game, they may look back to this catch and run by Mark Ingram."

Rushes by Anderson and Meggett gained six yards; so just a few minutes after Ingram's spectacular play, New York needed another clutch play on third down. Again, they got one.

Each third-down conversion on this game-defining drive had come by way of a different Giant contributing in his own unique way: Meggett outrunning a Buffalo defender, a powerful charge off tackle by Anderson, and the squirmy catch-and-run from Ingram. This time, they looked toward their multitalented quarterback to produce the key play.

When Hostetler took over in mid-December 1990, the Giants did not revamp their entire offensive game plan. But Parcells and his offensive staff knew that to succeed with their understudy performing in the lead role, they would need to take advantage of Hostetler's gifts.

"Except for a few plays like a quarterback sneak or a draw or a rollout, you don't design plays for the quarterback with the intent to run," Parcells told reporters two days after Simms was placed on the injured reserve. "But he does have the improvising ability to run and escape the rush. Will we change the whole offense for him? No. Will we put in things for him? Yes."

The "bootleg" was a perfect fit. On the bootleg, the quarterback fakes a handoff toward one side of the field, then pivots and runs to the opposite sideline where he looks for an open receiver.

With the athletic Jeff Hostetler and the Rodney Hampton–Ottis Anderson duo combining for thirteen touchdowns and more than twelve hundred rushing yards during the regular season, the bootleg was tailor-made for the new-look Giants.

A bootleg to the offense's right was the most effective way for the Giants to run the play. A right-handed quarterback, such as Hostetler, will make a more accurate throw running to his right instead of running to his left. Furthermore, faking a handoff to the left would likely draw in more defenders than if the bootleg was run to the opposite side: the left side of the Giants' line featured Pro Bowler William Roberts and Jumbo Elliott, fast becoming one of the league's best tackles. More often than not, when New York needed to move the football on the ground, the running back would follow Roberts' and Elliott's front-side blocks.

On three plays early in the game, the Giants successfully ran the bootleg—fake handoff to the left, Hostetler drifting right. Hostetler completed a thirteen-yarder to Howard Cross, a six-yard gain to Bavaro, and a twenty-two-yard grab by Ingram.

"[On] those bootlegs, I think Buffalo's backs were hanging," Parcells said. "They were not even flowing to the flow side, they got so paranoid about the bootleg."

But the fourth time that the Giants ran the play, Bills linebacker Cornelius Bennett was ready. Inside the Buffalo red zone, late in the second period, Hostetler faked a handoff left, rolled right, and fired a pass for Cross. Bennett recognized another bootleg was coming to his side—did not bite on the fake—and lunged at Hostetler. Although he couldn't get to the quarterback, he sprung into the air and swatted down the pass.

"He kept trying that bootleg against me early, and I told him, 'Look, you're not going to get outside against me,'" said Bennett. "I said, 'Don't try that to my side. I'm gonna knock that pass down or I'm going to stick you.'"

The Giants waited for a critical moment—third down and four from the Buffalo twelve—to accommodate Bennett's suggestion.

New York's offense had already eaten up sixty-three yards and more than eight minutes of game clock on this opening drive of the third period. And unlike the third downs they had faced earlier in the drive, they were now well within Matt Bahr's range. But forcing a field goal attempt out of the Giants offense—after such a productive and emotionally charged possession—would have sapped some of New York's high . . . and boosted the Buffalo defense.

As future Hall of Famer Steve Young—a man who would retire with three Super Bowl rings—would later say: "I always had this philosophy that every time you kicked a field goal, you were just that much closer to losing. . . . Field goals to me, especially in the second half, it's like kissing your sister: it's not gonna help you too much."

In the huddle, Hostetler called a bootleg to the left. He faked a handoff to Anderson and rolled away from Cornelius Bennett, right at Bruce Smith. Smith read the bootleg, sprung into the air to knock down the pass, as Bennett had late in the second period. Hostetler spied Howard Cross wide open on the Buffalo eight-yard line. All he had to do was get him the ball: not an easy task with athletic six-foot, four-inch Smith standing in front of him.

The former star shooting guard for Conemaugh Township, Hostetler fed his big man in the low post, softly floating the ball over Smith's fingertips into Cross' hands. The tight end lowered his shoulder into a defensive back before being dragged out-of-bounds at the three-yard line.

A dive up the middle pushed the Giants closer to the goal line. On second and goal from the one, Anderson carried the ball off tackle, ripped out of an arm tackle from Kirby Jackson, and chugged into the end zone.

The eighty-seven-yard touchdown march was as historic as it was thrilling. The fourteen plays run and the nine minutes and twenty-nine seconds used each set new Super Bowl records. Bahr's extra point gave the Giants a 17-12 advantage.

The five-point deficit did not worry Buffalo. They trailed by less than a touchdown with more than twenty minutes of game time remaining. Still, New York's methodical offense had cost the Bills more than the lead. A thirty-seven-minute-long halftime sandwiched in between two excruciatingly slow Giants' touchdown drives meant that (aside from a kneel-down to conclude the first half) Buffalo did not run an offensive play in an hour.

Such an unusually long layoff severely hurt Jim Kelly and the offense. Their offense relied on a particular pace and rhythm. Furthermore, part of the no-huddle's success was the result of wearing down the opponent: the Giants defense had now been granted an hour to rest and strategize.

"Bill Belichick is a genius, but I'm gonna tell you something. If we had had another quarter, we would have killed them," Buffalo center Kent Hull said years later. "They still didn't stop us; we just didn't have the time. Their offense was as good as their defense. That's what they were looking to do. They said 'our offense has got to keep them off the field.' And they did it."

Buffalo's first possession of the second half didn't go nearly how they planned. Rushes by Thurman Thomas and Kelly produced a quick first down. But an offensive pass-interference penalty, an incompletion, then Leonard Marshall's bull-rushing quarterback sack meant the Bills punted the football right back to New York, minutes after the Giants go-ahead touchdown.

As frustrating as it was for Kelly and the Bills offense, the tremendous difference in time-of-possession devastated the Buffalo defense more.

"We were on the field 10 minutes at a time," Cornelius Bennett said. "We'd rest for two, and then go back on. When that happens, there's no way you can keep up your intensity. You tend to start reaching instead of taking the proper steps. You start making arm tackles."

The seventy-one-degree weather and 76 percent humidity compounded their exhaustion. Aside from the regular-season finale, in which most starters did not play all four quarters, the Bills had played the previous five games in wintry conditions: the "miserable," snowy scene at Giants Stadium in mid-December, followed by three games at Rich Stadium in Buffalo. Although defensive coordinator Walt Corey didn't believe the humidity that night in Tampa bothered his unit, at least one of the men perpetually running up and down the field disagreed.

"We weren't used to playing in this kind of heat," Shane Conlan said. "This was training camp weather."

Buffalo's defense slogged onto the field and—by way of another bootleg away from Bennett and toward Bruce Smith—Hostetler again connected with Howard Cross for a ten-yard gain. A defensive-holding call against cornerback Nate Odomes during the play further irritated Buffalo fans.

The penalty advanced New York five more yards and gave Hostetler's unit a first and ten from the Buffalo forty-three. Because they had controlled the clock and tempo, a few more first downs punctuated by another score—even a field goal—would give the Giants a two-score lead with less than a quarter to play.*

Still, no matter how tired they were, the Bills defense did not give in. After the automatic first down due to Odomes' penalty, the Giants failed to gain anything on a run from Anderson and (yet another) bootleg to the left by Jeff Hostetler, who scrambled toward the sideline, unable to find an open man.

That left a third and eleven. Hostetler's Giants had been so prolific at coming up with big plays on third down. They fully expected another.

"We had a lot of talent on that offense: Mark Ingram, Steven Baker, Dave Meggett, etc.," Mark Bavaro remembered years later. "Combined with Jeff's throwing skills, vision, and scrambling ability, there was never a third-down situation that seemed unattainable."

From a shotgun, four-receiver set, Hostetler sat in the pocket and fired a quick strike to Mark Ingram. As he had on the incredible third-and-thirteen conversion, Ingram caught the ball well short of the first down line with plenty of open field to run. But instead of using the fast feet and spin moves that shook four Bills defenders one drive earlier, Ingram elected to try and bowl over would-be tackler Leonard Smith, who collided with Ingram. Using the sideline to his advantage, Smith stymied the ball carrier by pushing him out-of-bounds, two yards behind the marker.

Finally, the Buffalo defense came up with the third-down stop they needed. But for the Bills to take back the football and regain momentum, the job was not done yet.

FLASHBACK: SUPER BOWL XVII

"I'm bored, I'm broke and I'm back," John Riggins announced to a small gaggle of reporters outside a Washington Redskins' off-season practice on June 11, 1981. "What did I miss most? Besides the money? I missed the little kiddie atmosphere. If I quit football, I'd have to grow up."

---

*At this point in the game, with less than three minutes remaining in the third period, a Giants field goal would have made the score 20-12. With the two-point conversion play not implemented in the National Football League until the 1994 season, Buffalo could not tie the game by scoring a single touchdown.

Riggins—the ninth-leading rusher in league history—had walked away from the NFL the previous July. After one day of training camp at the team's facility in Carlisle, Pennsylvania, the ten-year veteran left, citing his desire for a new contract. The Redskins refused to give in to the demands of the thirty-one-year-old who, throughout the 1970s, embodied the prototypical bruising running back.

An all-American at the University of Kansas, Riggins was the New York Jets' sixth overall pick in the 1971 NFL draft. After a Pro Bowl season in 1975, Riggins, "the New Yorkers' curly-haired iconoclast," left the Jets, in search of a six-figure deal. Washington eventually gave it to him. But two seasons in George Allen's uncompromising offense, combined with a knee injury in 1977, suggested that Riggins hadn't lived up to his expensive salary.

"[I] never had a chance to earn what I was making," he said.

Jack Pardee replaced Allen after the 1977 season, and Riggins enjoyed the finest stretch of his career, breaking the one-thousand-yard mark in consecutive seasons and winning the NFL Comeback Player of the Year Award in 1978. With the start of the new decade, Riggins felt he had out-performed his $300,000 per year salary and demanded the Redskins raise it to half a million. He announced his "retirement" and sat out the entire 1980 season.

Without Riggins, the Redskins struggled mightily in 1980, and Pardee was fired three weeks after the season. But the club refused to increase his salary. Still, Riggins returned to the team in the summer of 1981. The man who helped rescue Riggins back from the wilderness (literally) was Washington's new coach, Joe Gibbs.

Five months into his first head-coaching job, Gibbs journeyed to rural Kansas and personally met with Riggins to see if he could coax him out of retirement:

> When I got the job, everyone said, "You got to get John Riggins back here." Of course, he sat out the year before in a contract dispute, and everyone got fired. I didn't want to get fired. Without saying anything to anybody, I got on a plane. Flew to Lawrence, Kansas. Got a rental car. Went to the first corner gas station and said, "Do you know where John Riggins lives?" They said, "Yes, I do. Out down the dirt road." I pulled up on the back of this farmhouse. I knocked on the door, and I always say, I knew I had a chance to get John Riggins back because his wife answers the door, her hair's up in rollers, kids are running through the house, and says she wanted to come back.

I said, "Get me an appointment with John Riggins. I'll be at this motel." Got up the next morning. The [voicemail] red light was on. It said I got a breakfast appointment at 10 a.m. I put my best stuff on. Young coach. I go roaring out there. Pull up to the back of his farmhouse. First time I laid my eyes on John, he's walking across the back of the courtyard. He's got a buddy with him in camouflage outfit. They had been hunting that morning. It's 10 a.m., and he has a beer can in his left hand. I said, "I can tell he's impressed with me!" I sit down at the breakfast table and man, I start my sales pitch.

Gibbs' charm worked on Riggins, and in July, he was back at training camp, ready to don the Redskins' burgundy and gold.

"I'm out here trying to act like a young kid, which I'm not, and it's not easy," said the ninth-leading rusher in NFL history. "I can't do that and learn the plays, too. I thought about using something to cover up my gray hairs, but I skipped that."

By October, Riggins regained the role of feature back, and in Gibbs' power-running system, he began to flash shades of his former self. During a Week Five win at Soldier Field, Riggins upstaged a sore-legged Walter Payton, rushing for 126 yards on twenty-three carries as Joe Gibbs notched his first win as Washington's head coach.

Three weeks later, Riggins gained only fifty-six yards on the ground, but his trio of rushing touchdowns was the difference in a 42-21 win over the Cardinals. St Louis' featured back—twenty-four-year-old Ottis Anderson—racked up twice as many yards on the ground, but failed to get in the end zone as the woeful Cardinals fell to 3-6.

Despite splitting the carries with Joe Washington, Riggins' thirteen rushing touchdowns tied for the most in the NFC. Gibbs rewarded Riggins with an increased offensive load, and he responded with a remarkable half season. (Nearly two months of the 1982 season was canceled by a players' strike from mid-September to mid-November.)

Riggins didn't post prolific yardage totals: barely sixty-one yards per game and only three rushing touchdowns during the nine-game schedule, but at age thirty-three, he shared the NFL lead with 177 rushing attempts.

With a running back on whom he could rely for twenty-plus carries per game and an offensive line, newly dubbed the "Hogs," plowing open huge holes, Joe Gibbs' run-heavy, ball-control offense excelled. Washington went

8-1, cruised through the playoffs, and earned a berth in Super Bowl XVII. In those three playoff wins, Riggins averaged thirty-two carries and 148 yards per game: the greatest cumulative postseason rushing effort in NFL history.

"I thought it was awesome," Hall of Fame football writer Ray Didinger remembered three decades later.

> I don't think that in terms of history, it's really given its due. At the time it was . . . I think there's no question that that [performance] put him in the Hall of Fame. But I do think that when people look back and talk about great postseason performances, it's hardly mentioned at all. It does kind of get lost—which it shouldn't.
>
> How many running backs in the history of the NFL have their best years in their thirties? It doesn't happen. . . . That's the amazing thing, is that he played as well as he played, and accomplished what he accomplished with that kind of workload as a thirty-three-year-old man.

On January 30, 1983, Washington battled the Miami Dolphins in Super Bowl XVII. The Redskins' hopes for a first world championship in forty years did not get off to a rousing start. David Woodley's seventy-six-yard touchdown pass to Jimmy Cefalo midway through the first quarter gave the ho-hum Dolphins offense an early lead. And while the Redskins had been proficient at gaining a first-quarter lead, then playing keep-away thanks to a stout defense, the Dolphins owned the lead and dictated the game's tempo from the outset.

"In our first couple of offensive series, I think we were just caught up in playing in the Super Bowl. It was hard not to be excited," left tackle Joe Jacoby remembered. "[Quarterback Joe] Theismann was probably a little hyper, but I'd say that was true for all of us. We moved the ball pretty well, but we were forced to punt when we let them sack Theismann a couple times on third down. Then all of us calmed down and began to play much better."

Late in the second period, a touchdown pass from Theismann to Alvin Garrett gave the Redskins their first touchdown, and Washington looked to head for halftime content with the 10-10 score. But while Theismann, Riggins, and the Hogs celebrated their impressive eleven-play, eighty-yard touchdown drive on the sidelines, Dolphins kick returner Fulton Walker stunned every one of the 103,667 patrons at the Rose Bowl.

The second-year defensive back accepted the ensuing kickoff at his own two-yard line, found a seam along the left side, and raced untouched into the end zone. The first kickoff return for a touchdown in Super Bowl history gave the Dolphins an unexpected 17-10 halftime lead.

"I almost swallowed my tongue when I saw Walker's run," linebacker Larry Kubin said. "When you see a play like that, sometimes you wonder if fate isn't smiling on the other side of the field."

As the second half unfolded, Kubin's fear did not manage to spread across the Redskins' sidelines.

"Nobody panicked. We knew what had to be done and we were ready to do it," said guard Russ Grimm.

Early in the third quarter, a trick play—a forty-four-yard reverse to Garrett—buoyed the Redskins with a first and goal inside Miami's ten-yard line. But after a short Riggins run, two passes failed to produce a touchdown, and Washington settled for a short field goal.

Not long after that missed opportunity, Theismann threw an interception and almost threw another: near his own goal line, Theismann himself broke up Dolphins lineman Kim Bokamper's attempt to haul in a pass batted down at the line of scrimmage. And when a flea-flicker from the Washington offense resulted in Theismann's second interception of the half, the game plan simplified.

"Joe [Jacoby] came over to me," offensive line coach Joe Bugel told reporters after the game, "and said, 'Hey, Bugs, let's stop running that trick stuff and let's start trying to run the ball. I made the suggestion to [Joe Gibbs]."

Riggins had already carried the football twenty-seven times for ninety-three yards that evening. Those totals were so often enough to put his team ahead, yet the Redskins still trailed 17-13 once they took over at their own forty-eight with under twelve minutes remaining in the game. Gibbs turned to Riggins again: "He's our bread and butter. We give it to him and make people take it away from him."

Consecutive carries by Riggins pushed the Redskins across midfield, setting up a third and two at the Miami forty-four. Trying to sneak Clarence Harmon through the middle of Miami's defense—a unit that surrendered the fewest total yards in the NFL that season—didn't pick up the first down, and the Redskins now faced a fourth and inches.

"We were on the sidelines, and coach Joe Gibbs and the staff were all debating whether to go for it and the urgency and time of the game and that if we were going to make a statement it had to be right then. So they decided to go for it," tight end Clint Didier recalled.

"Joe Gibbs was more of a conservative coach than that, but we went for it on fourth down but not that much. He wasn't a gambler. He played the odds: we were in the fourth quarter, we were behind, and it was time. You had to go for it. You had to make your stand. You had to show the other team that you were willing to risk it all right then and there to make a statement."

Gibbs made his decision and told the play to Theismann, who sprinted back onto the field.

"Goal line, I-left, tight-wing, fake zoom, seventy chip," he told the other ten men in Washington's huddle.

"Goal line, I-left, tight-wing" was the formation. "seventy chip" was the play call—a Riggins run off tackle. The Redskins relied so heavily on seventy chip that in order to perfect it, the offense ran the play in practice under very special conditions.

"[Redskins offensive line coach Joe] Bugel and those guys took great pride in never being stopped when they ran it," Ray Didinger said.

> Bugel told me that they practiced it all the time because it was such a key play in their arsenal. But Bugel said that when they practiced it, they ran it against a defense with thirteen men.
>
> Because they wanted to hone it to such a fine edge that when they would run short yardage or goal line in practice and they wanted to run seventy chip, they would actually put two extra defenders on the field and make it that much harder on the offense to execute it, that much harder for [Jeff] Bostic and Grimm and Jacoby and Otis Wonsley, who had to throw the key lead block. . . . And they were still making it in practice so when they got out to play in the game and they played against eleven, it almost seemed easy.

As proficient as the Redskins—and especially the Hogs—became at forcefully carving out holes in the defense, seventy chip was virtually unstoppable for one more reason: motion.

The "fake zoom" portion of the play call in "Goal line, I-left, tight-wing, fake zoom, seventy chip," meant that, prior to the snap, wing–tight end Clint Didier—who was aligned on the left side of the line—would go in motion to the right, then come back left. The purpose of the motion was to disrupt the positioning of Miami's Don McNeal: wherever Didier went, it was McNeal's job to follow.

"I can remember in the huddle thinking all I gotta do is make sure I get that safety that follows me to think that I'm gonna go clear cross the formation," Didier remembered. "I carried my motion further than I normally would, and I had good footing and I came back and [McNeal] slipped."

At the snap, Didier and each one of the Hogs neutralized Miami's six-man front line at the line of scrimmage, opening a huge hole for Riggins to run through. The last man in position to make the tackle was McNeal. A few steps out of position, the 190-pound McNeal had no chance of bringing down the 235-pound "Diesel."

The eleven-year veteran plowed over McNeal, continued on in the open field and chugged into the end zone. The forty-three-yarder gave Washington a 20-17 lead.

"It was amazing to see a guy that age do the things that he did over the course of that long season and then cap it off with the performance he had in Pasadena," Didinger said. "If he had played that whole game and scored that winning touchdown from the one-yard line, you still would have said 'Jesus, that's quite an accomplishment.'

"But for him to cap it off with that run, which was forty-plus yards, that's the really amazing thing: on that carry, at that stage in the game after all the wear and tear and all the pounding he had taken, that he could still break through the line and outrun the secondary. That's the one that just takes your breath away."

An immediate three-and-out from the Washington defense, followed by a seven-minute, twelve-play touchdown drive—in which Riggins toted the ball eight more times—sealed the Redskins' victory. And an hour later, in the victorious locker room, Joe Gibbs chatted with a satisfied commander-in-chief.

"I hope when you come back you can help me up on Capitol Hill with some congressmen," President Ronald Reagan told Gibbs during a postgame, congratulatory phone call.

Meanwhile, a never-shy John Riggins—"Ron is the President, but I am the King"—soaked up his share of the championship spotlight. Setting new records for rushing yards and carries made the sportswriters' choice for the

Most Valuable Player of Super Bowl XVII a no-brainer: Riggins garnered every single vote.

But for all those yards and all those runs, it was the longest run in Super Bowl history—a play on which he needed just a foot—that defined Riggins, the Redskins, and Super Bowl XVII.

"I felt like that was the game right there. That broke their backs," center Jeff Bostic told the Super Bowl press corps regarding Riggins' touchdown jaunt. "It wasn't so much what it did for our team, it was what it did to their team. It took all the emotions out of them."

With the third-quarter game clock showing just under a minute and a half, Bill Parcells did not hesitate about his approach to fourth and two at the Buffalo thirty-five. And why not: in the postseason, New York was five-for-five on fourth-down conversion attempts.

Hostetler and the Giants offense stayed out on the field while Parcells and Erhardt—speaking to each other through headsets—selected a play. It wasn't exactly "Goal line, I-left, tight-wing, fake zoom, seventy chip," but it was close.

There was no motion-man, and, instead of a lead blocker, the three–tight end formation featured a flexed-out wide receiver, Mark Ingram. Still, in another moment of Super Bowl déjà vu, thirty-four-year-old Ottis Anderson— the recently reborn power back—took the ball from his quarterback and spied a spot off left tackle.

Serving as lead blocker, front-side left guard William Roberts pulled around left tackle Jumbo Elliott, looking to block any Bills defender who crossed his path. But next to Roberts were tight ends Howard Cross and Mark Bavaro, and they couldn't quite figure out who to block: Pro Bowl linebacker and Buffalo's leading tackler that season, Darryl Talley, or the NFL's Defensive Player of the Year, Bruce Smith.

Fortunately for the Bills defense, they both chose to block Talley. That left Smith virtually untouched precisely at the spot on the field where Ottis Anderson was heading. Anderson had no chance. He couldn't bounce away from Smith—there was too much congestion, the result of his own blockers' miscue. And no running back—even a bruising load such as Anderson—could bowl over a 275-pound defensive end.

Two yards behind the line of scrimmage, Smith stood Anderson up, and with teammates Shane Conlan, Leon Seals, Nate Odomes, and Mike Lodish swooping in as reinforcements, the mob wrestled Anderson to the ground. While sitting on the ground, Smith, who, since recording his pivotal sack/safety, had been largely neutralized in his one-on-one battles with Jumbo Elliott, stared down and pointed to the nearby Giants' sideline.

"We contributed to our own demise there," Parcells remembered. "And it was a really important play. That could have provided more additional momentum than we already had. And we had an awful lot at that time."

Buffalo took over on downs at their own thirty-seven-yard line. Narrowly avoiding Lawrence Taylor's first sack of the game, Jim Kelly floated a short pass toward the sideline. Thurman Thomas made the catch, avoided a would-be tackler, juked away from another, and picked up nine yards.

Thomas had now carried the football on sixteen plays and averaged more than seven yards per touch. That, coupled with a hard hit that nose tackle Erik Howard delivered to his surgically reconstructed right knee, meant Thomas needed a short break. Backup Kenneth Davis took his spot. This time, rather than stalling with their main cog on the sidelines, the Buffalo offense continued to churn out yardage.

A quick dump-off pass to Davis gained four yards and pushed the football to the midfield stripe. The third-quarter game clock dipped under thirty seconds while Kelly assembled the K-Gun offense in place. Four receivers, along with running back Davis, spread across the formation, leaving Kelly alone in the backfield. He ignored a tame Giants rush and unloaded the ball a few yards past the line of scrimmage, where Davis made his second straight catch. Employing his own flashy moves, Davis took advantage of a key block from wide receiver Al Edwards and sprang upfield, gaining another nineteen yards.

The game had quickly shifted from the lumbering, measured pace of the Giants offense to Buffalo's frenetic, spastic style.

"Any time you're standing on the sideline and you run our type of offense, it's very frustrating because we know sooner or later, we're going to put the ball in the end zone," Kelly said. "When we have the ball, we're going to have to score because we're just not going to get that many opportunities."

Reduced to all zeroes, the third-quarter game clock meant a brief pause in the action and an opportunity for the defense to rest and Bill Belichick to ponder adjustments.

Once again, the Giants turned to their best weapon thus far in Super Bowl XXV—dwindling time—to stifle the Bills. But the momentary pause in action would serve as merely an immaterial impediment on Buffalo's fervid march to a fourth-quarter lead in Super Bowl XXV.

10

Buffalo's Bickering Bills

Sixty-one-year-old Marv Levy did not fit the stereotypical image of a football coach. He was a fine athlete in his day. A native of Chicago, Levy lettered in football and basketball at South Shore High School, then (after dropping basketball) added track to his list of activities upon attending Coe College in 1946.

Well into his seventies, he remained a health fanatic. He jogged, ate right, and camera crews routinely caught him doing multiple sets of push-ups on the sidelines of Bills' practices.

Still, at five feet, seven inches, and 165 pounds—he didn't intimidate anyone. At least not physically: Marv Levy was one of the most intelligent men ever to come through professional football.

Levy enrolled at Harvard Law School in the fall of 1950, but within a few weeks realized he'd rather coach football. He remained at Harvard, earning a master's degree in English history, then began a five-decade-long coaching career.

"There are moments," Levy said during Super Bowl week, "when I look out on the field and say to myself, 'What the heck are you doing here? What's so important about all these men banging into each other?' But I love the game and the challenge of it all."

Because of his unique background, he did not speak like a jock. In team meetings, he befuddled many of his players with words like "extrapolate" and "salient," or references to ancient Carthaginian military leaders and the Battle of Belleau Wood.

Stanford's James Lofton and Northwestern's Steve Tasker were the two Bills players appointed to translate specific portions of Levy's speeches.

"That kinda came out during Super Bowl week about how cool it was the way Marv ran his team meetings, listening to a great speaker speak rather than just a football coach laying out the day's events. We used to keep a list," Tasker said. "We used to keep a list. . . . Marv would throw these words out there and guys would look sideways and you write it down. I think one of them was 'inculcate.' There was maybe five of them on my list.

"It was a real treat to listen to him speak. The guy is a great speaker. He's very sharp, very well organized, and it was fun to sit there every morning and listen to him give us about five or ten minutes of the day in wisdom and put us all in perspective mentally."

On the night before the AFC Championship Game (and again throughout Super Bowl week), Levy told his team about the British Eighth Army and the war cry—"One More River to Cross"—they sang while marching into World War II battles. Levy then sang it for his players.

"He's a better coach than he is a singer," long-snapper Adam Lingner said.

Although that anecdote gave Buffalo an idea to rally around during the postseason, Levy's most brilliant piece of coaching that season did not come in the form of inspirational speeches. Even implementing the no-huddle offense approach full-time—an extremely unorthodox yet wonderfully prosperous change—was not the genius move that put the Bills in position to win the franchise's first world championship. There was no such masterstroke. But without the acumen and adaptability that Marv Levy displayed between the 1989 and 1990 NFL seasons, Buffalo would not have been in Tampa Stadium competing for the Super Bowl XXV title.

In early January 1990, it became clear to everyone who followed the National Football League that the Buffalo Bills needed change—especially owner Ralph Wilson, who phoned Levy and asked him to board a plane for Detroit.

"I wondered if, perhaps, he was so miffed that he might speak those words so many of us in my line of work hear with such demoralizing frequency at that time of year, 'Coach, you're fired.'"

After the 12-4 Cinderella year in 1988 that saw the Bills reach their first-ever AFC Championship Game, the Bills expected more the following September. The season opened with a 27-24 road victory over the hated Miami Dolphins. On the final play of the game, Kelly—operating in the no-huddle— capped the Bills eleven-point fourth-quarter comeback, by scoring a two-yard rushing touchdown.

"I know exactly how good Jim Kelly is," the quarterback said about himself, after leading the Bills to a pair of long scoring drives in the game's final four minutes. "I know I'm up there with the elite. I'm not bragging. I just know how good I am."

But they were beaten 28-14 the following week against Denver in the Bills' first home Monday night game in five years. During the nationally televised game, cameras caught Jim Kelly chastising a wide receiver on the sidelines, and an angry exchange between Cornelius Bennett and Bruce Smith only ended when an assistant coach broke it up.

Alone, those minor tiffs among players would not have made headlines. Every team—good or bad—goes through those squabbles; they usually are fortunate enough for them not to occur on national television. It was an incident that occurred off the field, and away from the "heat of battle," that earned the team its undesirable nickname, the "Bickering Bills."

"The 'Bickering Bills,' that came about because everybody in that locker room is so competitive. If we were playing tiddlywinks, everybody would be up on the floor," Darryl Talley said. "We were holding each other accountable for everything we did. And if we didn't hold each other accountable and fight with each other because we were so competitive and wanting to win, then we wouldn't have been the resilient team we were. We fought with each other more times than not. The way I looked at it, you fight with your brothers and sisters and that's all we were doing."

Two weeks (and two wins) after losing to Denver on Monday night, the Colts pounded Buffalo at the Hoosier Dome. Indianapolis led 23-0 late in the third quarter before the Bills finally scored. Kelly connected with Andre Reed on a sixteen-yard touchdown, but just as he released the pass, two Colts leveled him. Defensive end Jon Hand shoved Kelly to the hard AstroTurf, and the quarterback landed directly on his left shoulder.

"I knew, the very instant I hit the ground, that my shoulder was separated," Kelly later wrote. "I remember what my right shoulder felt like when I hit the ground in that Virginia Tech game in my senior year of college. It's a feeling you never forget."

Doctors recommended three to six weeks on the sidelines. A day after the 37-14 loss (which cost the Bills first place in the division), Kelly publicly blamed left tackle Howard Ballard for the hit.

"It should have never happened," he told the press. "[Hand] should have been blocked. Watching the film, I don't know what Howard was thinking. . . . I think four out of our five positions [on the offensive line] are very solid. I don't even need to tell you guys what position they might have to make a change in. I can't stand up here and say they should do it or shouldn't do it; I don't make the decisions. But something has to happen."

The comment set off a national controversy. Coaches, players, and commentators contemplated Kelly's right to publicly chastise a teammate. Through the press, several of Kelly's teammates expressed their disapproval.

"I told him . . . in the last two games, you've had some terrible games," Thomas said on the weekly *Sports Line with Paul Maguire*. "I felt somebody had to come out and say something because that's just the way I felt and a lot of the players felt and nobody was saying anything about it."

Kelly's shoulder injury put Frank Reich in the starter's role for three games, each of which Buffalo won.* The Bills' subsequent five losses in seven games sparked a debate that Reich gave the team its best chance to win. Such trouble might have been on the horizon since the previous year: during the 1988 play-offs, Robb Riddick told reporters that he was "unhappy with the quarterback situation" because he did not think Kelly sufficiently utilized the running backs in the passing game.

Even the coaching staff was not immune. During a film session after a 34-3 win over the Jets, a fistfight broke out between two assistants: linebackers coach Nick Nicolau allegedly punched offensive line coach Tom Bresnahan and "rammed his head through a plasterboard wall" during a film session.

The perceived quarterback controversy, a random scrap among coaches, and open airing of the team's "dirty laundry" compounded already shaky team chemistry.

The *Buffalo News* reported that African American players and white players occasionally argued over several issues: which race contributed more to the team's success, what music to listen to in the locker room (rap or country),

---

*Reich's statistics during those three games were impressive (60 percent completions, 482 yards, six touchdowns, one interception) and, in his first game, Buffalo beat the undefeated Los Angeles Rams. But the Bills' rushing game also averaged over two hundred yards per game during that stretch.

and inequality in endorsements deals. A story also surfaced that running back Ronnie Harmon "only allowed black teammates to autograph a football he brought into the dressing room one day and wouldn't allow a player [Andre Reed] whose parents are racially mixed to sign it."

Others insisted that, instead of race, the strife resulted from swelling egos.

"It wasn't so much about black guys, white guys as it was about great players and their role on the team," Steve Tasker later said. "The great players on the team like Bruce and Jim didn't really like each other that much, and it had nothing to do with black or white. Bruce had a huge ego and so did Jim. And Jim was a huge celebrity and Bruce wanted to be and was. But Bruce was really more of a celebrity outside Buffalo than he was inside. He was one of the big names in the entire NFL. Jim was a Buffalo icon."

Three consecutive losses at the start of December meant the Bills might not qualify for the 1989 playoffs. Fortunately, their opponent in the season finale was the 4-11 Jets. Buffalo clobbered New York 37-0, setting up an AFC wild-card game against the Cleveland Browns.

On that day in early January, the K-Gun was born. Four touchdowns and 405 yards passing from Kelly, along with the Thurman Thomas' playoff-record-tying thirteen catches for 150 yards kept the Bills in stride with Cleveland.

But Matt Bahr's forty-seven-yard field goal in the fourth quarter gave the Browns a ten-point edge midway through the fourth quarter. Kelly then drove seventy-seven yards in less than three minutes, cutting the Browns' lead to 34-30. The Bills defense forced a three-and-out to put Kelly and the offense back on the field.

From his own twenty-six, Kelly continued to pick apart the Cleveland defense. A string of completions—including a clutch fourth-down hookup with Don Beebe—had Buffalo inside the Browns' twenty. With sixteen seconds remaining, Kelly spotted Ronnie Harmon wide open in the left corner of the end zone. And, although he already caught four passes during that final period, the ball bounced off of Harmon's fingertips. One play later, Kelly's pass for Thomas was intercepted by Clay Matthews, and the game was over.

In the postgame press conference, Thomas hinted that Harmon's drop was the result of Kelly's hesitation—"Ronnie came back to the huddle and told Jim 'If you looked a little sooner, I could have scored a touchdown'"—then overtly said as much about the season-ending interception.

"I was open for a split second," he said about the final play. "Jim held the ball too long."

Both Harmon and Kelly refused to speak to the media after the loss.

Marv Levy may have served in World War II, began his coaching career long before any of his Buffalo Bills players were born, and installed the Wing T offense when the Kansas City Chiefs hired him in 1978, but he did not fear change.

"If you don't change with the times," he once said, "the times are gonna change you . . . for another coach."

Levy and General Manager Bill Polian reconstructed the Bills' roster during the 1990 off-season. Although Levy believed there were no "troublemakers" on the 1989 roster, Ronnie Harmon was not protected from Plan B free agency. Parting with two team leaders who spent a combined twenty-five years with the Bills was much more shocking. Offensive tackle Joe Devlin was coaxed into retirement, and nose tackle Fred Smerlas was allowed to leave via free agency.

"Joe Devlin and Freddy were the oldest guys in the locker room. And at that time in the league, age was a big factor in whether you were a leader or not. If you were there for a long time, if you were an older guy, you got certain perks and privileges. I think times were changing," Steve Tasker said.

"To Marv's credit he released both those guys, even though they both could still play. What that did was force Jim and Bruce—the great players on our team—to be the leaders. They were now the voice of team meetings and players-only meetings. It was Jim and Bruce who spoke; not Fred and Joe. And it really worked well in a group setting because the best players were the ones calling the shots and that's really the way it had to be."

In addition to their star quarterback and star defensive end, each of Buffalo's superstars was charged with a new leadership role upon the start of 1990's training camp. Levy assembled a nine-man players' committee (Kelly, Smith, Thurman Thomas, Kent Hull, James Lofton, Pete Metzelaars, Cornelius Bennett, Mark Kelso, and Darryl Talley) to help mitigate any locker room conflicts before they produced more headlines.

Levy didn't shelter his players, either: "I told the team coming into training camp to be prepared for all those magazine articles about 'the Bickering Bills,' that the term had a nice ring to it. I told them they had to overlook that kind of thing and concentrate on football."

"I think they were a divided team, an immature group that needed to grow up and needed to understand about working together," said Vic Carucci, the former *Buffalo News* beat writer.

To me, it was the best thing that happened to them. They definitely fought like brothers, but I also think that they needed to realize how much better they would be if the bond were tighter and if they worked together and did less of the backbiting. Sure [the media], always takes something and makes it bigger than it is, but it was pretty substantive. . . . They hit that crossroads in '89, that allowed them to be the team they were in '90 because they made such an effort. . . . There was almost a kumbaya effort once they got to camp.

In Week Two, the Bills lost their road opener to Miami. Headlines announced that little had changed in Buffalo during the off-season. Behind 30-7 with 7:54 remaining, Levy pulled his first stringers amid the sweltering south Florida heat. Bruce Smith complained about the move, saying, "We just fuckin' gave up."

Levy was angry and fined Smith $500. He also fined three defenders who refused to come off the field when the starters were ordered off. But the conflict did not escalate from there.

"The harmony has been great," Kelly said. "I know people will point to what Bruce said. Bruce says what he wants to say, but we are together as a team. Last week was a bummer. But teams go through that once in a season. Hopefully, this is ours, and we've gotten all that bad stuff out of the way in the second week."

Kelly's confidence in a new, controversy-free Bills team was valid. That off-season he took Marv Levy's vows of change very seriously.

"It was Jim, too, I think, figuring out that he needed to learn that he had to have these guys on his side—which he did," Vic Carucci noted.

They were behind him because they knew he was good. But when he came in, he came in kicking the door down, he was like, "Everybody get on my back, let's get going and you step up to my level," calling out offensive linemen. Linemen didn't love that, and their wives didn't love that, and their families didn't love that. They had issues with this cocky kid who seemed to have a free reign.

They got to know each other better; they figured out what he was about. He definitely was smart enough to—as he did with his own family—share with his team, his success and his attention. The only guy getting national notice at that point was Jim, but he shared the wealth.

Kelly—who signed the NFL's richest contract prior to the 1990 season—started including his teammates in photo shoots as well as his endorsements projects. And the postgame parties at his house, win or lose, became a bonding ritual for the entire team.

After the loss to Miami, the harmonious Bills promptly won eight straight. A loss to the Houston Oilers, on an eardrum-busting Monday night at the Astrodome, did not sidetrack the newly focused Bills. Wins over Philadelphia and Indianapolis meant the Bills were already guaranteed a better December record than they had posted in nine years. And with a Week Fifteen victory over the New York Giants, the Bills swept away all remnants of the "Bickering Bills."

"I told Vic [Carucci] don't print this, but if we beat this team, on the road in the Meadowlands, there's no stopping us. They were good, and that was a tough road game against a team we didn't see very often, a good defense and we beat them," Steve Tasker remembered.

That was the one locker room, after that game, when we knew we were good. We knew we were special. That was the happiest locker room I was ever in. . . . This one wasn't a celebration of "Hey we won this game."

That locker room was a celebration of convincing ourselves that we were special. And that was the first time—through '89, '88—when we beat that team in New York, that team for the first time believed it was special and believed it was great. I'll never forget that locker room. It was really something. I remember Teddy Marchibroda, the smile on his face, and Marv. We were just giddy. Everyone was giggling.

11

The Irresistible Force vs. The Immovable Object

On the first play of the final quarter of Super Bowl XXV, Thurman Thomas stole back the lead for the Bills.

Buffalo aligned in their standard three-receiver, single-back shotgun formation on first and ten at the thirty-one. As they had been most of the night, the Giants were in their two-down-linemen, four-linebacker front. Giants Carl Banks and Gary Reasons crept near the line of scrimmage, but at the snap, they didn't blitz.

From this read-and-react position, the two inside linebackers saw Kelly place the ball in Thomas' hands. A powerful surge by Buffalo's line—especially center Kent Hull and left guard Jim Ritcher, who teamed up to block Reasons and Banks—sealed off a huge alley for Thomas up the middle. He carried the football a full ten yards before anyone laid a hand on him.

At the twenty-four-yard line, cornerback Reyna Thompson and safety Myron Guyton converged on Thomas. They had him stuffed.

Thomas lowered his shoulder and plowed into Guyton, who tumbled to the ground. Thomas kept running. He sidestepped Thompson and darted outside to the sideline. Guyton's hit, though it didn't bring him down, did allow several Giant defenders to gain in their pursuit of Thomas.

Cornerback Everson Walls, who had begun the play on the opposite side of the field, raced to make the tackle. He was in position to bring the ball carrier down at the fifteen, and limit the run to just a first-down gain. Then, wide receiver Andre Reed approached him.

Reed had been severely punished by Giant defenders all day, taking shot after shot whether he caught the ball or not. Here was his chance to deliver the punishment. Reed dove at Walls' legs, cutting him down to the ground two steps from Thomas.

"That was a freakin' clip, man!" Walls remembered twenty years later. "That was an easy call to make. . . . He got me strictly from behind. I had the angle down on Thurman Thomas. I had made tackles before that. I was gonna make that tackle. I had him in my sights. Andre did a good job of hustling down the field, things of that nature, but the ref's gotta do his freakin' job as well. He's gotta drop that flag! That was a bad no-call."

With Walls safely on the ground, Thomas continued on to the end zone untouched. Lawrence Taylor came within a step of Thomas at the two-yard line, but by then, it was too late. Thomas crossed the goal line, pushing Buffalo ahead.

"It would be hard to argue that the best player on the field that day wasn't Thurman Thomas," Dan Dierdorf said in 2010. "His play was just exemplary. It was a joy to watch."

Scott Norwood's extra point made the score 19-17. Once again, Jeff Hostetler and the Giants offense would be called upon to produce. And once again—as they had done three times in the second half against San Francisco a week earlier and twice already this evening with consecutive, lengthy touchdown drives—they did.

The drive started in familiar fashion. First, Anderson grabbed a few hard-earned yards up the middle. Then, just prior to releasing a pass, Hostetler absorbed a brutal hit in the backfield: offensive tackle Doug Riesenberg had to peel his quarterback up off the ground. The incomplete pass set up third and long.

"Anytime, whether it's run or pass, you can make a third-down conversion, it's big," Ron Erhardt said. "You called it because you wanted to make the first down; if you didn't feel good about it, you wouldn't have called it. So when we did make one of those, it was because it was a good call or it was executed well."

Five times thus far, the Giants had successfully executed third and long situations (seven or more yards to go) during the game. The lone exception being Hostetler's completion to Mark Ingram, which came up two yards short and set up Ottis Anderson's failed attempt on fourth and two late in the third period.

"There was no panic," Jumbo Elliott said afterward. "We can pass when we have to. We're not one-dimensional."

Even when trailing in the fourth quarter and facing a third and seven deep in their own territory, panic never permeated the Giants' huddle.

Each of the Giants' skill players—Anderson, Ingram, Baker, Meggett, and Cross—had come up with a clutch third-down play. Now came time for Mark Bavaro to contribute to the Giants' incredible string of clutch performances.

Matched up man-to-man with linebacker Shane Conlan, Bavaro beat the all-pro to the outside, snagged a Hostetler pass, and made his way upfield to ensure the Giants' eighth third-down conversion in thirteen attempts.

"He is a money player," Frank Gifford told viewers.

Bavaro's seventeen-yard reception put New York near midfield. Hostetler soon turned right back to his "money player," hitting Bavaro with a play-action pass over the middle that netted nineteen. Wincing from the tackle of two Bills defenders, the already aching Bavaro—all week long, the twenty-seven-year-old addressed speculation about whether or not injuries would force him to retire—walked to the sideline, knelt on the ground, and was looked over by the trainers and the team physician. Thanks to a long television time-out, Bavaro returned to the field a play later.

"He's the toughest guy on our team," Jumbo Elliott said that week.

Even without the franchise's leading receiver from 1985 through 1990, the Giants' passing game continued to sparkle. Negotiating the Buffalo zone coverage, Hostetler threaded a pass to Mark Ingram, adding thirteen more yards. Ingram wisely decided against lateraling the football to a teammate at the end of the play: "I saw a few words come out of [Parcells'] mouth that you can't say on television."

Steely third-down heroics were soon needed again. An Anderson run and a short pass to Bavaro—his third catch of the drive—didn't get the Giants much. But offensive coordinator Ron Erhardt found the situation manageable. Needing only five yards for the first down allowed the Giants the option of running the football on third down, which they did.

A simple draw play—Hostetler dropping into the pocket as if he were going to pass, then quickly handing the ball to running back Dave Meggett—was the call. Only momentarily frozen by Hostetler's fake, Buffalo's linebackers reacted well, filling the running lanes. With the middle of the line too crowded, Meggett bounced to the outside. He ran away from the grasp of Cornelius Bennett, niftily eluded Leonard Smith, and dove toward the three-yard line.

Although Mark Ingram flashed the first-down arm signal, the referees were not as certain, and the yardage sticks were brought out for a measurement. As it turned out, Ingram was right. Meggett had made the first down by three lengths of the football.

First and goal at the three shifted the Giants into their standard goal-line offense of three tight ends and two backs. Because their offense had historically been very efficient inside the ten-yard line, New York seemed destined to put the ball in the end zone. Although surrendering a field goal would still cost Buffalo the lead, the difference between a one-point deficit (20-19) and a five-point deficit (24-19) was immense.

Along the left side of the line, Bavaro, front-side guard William Roberts, and lead blocker Maurice Carthon cleared a path for Ottis Anderson to fire through. But a split-second after Hostetler handed off the ball, nose tackle Jeff Wright lassoed Anderson's legs and brought him down four yards behind the line of scrimmage.

Anderson made up the lost four yards on the next play, following Carthon's lead block up the middle, returning the line of scrimmage to the three. Shane Conlan and Carlton Bailey teamed up to make the hit, setting up yet another immense third-down showdown.

Running the ball on third down near the goal line was too risky, so a pass play was the choice. Hostetler received the snap, stepped backward, and scanned the field. Rather than let Hostetler pick apart his zone coverage once more on third down, Bills defensive coordinator Walt Corey blitzed linebackers Darryl Talley and Cornelius Bennett. And with Bruce Smith occupying two Giants—Jumbo Elliott and Ottis Anderson—a pair of Bills defensive linemen penetrated. The pocket collapsing, Hostetler rolled right until he had no choice and was forced to get rid of the ball. Fortunately, his favorite receiver that evening, Mark Ingram, stood alone along the near sideline. But Bennett blocked Hostetler's passing lane and batted the ball down, snapping the quarterback's streak of eight consecutive third-down completions.

Even had Ingram made the catch, Leonard Smith was in perfect position to make the tackle short of the goal line. (Of course, that evening, Ingram's penchant for breaking seemingly certain tackles had already produced one impossible third-down conversion.)

Trailing by just two points, Parcells sent out the kicking unit. And for the second time in two weeks, his reserve kicker, Matt Bahr, stroked through a go-ahead, fourth-quarter field goal.

After a somewhat slow start, New York's carefully crafted offensive strategy of controlling both the ball and the clock—taking "the air out of the ball" — had yielded tremendous results. On four consecutive possessions, beginning with Stephen Baker's touchdown late in the first half and ending with Bahr's fourth-quarter field goal, the Giants produced seventeen points and ate up 259 yards.

But two additional stats were even more incredible. Over the course of those four drives, the Giants ran forty-three plays while consuming twenty-two minutes and forty-eight seconds of the game clock. (By contrast, during the entire game, Buffalo held the ball for just over nineteen minutes.) Win or lose, the offense more than met Parcells' pregame objective of shortening the game.

Parcells was glad to reclaim the lead, but he knew the Giants had missed an opportunity.

"We had had a real good opportunity to score a touchdown down on the goal line," Parcells recalled years later. "Had [Jeff Wright] not made that play, we would have walked in for a touchdown. But he did make it, and it forced us to kick a field goal. And that's what kept the game close."

From the moment Buffalo's offense retook the field, the Giants' lead looked even more tenuous. Back-to-back plays to Thurman Thomas—a run and a reception—garnered nineteen yards.

Thomas rested along the sideline, and, as was the case several times that night, the Buffalo offensive immediately stalled with him there. Short runs by Kenneth Davis and Kelly—he couldn't find anyone open amid the sea of defensive backs—pinned Buffalo with a third and long of their own. And while the Giants' 60 percent (nine of fifteen) third-down conversion rate at that point in the game had been magnificent, on third down the Bills were virtually anemic. Thus far, on that most critical of downs, Buffalo failed to convert each occasion.

When Kelly darted a perfect pass toward the left sideline, the third-down woes continued. Bills receiver Al Edwards was beyond the yardage marker and cradling the ball until a vicious hit by cornerback Perry Williams knocked Edwards backward on his heels. He dropped the football before hitting the ground: no catch, incomplete pass. The Bills would have to punt.

Less than six minutes now remained in the fourth quarter and the Bills still trailed 20-19. Given New York's ball hogging, the Bills knew they might not get the ball back. A few Giants first downs would mean the Giants could salt away the game.

Rick Tuten came out to punt for the sixth time. The Bills punt team wasn't accustomed to so much work: Buffalo punted only three times in their previous two games. Still, the kick coverage in Super Bowl XXV had been exceptional.

For a team that looked to generate yardage and points any way possible, Dave Meggett's contributions (he returned punts for touchdowns in both 1989 and 1990, and led the NFL in return yardage both those seasons) had been crucial for New York. But after Meggett began the game with a terrific twenty-yard return following the game's opening possession, the Bills punt team hemmed him in, coaxing four consecutive fair catches.

Meggett's sixth opportunity, however, nearly broke the back of the Buffalo Bills. He fielded the ball at his own fourteen-yard line, drifted right, then scurried upfield. A trio of well-positioned blocks from the punt-return team sealed off a wide lane, which Meggett saw. What he did not see—until it was too late—was Steve Tasker.

Tasker, the former Houston Oilers castoff, that year earned his first of a record seven Pro Bowl appearances as the designated special-team ace. And in the Super Bowl, he went head-to-head with his counterpart, the NFC special-teams selection, New York Giant Reyna Thompson. Along with Everson Walls, Thompson jammed Tasker at the snap, then ran downfield, attempting to keep him away from the returner.

"The two guys were doing a really good job of doubling me, they really had me and they did a nice job all night, but I ducked down low, like went to the ground and dove between them, their legs, and just tripped Dave up. I got a piece of him, enough to make the tackle," Tasker remembered years later. "When I got up to look I thought, 'Oh my gosh, it was a good thing I got that guy, 'cause he would have been gone.'"

With Tuten the lone player in position behind Tasker, had Meggett avoided the tackle, he might have stretched a sixteen-yard return into the eighty-six-yard touchdown that effectively ended Super Bowl XXV.

"Dave Meggett had a colossal hole if Tasker doesn't knock him down!" Dan Dierdorf noted on the broadcast.

"That could have [gone] the distance!" Gifford added.

Tasker's tackle saved the Bills from potential disaster. Still, two plays into the drive, New York's ground game started dealing Buffalo a slow death. Back-to-back rushes by Anderson bagged a first down for the Giants. Those fourteen yards pushed Anderson beyond the one-hundred-yard threshold and consumed time off the clock. Three minutes forty-five seconds remained when the Giants next snapped the ball. And after a third straight run (Meggett gave Anderson a brief rest on the sideline), Buffalo had to spend their first time-out.

Parcells and his "conservative" offense caught Buffalo off guard with a quick pass. Bavaro nabbed the reception, his fourth of the final period. The play picked up seven yards, creating another momentous third-down matchup between the Giants offense and Bills defense.

Knowing that a first down meant he could drain most, if not all, of the time remaining, Parcells did not want to make a hasty move. Hostetler let the play clock run down to one second, then called a time-out and headed over to the sideline to discuss their options. Running the ball would keep the clock moving but most likely would not gain the first down. Throwing the ball could gain the first down, but an incompletion would stop the clock and allow Buffalo to keep one of their time-outs.

New York's repeated success, throwing passes to Bavaro—especially in the fourth quarter—tempted Parcells.

"We really didn't want to give the ball back to them," Parcells said. "The decision came down to, should we try to win the game with that same play, because we thought that play was there, or should we try to run the clock and maybe make Buffalo use another time-out and run the shotgun draw."

Following the discussion with his offensive coordinator, Parcells asked his quarterback.

"What do you think about quarterback draw?" he asked.

Standing face-to-face—the two men who, for years, didn't see eye to eye—debated the issue. Pressed for a decision, they settled on the shotgun draw, a decision that caused Parcells great angst over the next fifteen minutes.

New York aligned in a four-receiver set, with Meggett beside Hostetler. During the cadence, Meggett motioned out, leaving an empty backfield. Upon catching the snap, Hostetler set up as if he were looking for a receiver. The Bills defense didn't succumb to the misdirection.

Defensive coordinator Walt Corey had chosen to pressure the Giants, rather than sit back and react. From their spots as defensive backs, Clifford Hicks and Kirby Jackson sprang toward the backfield. Hostetler ran away from Hicks' side and eluded Jackson, but with only five offensive linemen in position to block the six defenders, Buffalo had the edge. Leon Seals tripped Hostetler up, limiting the play to a minimal gain. The Giants had to punt.

To prevent the clock from reaching the two-minute warning, Buffalo called for their second time-out. Sean Landeta booted a kick downfield, high enough that Bills returner Al Edwards called for a fair catch at the ten-yard line.

Two minutes and sixteen seconds remained. The scoreboard read "Giants 20, Bills 19." Each unit's objective was simple: for Buffalo, score; for New York, keep Buffalo from scoring.

Throughout Super Bowl week, one topic of debate saturated west Florida. Who would emerge superior in the battle of what *Newsday*'s Bob Glauber called "the irresistible force of the Bills' offense versus the immovable object of the Giants' defense."

Fittingly, with the championship on the line, the outcome would be determined by one more showdown.

Kelly jogged into the huddle, called a play, and the offense spread out into the four-receiver formation. With Thurman Thomas to his left, Kelly stared down the defense; Lawrence Taylor and Carl Banks stared right back. Kelly barked out the cadence, caught the center's snap, dropped back, and set up in the pocket.

"Two minutes to go, you're the quarterback in a Super Bowl, you wanna lead your team down the field for victory," Kelly said years later. "It was a dream come true for me."

FLASHBACK: SUPER BOWL V

Upon assuming command of the Washington Redskins in 1971, head coach George Allen issued an unusual decree. He barred all rookies from his team.

"We're going to have an all-veteran team," Allen said. "There will be no rookies, and that's the way it should be."

Allen's contempt may have been extreme, but he was not alone in distrusting rookies. Jim Lee Howell, the New York Giants head coach from 1954 to 1960, would have applauded Allen's roster maneuvering: "I really think Howell hated rookies," Giants Hall of Fame linebacker Sam Huff wrote in his autobiography, *Tough Stuff.*

Andy Russell, another great linebacker from the premerger era, echoed the same sentiment about the man who drafted him, Steelers head coach Buddy Parker.

"He hated rookies," Russell recalled. "In fact in the year I was drafted, he traded away the first seven picks."

Back then, no one could predict that, by the twenty-first century, rookies would routinely earn more money than ten-year veterans. But even in the early 1970s, Allen's ideal vision of an NFL roster was becoming antiquated.

A season before Allen's rookie purge, the Baltimore Colts' locker room could have been confused for a college dormitory. By the end of 1970, nine men on their roster never played pro football prior to that season. Perhaps the head coach was partial to them: forty-nine-year-old Don McCafferty—an assistant throughout his entire collegiate and professional coaching career—replaced Don Shula that year.

But a rookie head coach and rookies comprising more than one-fifth of the roster did not hamper the Colts' season. With a pair of MVP quarterbacks, John Unitas and Earl Morrall, and veterans like John Mackey, Jimmy Orr, and Billy Ray Smith, the Colts were championship-hardened. And most of them had the scars to prove it.

"Super Bowl III was an obvious turning point in the history of the National Football League and what had been the American Football League," Colts center Bill Curry said. "There was such disdain from the NFL toward the AFL; there was such horror at the notion that one of us might eventually lose to one of them in the game. . . . We were about to be validated as the greatest team in the history of the National Football League: 15-1 going into the Super Bowl. I swear, I don't think we were complacent. We prepared well. We didn't just go to Miami and go to the beach."

Complacent or not, at the Orange Bowl in January 1969, the Colts lost to Joe Namath's New York Jets 16-7.

"It was one of the best teams I ever played with," linebacker Mike Curtis told NFL Films years later, "and we lost to somebody that we would beat eight thousand times after the Super Bowl. It was a humiliation."

Two years after the loss to the Jets, the Colts and their odd mixture of youth and veterans (in addition to the nine rookies, four second-year players were on the squad) cruised through the regular season, then the playoffs, earning a berth in Super Bowl V.

"They weren't relaxed going into the game," Curtis said. "I wasn't relaxed; I think a lot of it 'cause the guys put a lot of pressure on themselves, to push harder."

Not every Colt felt that way about the mid-January trip to Miami. Those nine rookies had been college juniors when Namath stunned the world in Super Bowl III.

"A couple guys and I rented a convertible," rookie kicker and fourth-string wide receiver Jim O'Brien remembered. "After being in the miserable weather in Baltimore for the past two or three months, we thought we would splurge a little."

Splurging also meant a fishing trip on the team's first full day in south Florida. Rookie running back Jack Maitland's parents lived in Fort Lauderdale, and his father's business owned a forty-four-foot striker fishing boat. Along with veteran Cornelius Johnson and second-year player Tommy Maxwell, rookies Maitland, O'Brien, Jim Bailey, Rick Herdliska, and Lynn Larson spent hours out on the Atlantic. Late in the voyage, one of the players hooked a mako shark, and the teammates traded off reeling it in.

"We were debating, thinking about putting it in [running back Tom] Matte's room, which we decided against. Then we were gonna take it down and put it in the swimming pool, which we decided against," Maitland remembered. "It was a fun time."

O'Brien's week wasn't all fun and games, however. Super Bowl V was to be the first played on artificial turf. In fact, prior to that 1970 season, not a single regular-season or playoff game had been played on a surface other than natural grass.

The twenty-three-year-old rookie, nicknamed "Lassie" because of his long hair, who wore bell-bottoms, liked to paint with acrylics, and read the book *The Sensuous Woman* that winter, was surprisingly old-fashioned. He was a straight-ahead kicker (not "soccer style") and didn't care for the new-age playing surface.

"To my recollection, we had played one game in our history on artificial turf," said Ernie Accorsi, Baltimore's young public-relations director and scout.

So we're down at the practice the day before the game, which is nothing but a walkthrough. And O'Brien did not have a good day of practice. He said to me, "I hope they're not counting on me Sunday." I said, "Why?" He said, "I can't kick on this stuff." He was a straight-ahead, conventional kicker. He said, "I take a divot like a 7-iron. The way I kick, my foot's bouncing into the ball; I'm kicking the top half of the ball."

You can imagine what my feelings were the rest of the day about the kick coming down to Jim O'Brien.

On Sunday, Accorsi's fears mushroomed. At the start of the second period, Baltimore scored the first touchdown. To attempt the extra point and give the Colts a 7-6 lead, Jim O'Brien marched onto the Orange Bowl's new PolyTurf surface.*

"I didn't have the experience," O'Brien said. "I'm thinking 'Oh, shit, here we are in the Super Bowl' . . . as opposed to concentrating and thinking about what I do and going through my routine. If I had gone through my routine like I should have, I wouldn't have been nearly as nervous."

Without that perfect concentration, O'Brien's timing was off. He hesitated in his approach and kicked the ball too low. So low that it hit Dallas' Mark Washington in the chest.

But by then, O'Brien's blocked extra point was just another wacky play in a game that would later earn the nicknames the "Blunder Bowl" and the "Stupor Bowl." In the first half alone, there were two interceptions, two fumbles, and ten penalties, two of which were personal fouls.

"According to the advance billing this was the Super Bowl, a titanic contest between two super teams playing super football," wrote Arthur Daley of the *New York Times*, "But this one came up strictly from hunger, a sandlot exhibition between a couple of ball clubs of Lilliputian dimensions and miniscule

---

*Although the term "AstroTurf" would eventually become synonymous with all artificial sports surfaces, Super Bowl V was played on PolyTurf, a product made by a rival company. Super Bowl VIII, played at Rice Stadium, would be the first played on AstroTurf.

skills. . . . At least the TV watchers could have escaped if they so desired. The folks here were trapped."

Even the Colts' lone score had come on a fluke. A pass from Unitas was tipped by Colts receiver Eddie Hinton *and* Dallas safety Mel Renfro, then hauled in by John Mackey. The Hall of Fame tight end galloped the rest of the way for a bizarre seventy-five-yard touchdown, the longest play in the Super Bowl's five-year history.

Still, for all the absurdities, the contest emitted a palpable intensity.

"A lot of the turnovers had a lot to do with that damn turf. People were slipping all over the place. It was a crazy game," Accorsi said. "But we played that game in a panic; it was desperation. I was on the sideline for most of the game; to this day, it was the most vicious football game. So they can talk about it being the 'Blunder Bowl' all they want. It was a vicious, physical battle."

"I think [Cowboys linebacker] Chuck Howley still wears my number on his forehead," rookie running back Norm Bulaich said years later.

The less-than-refined football didn't cease with O'Brien's botched extra point. After a grand total of nine turnovers and fourteen penalties, the score stood even at 13-13 with one minute to play in the fourth quarter. One final blunder remained. At his own twenty-seven-yard line, Dallas quarterback Craig Morton rolled out of the pocket and lobbed a pass over two rushing defenders, intended for running back Dan Reeves. The wobbly football fluttered above Reeves, who jumped for it but could not make the catch. It bounced off Reeves' fingertips directly into linebacker Mike Curtis' grasp.

Curtis' interception gave the Colts fantastic field position. Two Norman Bulaich runs—"just don't fumble," the offensive linemen told him—picked up a few yards, and with nine seconds to play, the field goal unit took the stage.

Although Jim O'Brien was admittedly a bit nervous, he wasn't nearly as flustered as some of his teammates would like to believe.

"Earl Morrall [says] I was trying to pick AstroTurf off the field to see which way the wind was blowing," said O'Brien.

But I did pick up wind because the AstroTurf fields aren't like the pure turf fields of today. They're pretty bristly and they catch a lot of lint off people's uniforms. So I would always pick up lint on an AstroTurf field to see which way the wind was blowing. That's all I really did. But Earl kinda embellishes, likes to make it more than it is. He uses that when he goes to all the speeches he gives. . . . It's half true, except it makes me look like an imbecile for trying to pick AstroTurf out, because you can't. You'd need a pair of pliers or a knife. Anyway, it's a funny story; we always laugh about it when we see each other.

Dallas called a time-out prior to the kick. And while the Cowboys players taunted him from across the line of scrimmage and the sidelines, the rookie barely noticed. For weeks, one of Baltimore's grizzled veterans had been hardening the mettle of the long-haired "child of the 1960s."

"Billy Ray Smith was inclined to want to cut my hair," said O'Brien. "All during that week in practice, he said, 'If we don't win this game, you're gonna get your hair cut.' . . . He did help me relax. From the time I got in camp to that last field goal, in practice, he was always talking and making it like the other team would do it: he would call time-out at the last second; he would yell stuff at me. So he trained me basically . . . to ignore the other team in that situation. And it paid dividends."

O'Brien's heightened concentration notwithstanding—this time, he fully went through his pre-kick mental routine—the short, championship-deciding kick remained in doubt even though it was only a thirty-two-yard attempt. After fifty-nine minutes and fifty-one seconds of a game that was supposed to showcase the elite of a newly merged league, not a single play could be considered routine.

"It was such a weird game, such a sloppy game," recalled Ray Didinger, the sportswriter covering the first of thirty-four consecutive Super Bowls.

What was going through my mind was, given the way this game has played out, I'm expecting a low snap, I'm expecting Morrall to drop the ball, or I'm expecting O'Brien—who's this rookie, who had been anything but consistent all year—he's gonna miss.

I was looking at it from the wrong perspective. I should have turned it over to the other side and said, "Everything has gone the opposite of what we expected it to go today; nothing's gone right. So O'Brien should miss this kick. But given the nature of the day it's been, I guess he's gonna make it!"

While his teammates prayed on the sidelines, O'Brien readied for the kick. Quarterback Earl Morrall gave him a final set of instructions—"Keep your head down and kick it straight"—then knelt at the thirty-two-yard line,

O'Brien three yards directly behind him. Veteran Tom Goode fired the snap back to Morrall, who spotted the ball. O'Brien, his chin strap inexplicably unsnapped, leaned into the hold and swiped through the ball. The perfectly straight kick sailed directly through the uprights. As soon as he kicked the ball, O'Brien knew it was good. The rookie repeatedly jumped up and down, then ran toward the Colts' sideline to rejoice with his teammates.

The Cowboys would have one last-second chance to score, but a desperation Craig Morton pass was intercepted, and shortly after, the Colts returned to the Orange Bowl locker room to celebrate.

"I remember Cornelius Johnson, offensive guard, number 61, he was just kinda bent over on a stool, actually crying," Jack Maitland said.

> He finally looked up in the air like he was praying and said, "Finally got the f-ing ring."
>
> But it was like the ring meant so much to a lot of those guys because many of them retired after that season. That was kinda their swan song. It was obviously a lot of joy and elation, but it was a tremendous amount of relief, it was kinda a sigh of relief. I don't remember popping champagne corks or anything like that. It wasn't a crazy celebration. The veterans, they finally made amends for that debacle two years prior. The rookies were obviously pretty ecstatic. For us, it wasn't a big deal: our rookie year we win the Super Bowl, no big deal. The longer you're around it, you realize how tough it is.

For the Colts' greener players—those who hadn't suffered through the Super Bowl III debacle—the victory was more enjoyable than poignant, especially for the Super Bowl hero, Jim O'Brien.

During the regular season, Ernie Accorsi had approached two of the lesser-known Colts players to represent the team at a series of charitable events. The gig paid a few hundred dollars per appearance. One of those players who Accorsi hired was Jim O'Brien.

"He wasn't any star at that point; he was a reserve receiver and a placekicker, not a famous placekicker by any means," Accorsi said.

When Accorsi walked into the winners' locker room after Super Bowl V, he quickly learned a replacement for O'Brien would be needed.

"After the game, they did not have press conferences with big tables and big rooms like they do now," Accorsi continued. "Everybody was in the locker room. It was a small locker room, and, obviously, everyone had surrounded [O'Brien]. They usually came to your locker. He wasn't at his locker; he was in the middle of the room, surrounded. And he spotted me, and he said, 'Ernie, I quit, I quit the job!'"

A couple hundred dollars for local charity events gave way to the national spotlight. With the headline "Jim O'Brien's Super Kick," a photo of the game-winning play appeared on the cover of Sports Illustrated, although O'Brien was barely visible in the image. Following a celebratory team vacation to the Bahamas, on Sunday he flew to New York City and appeared on the Ed Sullivan Show. A month later, he was traveling across the country, promoting candy: for his Super Bowl winning kick, the Life Savers Company presented him with their first "Life Saver of the Month Award."

The newly crowned sports icon soaked up the spotlight for months.

"Counting my $15,000 from the Super Bowl, that one kick has been worth $30,000 to me," O'Brien said in July 1971. "I made more money in two months than a lot of people make in a year. I want to make it now, so I can do the things I want to do later on. Society will get it back. I like playing football because it beats working, you know?"

On the field, the future turned out to be far more productive for O'Brien. Accounting for ninety-five points on field goals and extra points, he helped the reigning world champions reach the AFC Championship Game in 1971. The next season, O'Brien began to crack the lineup as a Colts wide receiver.

During an October Sunday afternoon at Shea Stadium, he caught five passes for ninety-one yards, and kicked two field goals and a pair of extra points. The second extra point came after he nabbed a thirteen-yard touchdown pass that gave Baltimore a 20-17 fourth-quarter lead over the Jets. He finished the 1972 season with eleven receptions, 263 yards, and a pair of touchdowns.

O'Brien retired after the 1973 season and eventually became a successful real estate and construction developer in California. Still, over the years, the image of the rookie kicker bounding through the air would be forever burned into sports history and into the minds of America's sports fans.

"People don't ask me how many touchdowns I had in college or how many whatevers in pro," O'Brien said forty years later. "It's basically, Super Bowl V and the game-winning kick. That's defined my whole career."

❧

"I remember Jim coming in [to the huddle] and saying, 'Alright boys, we gotta get to the thirty, at least.' And I remember thinking, 'God, I hope we get to the twenty-five,'" said Bills left tackle Will Wolford. "I had very little doubt that we weren't going to go right down the field, because our offense, it hadn't really been stopped in a while in that game. We had a lot of confidence."

Equipped with four receivers and the option of Thurman Thomas running a short route into the flats, Jim Kelly surveyed his options on first and ten. Against just three rushers, five Bills linemen surprisingly could not protect him. At the three-yard line, nose tackle Erik Howard almost brought down Kelly, who avoided Howard, found room to run, and by freezing linebacker Carl Banks with a ball-fake, gained eight yards. Pepper Johnson pulled him down from behind, and the clock continued to run. The clock soon stopped for the two-minute warning.

While ABC's television audience watched the gripping finish to Bud Bowl III—an homage to the Stanford-California "band on the field" play from 1982 featuring animated beer bottles in helmets—which gave Bud Light the win, Kelly, Marv Levy, and Ted Marchibroda contemplated the next play. Despite the long discussion about a second-down strategy, the play produced roughly the same results as their first-down performance. Kelly could not find anyone open, a trio of Giants defenders neared him, and he was forced to vacate the pocket. Erik Howard brought Kelly down, limiting him to one yard.

That brought up third down and less than one at the Buffalo nineteen. The frantic pace of the no-huddle allowed Kelly to try and sneak in a run. Given that the Bills had been zero for seven on third-down conversions—and each of those failed attempts came on passing plays—it was a welcomed change.

Kelly placed the ball in Thomas' stomach. The all-pro headed for the right side—his blockers had all crashed down that direction—but Pepper Johnson squeezed through a small hole and would have slammed right into him. Thomas' great instincts and tremendous change-of-direction abilities allowed him to shuffle to his left, where an enormous hole opened up before him.

Tackle Will Wolford's cut block held up Gary Reasons just enough for Thomas to run by the Giants linebacker. As the clock dipped below one hundred seconds, Thomas was sprinting down the field with seven Giants in pursuit. Only cornerback Everson Walls was ahead of him

"We came in there with those five linebackers and five defensive backs, we had so many lightweight people in there," Walls remembered.

> It was a *perfect* call. L. T. was upfield, Pepper had gotten walled off, and here I am, it's a cover two. So my first steps are backwards: I gotta cover James [Lofton] coming down the seam, I gotta cover Andre [Reed] trying to go down the sideline. I have to work on getting my depth so I don't get outflanked.
>
> As soon as Thurman got the ball, it was like he and I were looking right at each other. Once he made the move up the field, then that's when I made an aggressive step forward. But the thing that helped me was, when Thurman and I got real close to each other, we got within five yards, instead of me taking another step forward, I actually took a step backward and allowed him to commit. . . . It was much easier for me to read where he was going, and once he made his move, I just cut his legs out from under him. And we had to line up for another play, but I knew at that time that it was a huge play.
>
> With everyone trying to blame me for this and trying to remember me in history for something I did when I was just turning twenty-two years old, I went into that game thinking, "They are not going to blame me for this."

Walls' game-saving tackle limited Thomas' fantastic run to twenty-two yards. The Bills hurried to the line and ran another play—a short, across-the-field completion to Andre Reed (his eighth catch). The clock continued to roll—a minute remained.

On the two passing plays that began the drive, the Giants' three-man rush forced Kelly to scramble in order to avoid a sack. But on Reed's short gain, New York's front line could not put any pressure on the quarterback. And on the next play, Kelly again was untouched and not harassed as he looked for a receiver.

Although Hostetler was regarded as the mobile, western Pennsylvania quarterback on the field that day, Kelly employed a few nifty moves and darted through the line, picking up eight more yards. Repeated double (even triple) teams had begun to wear out the Giants' front line.

"I was gonna pass out," said Erik Howard, who, after Kelly's scramble, took off his helmet at midfield and signaled to the sideline that he needed a replacement. "That was the most tired I ever was after a football game. I felt like my heart was gonna explode."

Past the fifty-yard line, Kelly signaled for a time-out with forty-eight seconds left and went to the sidelines to consult with offensive coordinator Ted Marchibroda. Across the field, Marchibroda's former $25-a-week assistant, Bill Belichick, shouted out substitutions and alerts to his assistants and players. And like his current head coach, Belichick didn't panic despite several significant Bills gains. The Giants stuck to their game plan. On the play following the time-out, two down linemen, along with Lawrence Taylor, rushed the quarterback, while eight others dropped into coverage.

Again, there was no penetration by the Giants, and again, Kelly could not find a man open downfield. After a few seconds of waiting, he dumped the ball off to tight end Keith McKeller, who made a shoestring catch at the forty-yard line.

Officials wanted to make sure that the ball did not hit the ground prior to McKeller's bringing the ball up into his chest, so instant replay was called upon to verify the catch. Within a minute of review, referee Jerry Seeman announced the play stood. The twenty-two players on the field appreciated the extra seconds to catch their breath.

Seeman wound the clock and twenty-six seconds remained when Kelly began the next play, another shotgun draw to Thurman Thomas. It was the same exact play that gained twenty-two yards (and nearly went for a touchdown) earlier on the drive. However, instead of cutting back, away from his blockers, this time Thomas flowed to the right side. As he approached the line of scrimmage, two Giants stood hip to hip, ready to make the tackle: Lawrence Taylor and Carl Banks, whom one NFL Network analyst later called "as good an outside linebacker against the run as the league has ever seen." Thomas blew past both of them.

Free from Giants and near the sideline, Thomas was faced with a crucial, split-second decision. Continue trying to gain yards or make for the sidelines to stop the clock.

Neither choice could be wrong—or right. By avoiding the sidelines, he might gain more yards and shorten the distance to the end zone. It also meant that he would most likely be tackled in bounds and the clock would roll. With no time-outs, the Bills would be forced to spike the ball and not have another chance to run an offensive play.

Thomas could have opted to run out-of-bounds in an attempt to preserve time (twenty seconds would have been left, time enough for at least one more offensive play). But doing so would have sacrificed a chance to gain more yardage. He made the aggressive choice, shunning the sidelines and continuing upfield to gain six additional yards. Mark Collins tackled him, in bounds, at the twenty-nine-yard line.

"Bill [Belichick] said to me 'We may have just lost the game on that play,'" Parcells recalled. "He said, 'We were in the wrong defense for that one.'"

The clock rolled—twelve . . . eleven . . . ten . . .—while an official spotted the ball. At the nine-second mark, Kelly (under center for the first time in the second half) took the snap and fired the ball into the ground to stop the clock.

Only eight seconds remained. The Bills could not risk running another play. If the ball carrier were tackled in bounds, that would surely end the game. They had to attempt the field goal. Scott Norwood jogged out on the field to attempt the Super Bowl–winning field goal. As both teams began to line up for the kick, Parcells gestured and shouted to the officials: he wanted a time-out to "ice" the kicker.

Norwood's strong suit was accuracy, not distance. Because the Bills played their home games on the AstroTurf of Rich Stadium in 1990, Norwood had attempted only one field goal on natural grass. And throughout his entire seven NFL seasons, he had never attempted a kick that long on natural grass.

This championship-deciding kick would be a forty-seven-yarder, which, if good, would be the second-longest field goal in Super Bowl history. He remained focused and confident.

"I thought about the mechanics, about getting a good plant, going into it slow, hitting the ball solidly, probably taking the breeze into consideration a little bit, whether or not to get a draw on the ball, and following through," Norwood said. "I don't back away from that type of kick. It's something I've done all my career."

Meanwhile, New York's field goal block unit remained on the field as well, stretching out, encouraging one another to block the kick.

"It's an emotional roller coaster," said Erik Howard, who recovered enough stamina to return for the field goal.

Everybody out there is thinking, "I'm gonna be the one to block this kick" or "I'm gonna be the one to make this play." And there's a bit of willing it to happen, a bit of prayer, whatever you want to call it. But for those guys that are out there on the field, it's the culmination of what they've done their entire lives. It's hard for people to probably grasp that. But think about all the blood, sweat, and tears of an entire lifetime and trying to get to that one moment and it comes down to [eight] seconds and a field goal. I don't know that you can describe that or bottle that emotion.

That emotion so overwhelmed at least one Giants player, that it nearly cost New York five critical yards.

Lawrence Taylor had a fairly quiet Super Bowl. Taylor was matched up with Pro Bowl tackle Will Wolford throughout most of the game. And Wolford limited the three-time Defensive Player of the Year to just one tackle. With several Giants coaches distracted amid last-second preparations during the time-out, Taylor decided he would not be a spectator on the Super Bowl's decisive play.

"Out of the corner of my eye, I see Lawrence Taylor run on the field," Giants special teams coach Mike Sweatman said.

Now, Lawrence is not on the field-goal block team. I'm thinking, "Oh shoot, here goes Lawrence, we're going to have twelve on the field." But Lawrence sends somebody off. So now we've got eleven on the field, I think, I can't really tell . . . but we've got Lawrence out there, who's not on the field-goal block team. I'm thinking, "I'm gonna let this pass, I'm not gonna make a big deal of this." It wasn't like Joe Schmo the Ragman.

After the game, I go up to Lawrence and I say, "Lawrence, what were you doing out on the field on the field goal block team when you're not on it?" He says, "I wanted to be on the field when the game was decided." I thought, "What a great answer."

For Matt Bahr's last-second game-winner in the NFC Championship Game against San Francisco, Taylor had been on the field as the kicking unit's left wing. Perhaps, he simply wanted to be in the same place, on the field, rather than on the sidelines.

Coincidently, a handful of his teammates also assumed a spot resembling their place along the sideline a week earlier at Candlestick Park. At least one bended-knee prayer group—Pepper Johnson, Greg Jackson, Mark Collins—was too nervous or too antsy to view the fate of a game-winning field goal attempt. Their anxieties were slightly eased knowing that no one would be there to narrate the moment. Everson Walls was part of the unit trying to block the kick.

Parcells, however, felt no comfort. His mind was clouded with one lingering regret: the decision during the Giants' previous offensive series, on third and one, to run the shotgun draw with Jeff Hostetler instead of throwing a pass to Mark Bavaro.

"When they were lining up to kick that field goal," Parcells remembered twenty years later. "I'm saying to myself: 'You know Parcells, if you just had a little more balls you might not be in this situation. Nobody knows that—no one. Not any of the [assistant] coaches don't really know it. But when you're alone with your innermost thoughts and you're trying to think about things that you did and didn't do, that's the major play decision in that game, for me.'"

As Parcells stewed, more than a dozen Bills players and coaches—Kelly, Lofton, Levy, Smith, Reed, Tasker, Carlton Bailey—joined hands. Others peeled off, away from the group to be alone.

Norwood, standing far from the other ten Bills players on the field-goal unit, continued to focus and practice. Eventually, the unit broke the huddle, and Bills long-snapper Adam Lingner—who spent his off-seasons pursuing a modeling career—bent down and gripped the football with both hands. His teammates crowded beside him, forming a human fence to protect against the soon-to-be charging Giants defenders. Seven yards behind Lingner, holder Frank Reich knelt and tamped down a small patch of grass on the field's chewed-up sod. This was where he would place the ball.

Norwood marked off his precise starting point—three paces backward, two to his left—then angled himself toward Reich. Slightly bent at the waist, Norwood shrugged out his shoulders and nodded at Reich. He was ready.

"The quiet man of this football team, Scott Norwood, he can fire 'the shot heard 'round the world' now," shouted play-by-play voice Van Miller, as he set the scene for tense Bills fans listening on radios back in Buffalo. "Here we go, with eight seconds to play, high drama here in the Super Bowl."

Norwood nodded to Reich, who, in turn, shouted out a signal to Lingner, letting him know to snap the ball momentarily.

Lingner fired the ball back to Reich. Instantaneously, a swarm of Giants bolted across the scrimmage line. Reich could see them out of the corner of his right eye, desperately trying to stop the kick. The Giants' Roger Brown eluded wingman Steve Tasker while Dave Duerson had bowled over Bills blocker Butch Rolle. But neither came close enough to disrupt the kick. The Bills' barrier resisted. Reich handled the snap cleanly, placed it on the ground—precisely to the desired "eighth of an inch"—and Norwood swiped at the football with his powerful right leg.

Seeing the ball spotted right on target, right on time, Norwood stepped into the kick. With the snap, spot, and kick unimpeded, all the Giants had left to influence the outcome were the upright arms, hands, and fingertips of two defenders just past the scrimmage line. New York safety Myron Guyton and tall nose tackle Eric Dorsey leapt into the air, attempting to block the kick once it had been launched. But Norwood had hammered the ball with such force that it kept climbing higher and higher, far out of anyone's reach.

"He absolutely crushed the ball," Reich remembered. "That kick probably would have been good from about 55 to 58 yards. I'm sure he was thinking it was probably going to come in a little bit. But it just stayed straight. Usually, with a soccer-style kicker, you plan on the ball coming in a little bit."

Approaching the right goalpost, the ball appeared on target.

"As the ball was kicked," said Bill Polian, "I said to one of my colleagues, 'We're World Champions! We're World Champions!'"

But the perfectionist kicker knew he didn't hit it precisely.

"I left it out right," Norwood said that evening. "I may have put a little too much emphasis on striking the ball hard. I hit it good and solid. Again, maybe too much emphasis on trying to get a good, solid kick. And it was a good, solid kick. I hit it solidly. I didn't get the draw coming from the right."

Upon crossing the plane of the crossbar, the ball stubbornly sailed outside—not inside—the right upright. Two zebra-clad officials beneath the kick waved their hands to the right, indicating the kick was wide.

Reich and Norwood just stared at the ground. So did all their teammates along their sideline. A despondent Marv Levy let out a sigh of acceptance.

"That was the most emptiest feeling that I ever had in my life," said Kent Hull.

For a moment, Bill Parcells began to celebrate. He hugged Pepper Johnson and Carl Banks, then asked them for a favor.

"Take me for a ride," he asked. "Will you guys take me for a ride?"

"Let's take this mother fucker for a ride!" shouted Banks.

Banks and Johnson bent down to pick up their coach onto their shoulders, but because four seconds remained, Parcells told them to stop. Instead of "going for a ride," he shouted to those players celebrating, begging them to get off the field so the Giants offense could run the clock out. Linebacker Steve DeOssie was too busy filming the crowd with his portable video camera to hear the coach screaming. Parcells and his staff were furious with the photographers and *professional* cameramen. They hollered incessantly to clear the field. During his fiery tirade, Pepper Johnson doused Parcells with a second "Gatorade Shower" in five years.

"We got you two, that's what we wanted," Lawrence Taylor said, embracing Parcells. "We got you two, you're the best."

"I'm going for a ride, you're gonna take me," Parcells told Taylor.

The offense assembled into the so-called victory formation—"six tight diamond," as the Giants called it—and Hostetler pulled in the snap, touched a knee to the grass, and the game was over.

Hostetler had been stoic in the seconds following the kick. He watched Norwood's attempt from the sideline with one knee on the ground. Upon seeing the officials gesture "wide right," his teammates burst into celebration. Hostetler remained frozen.

"I remember looking back into the stands and looking at the Buffalo players and looking at our players, and trying to take in all of the reactions, and I just kept kneeling there for a few seconds," Hostetler wrote. "I think I was lucky that I caught a moment in our lives that a lot of guys missed because they were celebrating so much. I was celebrating, too. I couldn't have been happier. But in one way that I've always been glad about, I was a spectator. I held back and watched it. I may never know another moment quite like it."

Taking the final snap of the Giants' Super Bowl win shocked Hostetler back into the moment. With the game now officially over, Hostetler exploded.

"I was drunk with emotion."

So were his teammates. As Frank Sinatra's "New York, New York" blasted over the public-address system, several Giants hugged each other and high-fived their teammates. Just as many rushed onto the field to congratulate Bills players and coaches on a terrific game, a game that set two Super Bowl records, which will never be broken. Neither team committed a single turnover, and the one-point scoring difference was the closest championship contest in NFL history.

"That's the best way to end that one right there," Dave Meggett told Thurman Thomas. "Couldn't have a better way than that."

From the sidelines, tackle Doug Riesenberg blew kisses to the stands. At midfield, Gary Reasons held his son, Nick, in one arm and an American flag in the other. At the center of the field, surrounded by cameramen, Johnson, William Roberts, Myron Guyton, and Lee Rouson broke into dance.

"We heard all the talk about putting the game off," Pepper Johnson told a reporter. "I think that would have hurt more than helped. Hopefully (soldiers') families taped the ball game so when their loved ones come back, they can watch us. They can watch us dance."

Back on the sidelines, Parcells' request was being fulfilled. Taylor holding the right leg, Banks the left, they hoisted the head coach into the air for a few seconds. They let him down to continue handing out thanks and congratulations to his players and assistants.

Heading off the field, moments later, Parcells once again encountered Lawrence Taylor. He threw his right arm around Taylor and the two legends, who had now earned a pair of world championships during their ten years together, jogged into the locker room to continue the celebration.

"Tell ya, boys," Parcells said the following morning. "Nothing beats winning. Nothing. It's better than sex. It's better than Christmas morning. It's like all the Christmas mornings you've had wrapped up into one."

A few hundred miles southeast of the Bahrain Peninsula near Saudi Arabia, the USS *Theodore Roosevelt* was churning through the Persian Gulf. At the precise moment that Scott Norwood's game-winning attempt sailed wide right of the goalpost, it was early morning aboard the Nimitz-class aircraft carrier. That day, the "*T.R.*" and its crew of six thousand sailors would continue her first combat mission: supporting operations in Kuwait and Iraq.

"The war actually started on the seventeenth of January and the *Theodore Roosevelt* was still steaming at thirty knots around the Saudi Peninsula to get into the Persian Gulf and arrived on the nineteenth of January and began to fly combat sorties immediately," Admiral C. S. Abbot said in 2010. "We worked every day until the air war ended, which was essentially at the end of February. People felt very good about what they were doing."

The ship's commanding officer, then-Captain Abbot, knew that for most of his young sailors, this would be the first brush with combat. Worse yet, no one knew quite what to expect from the enemy as the ship cruised throughout the dangerous region. Ten days into the mission, Abbot decided to provide his officers and sailors with a small piece of home and devised a plan to let his men experience the ultimate taste of Americana (albeit, a day late): Super Bowl Sunday.

Although live television feeds were not standard in 1991, that did not discourage Abbot.

"There were probably sailors who were trying to determine the outcome of the game," Abbot said. "But I think the crew, broadly speaking, was waiting until we could get the tape aboard and enjoy watching it through the closed-circuit TV system."

Hundreds of television monitors were scattered throughout the ship. A videotape of Super Bowl XXV could be obtained, and the game could be transmitted through the closed-circuit television so crew members would be able to see the Giants face the Bills.

Abbot dispatched the ship's public-affairs officer, Lieutenant Tom Van Leunen, to retrieve a video copy of the game. Supply runs between the *T.R.* and a base in Saudi Arabia were flown daily. So, several hours before kickoff, Van Leunen boarded one of the C-2 "Greyhounds" headed for Bahrain. There he would watch the game, inside the Armed Forces Radio and Television trailer, while a taped copy was made.

But simply showing the game to his crew was not the sole objective of Captain Abbot's plan. He hoped that the crew might watch the game as other Americans had: captivated with suspense, unaware of the game's outcome. To do that, outside communication needed to be suppressed. The ship's closed-circuit radio was shut down, and updates from the action in Tampa were intercepted.

"Three times a day, we took one of our radio antennas and got a feed in of all the day's news," Lieutenant Tom Van Leunen recalled. "It was the old ticker, the old letter ticker. We still needed to get that because we still had to do the rest of the world news and sports for the crew. And we did that every night live. So we had one of the ship's journalists who worked for me actually go up there, when the stuff was coming in and tear it off so the INTEL and COMS guys wouldn't get it and send it around the whole ship."

Van Leunen watched the game in the AFRT trailer and then flew back to the *Theodore Roosevelt* only to return and discover that news of the Giants 20-19 triumph had leaked through.

"There are some things you can't stop. When you've got a crew of six thousand people, there are probably one hundred short-wave radios, those little portable short waves. It was routine that guys had those. You're never gonna make an aircraft carrier, even in the middle of an ocean, information-free. Sailors are pretty good at getting around roadblocks."

Nevertheless, a Super Bowl party still took place later that day. Through the closed-circuit television system, the game was screened in bunk rooms and offices. And on two of the mess decks, the tape flown in from Bahrain was projected onto a large television, and the crew viewed the game. Along with hot dogs, hamburgers, popcorn, and sodas, a large cake decorated to resemble a football field was served. Beer—O'Doul's 0.5 percent-alcohol beer, a.k.a. "near beer"—was also provided.

"We tried to make it like they were sitting in the living room with their high school buds or their college buds," the ship's executive officer, Commander Ron Christenson said. "And I think it really helped."

The game's broadcast—throughout the ship's closed circuit and on the mess decks—was such a comfort to the thousands of sailors that another screening took place later that day for the sailors who had been on duty at the time.

"When you go to sea for six months at that time [of war], those are the things you really miss," Lieutenant Ron Christenson said. "You miss being with your family, but you also miss those things that you traditionally do, like watching a football game or a special football game like [the Super Bowl]. When you get to watch it . . . it's very special, for the whole crew."

12

Who Are the Champs Here, Anyway?

"There are occasions when a coach's words—and even his eloquence—are meaningful to his players," Marv Levy wrote years later. "This was not one of those times."

Still, upon his arrival in the quiet, deflated Buffalo locker room, just minutes removed from the bitter end of Super Bowl XXV, Levy opted to address his team.

"Yet I knew that to refrain from all communication would have been a gesture that they could rightly interpret as a display of anger and disdain toward them. No feelings were further from my heart than those. And so I spoke briefly and sincerely."

"There is not a loser in this room," Levy told his players.

As Levy expected, his words were little consolation to the team. But soon, amid the sounds of players removing athletic tape, unstrapping shoulder pads, and filing into the showers, two distinct sentiments swirled through the visitors' locker room beneath Tampa Stadium.

One after another, Bills players and coaches approached Scott Norwood, eager to console their kicker. They knew that his missed kick—no matter how long or how difficult—was destined to become the freeze-frame image of Super Bowl XXV and of Super Bowl defeats.

"His portrayal as some sort of a villain by media outside Buffalo couldn't be more wrong," Bill Polian said twenty years later. "It's not only unfair, it's disgraceful."

The other forty-six Bills players in that locker room realized that the best way, the most honorable way, to try and ease Norwood's pain was to share it. Accept it. Absorb it.

"I said, 'Scott, keep your head up, that game should have never come down to a field goal,'" Will Wolford said. "You can never hang a loss on one play. Regardless if it's a field goal attempt in the end or whatever it may be."

In addition to privately reminding Norwood that this was a *team* loss, several players did so publicly.

"I remember Darryl Talley sitting up there, and Jim was there up at the podium; we had a bunch of guys that were up there answering questions," said Mark Kelso. "Everyone has responsibility for the loss. It doesn't fall on Scott's shoulders; it doesn't fall on anybody else's shoulders. I missed a tackle on third down; I can remember saying that. Had that drive ended up in a field goal. . . . And I wasn't the only one that missed it on that play, two or three others guys. I remember them all standing up and saying there were plays that we could have made that we didn't make; and that was the most poignant, how unified we were as a team."

"I'll tell you this," rookie defensive tackle Mike Lodish said. "There was no 'Bickering Bills.' No one pointed the finger at anybody. And I thought that was a testament to a lot of classy guys that had learned."

For Norwood, his teammates' words were not enough.

During the course of its first quarter century, the Super Bowl had featured several courageous performances by fearless performers.

Joe Namath's guarantee in front of the Miami Touchdown Club prior to Super Bowl III projected a boldness never seen before (or since) in NFL history.

In Super Bowl XXII, Redskins quarterback Doug Williams' return to the field—minutes after a hyperextended knee forced him out of the game—flashed extreme grit. Throwing a touchdown pass (his first of four during a 42-10 romp of the Denver Broncos) on his first play back from the injury only made Williams' comeback that much more storybook.

Even Jeff Hostetler sniffing ammonia capsules, then retaking the field to endure another string of savage Buffalo hits, epitomized toughness.

But no player in NFL history ever displayed more courage and more dignity than Scott Norwood did in the moments following Super Bowl XXV.

Outside the Buffalo locker room, ABC's Lynn Swann conducted separate live interviews with Levy and Jim Kelly. Both answered Swann's questions with poise and honesty. After a glimpse into the victorious locker room— Brent Musburger's interview with a grinning Lawrence Taylor—Swann returned on camera to speak with Norwood.

"I know your teammates do appreciate the effort, they're not down on you, they want you to come back and play strong," Swann stated to Norwood. "It's a tough time to go through. . . . You did a good job."

"Thanks Lynn. Again, I missed an opportunity for this football team. I feel badly, let a lot of people down," Norwood said. "But as you said, you realize in this profession that you've got to come back off of times like this, and I'm certain I'll do that."

The ABC audience saw the heart-wrenching, eighty-second interview, then moved on. Some viewers turned off the television and went ahead with the rest of their lives. Others stayed tuned-in to see more from the victorious Giants' locker room (after the network inexplicably cut to the series premier of their short-lived sitcom *Davis Rules*, starring Jonathan Winters and Randy Quaid).

Norwood continued to address the media.

"I asked him a couple times, if he'd had enough," special teams coach Bruce DeHaven said. "No, he wanted to answer all the questions. I felt like in that situation it would have been so easy for him to have ducked in and out of the locker room and just went on his way and not answered the questions. And he answered every one of them as long as someone wanted to ask.

"When we adopted our son a few years later," DeHaven said. "His middle name is 'Scott' and that is derived from Scott Norwood. I just felt like some day I'd be able to tell my son, 'You're named for a guy that suffered one of the greatest defeats you could have in a sporting event, and the loss was put on him, and he conducted himself with such incredible grace that, well, this is a great lesson on how you want to conduct yourself as you go through life."

Each time DeHaven approached the Bills kicker, Norwood rebuked him and turned back to give his interviewer a reflective, thoughtful response.

"I'm sure it will never get to a point where I'll ever forget it," he said. "It's something I know I'll carry with me in the future, but when I take future kicks, this won't matter. I'll just try to give each one of my best. Unfortunately, there are no guarantees out there."

For many of Norwood's teammates, the future was also on their minds. Confident that that night in Tampa would not be their last taste of championship football, they looked ahead to training camp in July, the 1991 regular season, and a berth in Super Bowl XXVI to be played at the Hubert H. Humphrey Metrodome in Minneapolis.

"To say it's very disappointing is an understatement," said linebacker Ray Bentley. "But life will go on. It's just a football game. We're already talking about coming back. We know now what it takes to get here and what it takes to win here. We've already got our sights set on Minnesota."

Not every Bills player shared those feelings of optimism—at least not in the minutes and hours following the narrowest defeat in Super Bowl history.

"I was really physically sick afterwards. I felt awful because I had been there since '86, and I knew what it took to get there," Steve Tasker said. "It seemed to me like we had climbed Mount Everest and been about ready to plant the flag in the top of it, and we slide all the way to the bottom. We had to start over again."

Seventy-two-year-old Bills owner Ralph Wilson had waited a quarter century just to see his team reach the Super Bowl. He was just as forlorn as Buffalo's players and coaches; thoughts of a repeat journey were too exhausting and of little comfort.

"Who knows what's going to happen next year," Wilson said the following morning. "I don't know whether we're going to be back in the Super Bowl next year. We may never get back again. That's just the nature of this crazy game."

Beside the Giants' feuding co-owners Wellington and Tim Mara, and General Manager George Young, Bill Parcells accepted the Lombardi Trophy from Commissioner Tagliabue.

"I realized a long time ago that God's playing in some of these games," Parcells told ABC's Brent Musburger. "And he was on our side today. I thought both teams were valiant. I thought we played as well as we could. I don't think there's too much to choose between the two teams. If we played tomorrow, they'd probably win 20-19. But I'm very proud of my guys."

Super Bowl championship tee shirts and hats circulated the Giants' locker room, as did dozens of reporters, interviewing anyone and everyone. Lawrence Taylor, Carl Banks, Pepper Johnson, and the rest of the Giants defense explained how they limited the Bills offense to just seventeen points. Members of the Giants offensive line talked about dominating the line of scrimmage during the third quarter.

Stephen Baker gave a shout-out to his seventh-grade history teacher, Mr. Hughsley, the man who told him he would never grow up to be a football player. Matt Bahr talked about his kicking (what amounted to be) the game-winning field goal for a second-straight week. He then expressed empathy for Scott Norwood.

"I wanted anything else to happen than for Scott to miss that kick, simply because it would've taken on and did take on the focus that it seemed the whole game. Really a great game on both sides of the ball, players making tremendous plays all over the field, all during the game—to have that reduced to the sentence of a missed kick is a disservice to everyone who played in the game and unfair to Scotty," Bahr said years later.

"So even at that [the end of the game], I was standing there on the sidelines with my arms crossed hoping for a fumble, an interception, a bad snap, a bad hold, anything than for him to have the stigma of a missed kick. . . . Unfortunately, that's kinda the way it turned out. Turned out good for us."

But the obvious choices for interviews were the pair of former backups who guided the Giants to victory. Holding his two boys, Jason and Justin, one in each arm, and with his pregnant wife Vicky next to him, Jeff Hostetler spoke about the nasty hits he took, his streak of marvelous third-down completions, and becoming an unlikely Super Bowl legend.

"Everybody wrote us off, and we kept fighting, stayed together, hung tough, and this is just a great victory for us," he told one reporter. "I've heard so many guys say that I'd never be able to do it, and, thank the Lord, it's done and nobody can take it away."

Hostetler finished the game with twenty completions in thirty-two attempts, 222 yards passing, and the touchdown pass to Stephen Baker. His string of eight consecutive third-down completions, along with the brilliant second-half performance (eleven for fourteen, 117 yards), earned him four-and-a-half votes for the Most Valuable Player Award. But Ottis Anderson's go-ahead touchdown and 102 yards on twenty-one carries earned him seven-and-a-half votes. The inaugural Pete Rozelle Trophy, which came with a brand new convertible, went to the thirty-four-year-old veteran. *

"How he was never the MVP of the Super Bowl is beyond my wildest dreams," Don Nehlen said years later. "That was the biggest farce. And I have nothing against that Ottis [Anderson], 'cause he played very well. But without Jeff Hostetler, the New York Giants do not win that Super Bowl game. That I'm sure of."

Other, less-biased observers agreed with Hostetler's father-in-law.

"Hostetler, of course, deserved the award," John Markon of the *Richmond Times-Dispatch* wrote. "As for why he didn't get it, we can only surmise that there's a reluctance to bestow a major award on a player with only minor credentials. If the injured Phil Simms had played the same game as Hostetler, Simms would be tooling in that Buick Reatta today."

Despite second-guessers, the choice of Anderson made sense. The Giants won the Super Bowl by executing—to near perfection—their ball-control, run-heavy game plan. Anderson's punishing rushes allowed the Giants to eat up time and consistently gain yards via the play-action pass. (Still, at least one columnist suggested the entire New York offensive line should win the award.)

The MVP Trophy and the car (which General Motors announced five weeks later was to be discontinued due to poor sales) were not the most significant accolades lavished upon Anderson that evening. Words from his head coach carried much more weight than those material objects.

"He's going to Canton (the Pro Football Hall of Fame)," Parcells told reporters. "I don't see how they can keep the kid out. He's got too many pelts

---

*At the time, a fourteen-man committee of sportswriters voted for the game's MVP. Ballots had to be turned in late in the third quarter. Several sportswriters later believed that Thurman Thomas' performance (fifteen rushes for 135 yards, five receptions for fifty-five yards, and his go-ahead, thirty-one-yard fourth-quarter touchdown) was worthy of the award. Despite averaging 9.5 yards per touch, he earned just one vote. Only once before (Chuck Howley in Super Bowl V) did a player from the losing team win the Most Valuable Player, and Thomas himself didn't think he deserved the award: "We didn't win the ball game, so you have to say that someone on their team deserves to win the Most Valuable Player," he said that evening. "If we would have won, it would have been different. In my opinion, you always have to give that award to a player on the team that won the game."

on his horse. The mettle is the test of time and he's met it. He's one of the top eight rushers in the history of this league. He's got to go. He's got to go." "They brought Parcells into the interview tent," recalled Ray Didinger.

[I remember] asking him about Anderson; and Parcells, the affection that he showed for Anderson when he began talking about him—the respect and the affection that he showed for him.

He talked about him differently than he talked about other players. You could tell that he really admired the guy. He admired his career; he admired the fact that when Ottis came from St. Louis to the Giants, he had a couple of years where he basically didn't play almost. And he went from being a star in St. Louis to being this forgotten man in the corner of the locker room with the Giants.

And apparently he never complained about it. I guess he accepted the fact that that was his role, and he went out and practiced hard every day and was a good team guy, and whatever they asked him to do, he did. And kinda just waited his turn. And when they needed him and they gave him the ball, he played great, to the point where he's the MVP of the Super Bowl. The way Parcells—who can be sort of flippant in talking about even his own players—there was just a different tone in his talking about Ottis Anderson. I picked up on it. You just got the feeling he genuinely liked this guy and respected what he had been to that team. And what a pro he was.

Eventually, reporters working on deadline had their fill of quotes and let the players and coaches continue their celebration. Buses bound for the team hotel carried Giants players and their families—except Johnie Cooks' mother, who boarded the wrong bus and was eventually driven there by a Good Samaritan—back for more celebration.

"The third floor kept rocking until 6:30 a.m.," Mark Ingram said.

Separately, Parcells threw a party for his assistants, trainers, the equipment managers, and their families.

While Giants players drank champagne and their shouts filled the Hyatt Westshore Regency, their field general was nowhere to be found. The battered quarterback preferred the company of his family . . . and a soft bed. In his hotel room with his wife and children, brothers Doug, Ron, Todd, sister Cheryl and brother-in-law Steve, his father Norm, and his mother Dolly— who would pass away unexpectedly six weeks later—Jeff Hostetler sat very still, bags of ice affixed to his entire body.

"My elbow is killing me and I still have a headache," he said. "I'm probably as sore as I've been in some time. But it's a good sore."

The following morning at 9:30, Hostetler gently rolled out of bed and took the elevator down to the lobby. There, he and most of his teammates—the seven Pro Bowlers boarded a plane for Honolulu hours earlier—waited for their ride to the airport. A few sportswriters waited with them.

"A couple of us were standing around at the desk," said Ernie Palladino, the Giants beat writer for the Gannett Suburban Newspapers. "We were talking to Mark Collins, the safety, and we were asking him about a particular play in the game. He stopped in mid sentence and he said, 'Damn, wasn't that a great game?'"

At around five o'clock that evening, the team plane landed at Newark International Airport. Three buses then drove the team to Giants Stadium in East Rutherford, where players and coaches could clear out their lockers.

And that's when the Giants' Super Bowl honeymoon ended.

Over the previous ten days, the Giants had won two of the most physical, grueling, closely contested playoff games in NFL history. And they had flown just under twelve thousand miles to do so. The tired players just wanted to finish their final task of the 1990 season and head home. Therefore, the buses zipped through the parking lot, headed into the stadium, and unloaded the players inside the stadium.

The nine hundred fans that waited for hours in parking lots number nine and eleven expected a little more pomp and circumstance upon their arrival.

"You'd think it would be a little more personal than this," Newark's Roger Sanders—who had brought with him his two sons—told a reporter. "I took the day off from work for this. And what do you get? Buses. I wanted to see Bill Parcells and Jeff Hostetler give speeches."

"What they did is rude," said New Jersey resident Lisa Teichman. "It's like we didn't exist. They could have at least said something."

Those few disgruntled fans could at least look forward to the standard public celebration: a parade or rally to honor the team. But New York City Mayor David N. Dinkins—who had promised to "do something" should the Giants win—decided that there was no room in the budget for a ticker-tape parade. (Similarly, no ticker-tape parade was thrown when the Giants won Super Bowl XXI. Because the team played its home games in New Jersey, Mayor Ed Koch remarked "Let Moonachie [New Jersey] throw them a parade." At least

Dinkins had previously told a local television station, "They may be housed over in New Jersey, but we see them as ours.")

"You have to throw a party for your people," Everson Walls said. "You have to throw a party for Super Bowl winners of the most exciting Super Bowl in history. For them not to celebrate that, it was one of the biggest disappointments of my career."

"There wasn't a whole lot of love there," Erik Howard added.

Dinkins did offer to honor the team with a rally at the steps of city hall. According to published reports, the Giants accepted the invitation and even helped plan the January 30 festival, a statement the team's front office denied. While city workers set up a stage and chairs, and officials prepared "keys to the city" for Bill Parcells and the organization's co-owners, the Giants issued a press release. Given the fighting in the Persian Gulf, Wellington Mara decided that a citywide celebration was not appropriate.

Many in the press also sapped some of the newly crowned Super Bowl champions' joy. Most tossed around praise for the underdog team's stunning upset over the flashy and seemingly unstoppable Bills. But a few less-impressed media figures summarized the game by saying the Bills *lost* Super Bowl XXV, not that the Giants won it.

"There were some who said that Parcells and the Giants got lucky that day, something he would continue to hear about for years," Bill Gutman wrote in his 2000 biography about the head coach.

"It would have been a shame had we lost that game," Parcells later said. "Because—and I am prejudiced because I was the Giants coach; I'm sure Buffalo feels like they should have won the game—but when you really look at that game, I don't think there's any doubt who played better. I think our players played better than Buffalo's players."

Naysayers and the absence of a lavish parade and/or rally hardly dimmed the jubilant spirit of Giants players and fans. But less than a week after the Super Bowl XXV win, questions about the 1991 edition began to overshadow the 1990 World Champion Giants. In the eyes of many "experts," the loss (or expected loss) of coaches and players cast great doubt over the team's repeat possibilities.

The coaching staff was slated to lose two assistants: wide receivers coach Tom Coughlin had already accepted the head-coaching job at Boston College, and running backs coach Ray Handley planned to leave the NFL to enroll in law school at George Washington University.

But the architect of two Super Bowl–winning defenses, Bill Belichick, garnered the most attention. Both the Tampa Bay Buccaneers and Cleveland Browns hoped to hire Belichick as their next head coach. In the week following the Super Bowl win, Belichick met with both teams' officials. At the front desk of downtown Cleveland's Ritz-Carlton, he registered under the name "Andy Robustelli," the New York Giants' Hall of Fame defensive end from 1956 to 1964.

On February 4, Tampa promoted interim head coach Richard Williamson. The next day, Cleveland's general manager, Ernie Accorsi—still high on Belichick from their interview in 1989—made the thirty-eight-year-old the league's youngest head coach. An endorsement from University of Indiana Basketball head coach Bob Knight and (because of his youth) comparisons to Don Shula also helped.

"Bill is bright, competitive, intense and dedicated to the game. He knows what it takes to win in this league and he's going to help get us back to where we expect to be in the play-offs, fighting to win the Super Bowl," Cleveland owner Art Modell told the press upon the hiring. "I've been disappointed before. I don't expect to be disappointed this time. Nor will our fans be disappointed."

To fill out his staff, Belichick picked out his own young, fresh assistants, including thirty-three-year-old special teams coach Scott O'Brien, defensive line coach John Mitchell, and University of Toledo head coach Nick Saban. Although the New York press worried that Belichick would poach assistants from the Giants' already-depleting coaching staff, none of Parcells' lieutenants moved to northeast Ohio for the 1991 NFL season.

Around New York and New Jersey, Belichick's departure was met with apprehension.

"Belichick is probably the best informed and most imaginative defensive coach I've ever had," retired Giants linebacking great Harry Carson said the week Belichick left for Cleveland. "I honestly don't know how the Giants are going to recover from losing him."

The loss of Belichick was inevitable. For several years, he had been dubbed a "defensive genius." Given his two Super Bowl rings, a tremendous passion for the game, and the pedigree (a lifelong football coach as a father), NFL teams strongly pursued him.

The sports world was just as eager to know about the head coach's future as well. Within an hour of walking off the field at Tampa Stadium, Bill Parcells was answering questions that had nothing to do with the team's 20-19 victory over Buffalo.

"The last time we won one of these there was a little controversy about me and it didn't allow my owners and general manager to enjoy this very much," Parcells said at the podium. "They're going to enjoy this one, I promise you. There's not going to be any controversy."

Nevertheless, controversy arose.

As early as the 1989 season, Parcells contemplated leaving the Giants.

"The way I feel is if I win another Super Bowl, I'm gone. No chance of coming back. No chance," Parcells said prior to the Giants' critical Week Thirteen game against Philadelphia. "If it wasn't for games like this, I wouldn't be here. You know what I'd want if I quit? I'd take a year off."

The forty-nine-year-old coach allegedly repeated that sentiment prior to the next season.

Health concerns—apart from the kidney stones in late December—contributed to the chatter. Following Chicago head coach Mike Ditka's mid-season heart attack in 1988, Parcells told the press: "Any of us in this business can identify with it. I drink coffee, I smoke regularly. I'm 30 pounds overweight. Real smart."

A perceived burnout potential clouded Parcells' future.

"It's tough to be a head coach in this league for 10 years," he said prior to the 1990 season, his eighth as Giants head coach. "I don't know if I can make it for 10 years in this league."

Nearing the end of another long season, his outlook hadn't changed: "It's becoming more difficult to do. There doesn't seem to be any respite in this game," he said during Super Bowl week. "If you're in the playoffs, or in this game, you don't get any break until the end of May. It's just go, go, go, go, go."

A reportedly unhealthy relationship with George Young contributed as well: they often disagreed on personnel choices. Furthermore, only one year remained on Parcells' contract with the team. History—which Parcells hinted at during his postgame press conference in Tampa—also suggested the coach might not return to spearhead the Giants title defense. Days after winning Super Bowl XXI, newspapers across the country reported that Parcells was trying to break his contract with the Giants so that he could coach the Atlanta Falcons for a substantial raise in salary. An angry Parcells openly dismissed the claim.

Four years later, Parcells was answering the same questions. Prior to Richard Williamson's hire, some media outlets stated that Parcells would take the job in Tampa Bay.

Rumors spread that he might retire, then return—with another franchise that would let him be head coach *and* general manager—the following season. An analyst job, at ESPN, the Madison Square Garden network, or one of the major networks, was also mentioned. By March, his agent, Robert Fraley, began preliminary talks with NBC, and later that month, the network's play-by-play announcer, Don Criqui, made an audition tape with Parcells.

"Everything that's been written about me is a fabrication," he said at Monday's post–Super Bowl press conference in Tampa. "There's no basis for any of those rumors, I can assure you. I've talked to no one in connection with any other possibilities in any other field."

His players wanted him back. So did Giants fans, to whom he had now brought two world championships after more than two decades of mediocrity. On the Tuesday night following the Super Bowl triumph, hundreds of New Yorkers crammed into Gallagher's Steak House on West Fifty-Second Street to see Parcells appear on his weekly radio show for WNEW-AM.

The crowd repeatedly interrupted him with applause. As the *New York Times* reported, "The fans made clear they were not there simply to celebrate the 20-19 victory over the Buffalo Bills Sunday night but to urge their adored maximum leader to stay at his post next season."

Despite all the turmoil and suggestive evidence, the notion that the New Jersey native would leave his self-described "dream job" seemed ludicrous.

"He'll be coaching the Giants next year, I guarantee that," his mentor Mickey Corcoran said the day after Super Bowl XXV. "He'll never coach anywhere else. He's a Giant. He's got the greatest job in football."

Aside from the health issues, reassembling his coaching staff, bristly interactions with his general manager, and potential burnout, another factor rubbed some of the luster off "the greatest job in football." The Giants' roster was ready for major reconstruction.

The multiple surgeries endured by Mark Bavaro in recent years (two on his left knee, along with wrist, toe, and shoulder operations) took a toll on the veteran Giant. During their playoff run, one Giant quietly told *Newsday* that retirement "would be the best thing for Bavaro. It's pretty bad. I don't know how he keeps doing it." Super Bowl XXV was his final game in a New York Giants uniform.

At another key position, the Giants also faced major concern regarding one of their proven veterans. Bart Oates—the only New York lineman to start both Super Bowl victories—had already graduated from Seton Hall Law School and passed the New Jersey state bar. During Super Bowl week, he acknowledged that after the season, he would consider retirement. The thirty-two-year-old had recently accepted a summer position at the Morristown firm Ribis, Graham and Curtin.

On the other side of the ball, four of the defensive starters (Lawrence Taylor, Everson Walls, Perry Williams, and Leonard Marshall) from Super Bowl XXV would be thirty or older by the middle of the 1991 season. And L. T.'s arrest—while in Hawaii for the Pro Bowl, during a traffic altercation with a taxi driver, he allegedly struck the cab with a metal pipe—again frustrated the Giants' front office.

The identity of next year's kicker was even in question. Thirty-four-year-old Matt Bahr had kicked eight tremendously important field goals during the postseason, including three clutch fourth-quarter kicks in the NFC Championship Game and Super Bowl. But in training camp, previously incumbent kicker Raul Allegre would be back to reclaim his job.

"I think [Parcells] saw what was going on with the franchise," said Hank Gola, a *New York Post* sportswriter during the Parcells' era. "He always used to say, 'God takes it away from you, with players.' And I think he saw that God was going to take it from a lot of players . . . that was kind of the last hurrah."

Even Ottis Anderson could not sidestep widespread consensus that the Super Bowl had been his swan song. Within seconds of being named the game's Most Valuable Player, ABC's Brent Musburger asked the thirty-four-year-old about retirement: "No way, I'm coming back again. I still got work to do."

"It's the player that determines when he's going to retire," Bart Oates insisted at the post–Super Bowl press conference. "What he has left, and how he's going to perform. [Ottis is] a tremendous role model for anyone out there that has somebody telling them they can't get the job done, that they're washed up. He was supposed to be washed up when he first came here, before the first Super Bowl. Another five or six years, and I think he'll be ready to retire."

Anderson may have refused to walk away, but that did not mean his place with the 1991 New York Giants was guaranteed. Five days after the win in Tampa, the Giants would have to submit to the league a list of thirty-seven players whom they did not want to become a Plan B free agent.* Each of the previous two off-seasons, Anderson had been left off the protected list. Given that Rodney Hampton would return, as would Dave Meggett—who had been a major contributor to the Giants' Super Bowl victory—Anderson was not protected. Jokingly, Anderson said he "would be insulted if they don't do it again."

But one uncertainty eclipsed all the others. Jeff Hostetler's exceptional performance in the playoffs, and especially on Super Bowl Sunday, had created a quagmire at the quarterback position.

Like Hostetler, Phil Simms had also brought the Giants a Super Bowl championship, just a few seasons earlier. The 1991 New York Giants depth chart would be the first in history with two quarterbacks to start and win Super Bowls. And Giants players did nothing to settle the issue either.

"Jeff Hostetler is a great quarterback," Mark Bavaro said. "He took over for Phil (Simms) when we needed him and filled in great. This Super Bowl was his game. We're just very thankful for him, that he was on our team. And I'm not taking anything away from Phil. Phil's a great quarterback too, but so was the Hoss. They're both great. We love them both."

"[It] doesn't matter to me which one of them is playing," added Bart Oates, "unless one of them has really cold hands."

Even more so than about his *own* future, the Giants head coach was non-committal about who would quarterback the team next season.

"I've got two pretty good quarterbacks, that's not a controversy," Parcells said. "I'll go by what I see at the start of training camp. That doesn't mean the quarterback's job is wide open. Quite obviously, Jeff Hostetler has earned a tremendous amount of consideration. But, hey, I've got a great veteran quarterback. He's one of my guys."

Simms scoffed when approached about retirement—and with good reason. Although Simms would turn thirty-seven that November, prior to the foot injury, he was enjoying the finest season of his career.

---

*A Plan B free agent was allowed to negotiate freely with any other NFL team until April 1.

But to earn their second Super Bowl championship, New York had won its final five games, two in the regular season and three during the playoff. Hostetler took all the key snaps, made all the big throws, and endured all the nasty hits in each of those wins. And without his clutch third-down passing the Lombardi Trophy would have been on a plane back to Buffalo instead of New Jersey.

"I like Phil Simms, and I don't wish him any bad luck," Hostetler wrote in his 1991 autobiography, *One Giant Leap*, coauthored with Ed Fitzgerald, "but I'm the one who sat on the bench for six and a half years and I hope I don't have to do it anymore. I think I've proved that I can not only hold the ball while somebody kicks it, but I can throw it, too—and run with it."

A pair of experienced Super Bowl winners was not the abundance of riches it seemed. Neither one wanted to return to the sidelines.

As spring approached, the front office submitted designs for diamond-encrusted Super Bowl championship rings, "Mr. and Mrs. W. Jeffrey Hostetler" attended a White House state dinner (Vicky sat with President Bush and the Guest of Honor, Denmark's Queen Margreth II) in February, and the New York Giants looked toward next season.

"For more than an hour, Bill Parcells and Ottis Anderson were center stage yesterday, with the Vince Lombardi trophy and the new Pete Rozelle Trophy," *New York Times* columnist Dave Anderson wrote upon attending the Monday press conference after New York's triumph over Buffalo. "But not once was the word 'dynasty' mentioned in asking about the Giants' future. Not once were the Super Bowl XXV champions described as the 'Team of the 90's.' Maybe people are finally learning that dynasties don't exist in sports anymore."

Beneath a gray sky and light rain, Pan Am Charter Flight 8207 took off from the runway at Tampa International Airport. Somewhere along the route from Western Florida to Buffalo, New York, Marv Levy left his seat and walked down the aisle to look over his team. His somber, silent players turned away from the in-flight movie, *Ghost*, starring Patrick Swayze and Demi Moore, and looked up at their equally somber head coach.

Returning to his seat, Levy leaned back and looked out the window.

"I recalled a poem that was in a slim volume of English poetry that my mother had given me way back when I had joined the Army Air Corps during World War II," Levy said years later. "It was by an unknown British poet in the 15th century about a Scottish warrior. It went just four lines":

> Fight on, my men, Sir Andrew said.
> A little I'm hurt, but not yet slain.
> I'll just lie down and bleed awhile.
> Then I'll rise and fight again.

The plane eventually touched down at the Greater Buffalo International Airport, where the team embarked on its final obligation of the 1990 season. Although no players really wanted to attend, the city had organized a rally to thank them for a great season. None of the players or coaches aboard the team buses knew what to expect.

Trailing behind ten police cars and beneath two helicopters, the team buses traveled across New York State Route 33, then reached Niagara Square, the center of downtown Buffalo. At city hall, the buses parked, and players and coaches took the stage. Before them, thirty thousand fans stood in subfreezing temperatures cheering, "Thank You Bills, Thank You Bills." The rally, scheduled for 3 p.m., was just about to commence when a new chant—"We Want Scott, We Want Scott"—started then billowed into a full-fledged deafening roar. Encouraged by his teammates, the modest Scott Norwood reluctantly walked to the podium.

"I've got to tell you that we're struggling with this right now," he said, fighting back tears. "I know I've never felt more loved than this right now. We all realize the sun's going to come up tomorrow, and we're going to start preparing this football team."

"The reception that he got from the fans was indicative of how they feel toward him and how much football they know," Bill Polian said. "They knew exactly what had taken place. And they knew that Scott did his best, and that's all he could do. That's all you can ask of any athlete. It's just unfortunate that people who don't know football as well as those fans have cast him as some sort of a goat because it's easy to do."

The master of ceremonies, Buffalo's Chamber of Commerce President Kevin Keeley, eventually began the scheduled portion of the rally, which included several local dignitaries addressing the crowd. From the Bills, owner Ralph Wilson, James Lofton, and Mark Kelso spoke, along with Marv Levy, who—as he had to his team a day earlier—told the crowd that not a single loser resided in Buffalo. The sea of Bills fans erupted.

"[We] get back to New Jersey," Giants cornerback Everson Walls later said, "and no one wants to foot the bill for a parade. Then I look on TV, and I see the Buffalo Bills got a freakin' parade. Come on, man! That was so disappointing, extremely disappointing."

New York Governor Mario Cuomo also took the stage. Earlier that week, Cuomo dodged the obvious question about which team he would cheer for. And although Cuomo's office later sent a telegram to Giants Stadium that read, "It was a great game between two great teams and you are deserving champions. Congratulations!" he appeared on stage at the Bills' rally at Niagara Square.

"They have made the entire state proud by their performance this year," Cuomo declared. "They showed more class, more character coming up one point short than most teams show in victory"

Those words didn't rile up the crowd nearly as much as his wardrobe: underneath his overcoat, the governor sported a sweatshirt that read "Buffalo Bills: Champion Super Bowl XXVI, Minnesota in 1992."

"It was off the charts, yelling and screaming," Carlton Bailey said twenty years later. "What more can you say about Buffalo? They understand and support their football team. It's in their nature. It's in their blood. It was outstanding. You would have thought that we won the Super Bowl."

13

January 15, 1994

Newspapers wrote about the story with zeal and intensity. Each of the major news magazines—*Time, People,* and *Newsweek*—ran cover stories about it. Correspondents from all the major television networks were dispatched so that live reports would be available for the evening news. And considering the international implications, detailed updates quickly spread to nations around the world.

But Americans were the most invested in the strife. And throughout the winter, they desperately wanted to know: Had ice skater Tonya Harding really hired her ex-husband to break the leg of her figure skating rival, Nancy Kerrigan, in order to force Kerrigan out of the 1994 Winter Olympics in Lillehammer?

Less than a week passed before the truth began to unfold. On January 12, 1994—exactly three years removed from the day when the House and Senate voted to authorize force against Saddam Hussein and Iraq—warrants were issued for the arrests of Harding's ex-husband, Jeff Gillooly, and her bodyguard, Shawn Eckardt. Harding herself would agree to a plea bargain, after admitting her complicity. Still, Harding was allowed to compete against Kerrigan in the Olympics later that winter, and the television broadcast of the women's short program in late February would attract a greater audience than any Super Bowl in history.

Somehow, the NFL managed to carry on with its postseason. And on the third Saturday of the new year, anyone who took a break from the mass-media coverage—right when the scandal was at its juiciest—to tune in for the second round of the 1993 NFL playoffs, was treated to a compelling and eerily familiar doubleheader of playoff football.

On May 15, 1991, television crews and sportswriters filled the press box at Giants Stadium. Bill Parcells took the podium to announce his resignation.

"I just think it's time. That's all there is to it. My instincts are usually good. I just think it's time to move on," he said.

"It's been a great experience. Who's been luckier than me? My hometown, my home team, my family and friends here. Nobody could have had a better job than me."

As early as March, the New York media had speculated that Parcells might step down. The *New York Times* reported that he was experiencing chest pains in the months following the Super Bowl—a December 1991 angioplasty revealed an irregular heartbeat.

Still, the news shocked many of his assistants and players.

"I was just in [Giants Stadium], talking with Bill a day ago," Ottis Anderson said. "We talked about the coming season. We talked about him losing weight and getting in shape. He looks good. I had no indication he was quitting."

Offensive coordinator Ron Erhardt and quarterback Phil Simms had virtually the same stories. But at least one person very close to Parcells saw his resignation on the horizon.

"I had a pretty good idea it was going to happen, just because I knew him," Parcells' personal secretary Kim Kolbe recalled years later. "I knew a lot of it was his health. I kept praying it wasn't gonna happen, but I was kinda thinking it might. I was actually on jury duty the day of his press conference. I was crying so hard they let me go."

Even after the announcement, rumors continued to swirl. Considering that in February, Tampa Bay had hired Richard Williamson, a low-profile coach, the Parcells-to-Tampa idea was a possibility, as were whatever coaching options opened after the 1991 season. Dismissing the notion that he was leaving the Giants because of a strained relationship with the team's general manager, Parcells told reporters at his farewell press conference that he enjoyed working beside George Young. Parcells' resignation inevitably produced more acrimony between the two.

"I knew something was wrong [with my health]; I didn't know what it was. I asked George Young when both [Bill Belichick and Tom Coughlin] left, 'Do you want to keep them here?'" Parcells said in 2010. "George said 'No, let them take their opportunities.' What he was telling me was that he knew there was a chance I was gonna step down. He knew because I was very clear to him: 'Do you want to keep them here?' He said no. He had made up his mind what he would do if I left.

"After the fact, that never came out. He never admitted to that. He said, 'Had I known . . .' That's not true. He did know."

An hour after learning of Parcells' intentions, Young promoted running backs coach Ray Handley to fill Parcells' spot.

The Ray Handley era began auspiciously. In Week One, the Giants trailed San Francisco 14-13 at Giants Stadium. And thirty-two weeks after his field goal erased a one-point deficit to win the NFC championship, Matt Bahr nailed a last-second thirty-five-yarder to defeat the 49ers 16-14.

From that point, however, the Giants were wildly inconsistent during an 8-8 season.

"When the [1991] season started, we played the 49ers and we're like 'Wow, we're back to where we started, we can do this again, let's try to run the table,' Stephen Baker recalled.

We had great chemistry the year before. The following year—and that's so important in sports, chemistry—it was all gone. Not to discredit Ray Handley, he did the best job that he could. But we'd lost the chemistry. It was very frustrating: from being the Super Bowl champion to playing how we played. It was probably the worst time in my life playing football.

I thought we were working hard and the practices were all going well, but maybe it was Parcells. I wish I could put my finger on it, but we were doing the same plays. . . . Change in chemistry messes up everything.

Losing Parcells and Belichick certainly hurt the Giants defense those two seasons. Even with the same starting lineup that finished 1990 tops in the NFL in points allowed, they slipped to twelfth, then twenty-sixth, over the next two seasons. On the other side of the ball, the Giants offense—which featured mostly the same faces, aside from Mark Bavaro who sat out 1991 and signed with Cleveland the following season—also tumbled.

Transitioning from Ottis Anderson to Rodney Hampton went smoothly. By Week Three of the 1991 season, Hampton became the feature back, and Anderson never started another game for New York. After playing thirteen games for the Giants in 1992—carrying the ball only ten times—the MVP of Super Bowl XXV retired from football. Hampton subsequently became a Pro Bowler. But the offense never approached the level of consistency that produced dozens of wins under Parcells.

"When Ray Handley took over that team, I never really thought much about it," said Bob Mrosko.

And then I remember Handley, when we got to minicamp, talking to a lot of players. He always said in the papers, "This is my team now; it's not Bill Parcells' team." It began to get apparent that he was gonna have a different philosophy. And I always equate it to the way Bill Walsh left the 49ers and George Seifert took over. He just stepped in and took over the team, and didn't miss a beat. He kept the same team, same philosophy, and he won football games.

And I felt when Handley came in and took over, he wasn't gonna be content with going in there and winning and having people say, "Oh, that's Bill Parcells' team." He wanted to put his own mark to it. By doing that, he decimated an un-believable good team, a team that was still poised to win more football games. He created a lot of dissension.

The identity of the Giants starting quarterback created the greatest dissension. Jeff Hostetler arrived at training camp a day late in the summer of 1991, while the final details of a two-year, $1.8 million contract were negotiated. The ensuing battle between Hostetler and Simms would essentially produce a draw during the next two seasons.

Hostetler won the job in training camp, surprising many teammates and members of the media: "In my mind without a doubt," Mrosko said, "Simms was the winner in that competition; he had an unbelievable preseason."

Beginning with the opener against San Francisco, Hostetler played fairly well. But the Giants offense struggled to score: after nine games, the 4-5 Giants scored just thirteen touchdowns. And in a stroke of irony, a devastating late-season, season-ending injury to Hostetler—a crushing hit by the Buccaneers Broderick Thomas fractured three vertebrae in his lower back and he left the game on a stretcher—enabled Simms to reclaim the starter's job.

Handley returned to Hostetler for the beginning of 1992, a season that saw even more of a quarterback carousel. Simms, Hostetler, and rookie Kent Graham each started at least three games. New York's 6-10 record was the team's worst since Parcells' rookie season as head coach.

"[1991 and 1992] were two of the most surreal years I've ever been through. It was like it came out of another dimension," recalled Ernie Palladino, the beat writer who covered the team for twenty years. "You always had the image of Parcells sitting at home laughing about this."

Parcells didn't sit around to watch the Giants crumble for long. Successful bypass heart surgery and a new healthier lifestyle convinced both Parcells and the New England Patriots to agree on a partnership. In late January 1993, the New England Patriots gave him a five-year, $5 million contract to rebuild their inept franchise.

"I started my coaching career here in New England, and I am going to end it here. This will be my last coaching job," Parcells said.

On the day that the governor of Massachusetts publicly welcomed Parcells during his introductory press conference at Boston's Westin Copley Hotel, George Young and the Giants' front office worked feverishly to sign *their* next head coach. Ray Handley was fired at the end of the 1992 season, and, five days after Parcells signed with New England, Dan Reeves took over the Giants. Reeves quickly settled on Simms as his starting quarterback.

"I didn't need that kind of controversy here," Reeves later said.

For the first time since leading the Giants to victory in Super Bowl XXI, Simms started all sixteen games in 1993. At age thirty-eight, Simms earned his second Pro Bowl invitation as the resurgent New York squad opened up 5-1. NFC East champions, the Giants hosted Minnesota in the opening round of the playoffs. Trailing at halftime, a pair of second-half rushing touchdowns by Rodney Hampton—who finished with thirty-three carries and 161 yards—propelled the team to victory.

"Maybe we're not as flashy, but we can control the clock," Hampton said afterward. "If we control the clock, we can keep those other teams that score a lot of points off the field."

The win earned New York a place in the second round and a cross-country trip to San Francisco. Since their unforgettable showdown in the 1990 NFC

Championship Game, the 49ers had also undergone a series of changes to their lineup. Gone was Joe Montana, replaced by Steve Young, the league's Most Valuable Player the previous season. And like the Giants, the 49ers boasted a new, younger model at running back: Pro Bowler Ricky Watters took over for Roger Craig.

But the apparent upgrades at those prominent positions were the only similarities between the two teams. Despite a shaky end to the regular season, the 49ers won the NFC West and earned a first-round playoff bye, largely because of an incredible offense that averaged nearly thirty points per game, twelve more than their divisional round opponent.

Against a revamped, yet still powerful, 49ers offense, the Giants would have to do battle without many of the stars from their vaunted 1990 defense. Pepper Johnson was gone, having left that off-season to join Bill Belichick in Cleveland; Carl Banks, who signed with Washington for the 1993 season, would join them both the next year. Everson Walls, Gary Reasons, and Leonard Marshall, the great pass rushing defensive end, weren't there either.

Within seconds of the opening kickoff, it became clear that this Giants team would not produce another thrilling upset by the Bay. Four and a half minutes into the game, San Francisco completed an eighty-yard touchdown drive.

By the first snap of the second period, the 49ers scored again, and when Ricky Watters added his third rushing touchdown of the half, late in the second period, the Giants trailed 23-0. The field goal New York kicked just before halftime proved to be meaningless. The Giants were manhandled in the second half, as three more rushing touchdowns (including Watters' fourth and fifth of the day) gave the 49ers a dominating 44-3 victory.

"Some of the guys were saying, 'Man these guys are good,'" safety Greg Jackson said. "I was so mad. I couldn't believe it. I wanted to slap some of those guys. I think a lot of the young guys weren't used to that kind of competition. They were shellshocked, scared. Some of them probably thought we were beat right from the start."

As bad as the Giants defense played—six touchdowns, 413 yards allowed, 79 percent pass-completion percentage—the offense was worse. The running game—which helped the Giants control the clock for more than thirty-five minutes in their playoff victory against Minnesota—managed just forty-one yards on nineteen carries. With their Pro Bowl running back, Rodney Hampton, gaining just twelve yards on seven carries, the Giants offense sustained only one drive of any length. New York converted just two of twelve third-down situations.

"Maybe the key to the game was the coin toss," Dan Reeves said. "They got the ball and it was 7-0. We were never able to play ball control. We were never able to get our running game going. We had to play catch-up all day. We didn't execute and they kicked our butts physically."

Phil Simms had a rough afternoon too. Without the team's clutch receiving duo of Mark Ingram (free agency) and Stephen Baker (released during preseason), Simms completed less than half of his passes and tossed two interceptions. It wouldn't become official for more than a year, but the crushing loss to San Francisco turned out to be his last NFL game.

"They were just way too good for us," Simms said. "If we could have kept some drives alive, we might have been able to hang in there. We tried but we just weren't good enough."

Another Giants Super Bowl hero joined Simms in ending his career on this sourest of notes. Within minutes of leaving the field after the worst defensive performance in team history, Lawrence Taylor addressed a group of reporters.

"I think it's time for me to retire," he said. "I've done everything I can do. I've been to Super Bowls. I've been to playoffs. I've done things that other people haven't been able to do in this game before. After 13 years, it's time for me to go," Taylor said that day.

After playing the entire season on a surgically repaired Achilles tendon, the Giants re-signed him for the 1993 season. They didn't want him to join Bill Parcells and the New England Patriots.

"I'm fortunate the Giants allowed me to come back and be on the ground floor of something big. In the years to come, I can always say I was there when this team started to make its rise to the top."

Seven hours before Lawrence Taylor, Phil Simms, and the Giants dynasty of the 1980s bid farewell to the National Football League, the Buffalo Bills sprinted out of the tunnel at Rich Stadium. They too had a rematch with an old foe from January 1991's conference championship Sunday. The Los Angeles Raiders came to town for the AFC divisional playoff round.

Unlike their Super Bowl XXV opponent, the Buffalo Bills did not stray off course following the epic showdown in Tampa on January 27, 1991. They opened the 1991 regular season on a roll, winning five straight, on their way to a fourth-consecutive AFC East title.

An all-pro year from Jim Kelly (he paced the NFL in touchdown passes) was eclipsed only by his running back. Thurman Thomas led the AFC in rushing yards: had he not sat out the meaningless regular-season finale, he might have won the NFL rushing title. He was just as vital to the Bills' passing attack, adding 631 yards on sixty-two receptions. Thirty-nine of the eighty-two first-place votes for league MVP went to Thomas; Kelly finished second with eighteen.

The Bills crushed Kansas City in the divisional round, then faced the Broncos in the AFC Championship Game.

As they had a year earlier, Buffalo turned in an incredible defensive effort, shutting out Denver through fifty-eight minutes. Pro Bowlers Darryl Talley and Cornelius Bennett, along with Bruce Smith—who missed most of the regular season with a knee injury—suffocated John Elway to the point where he was replaced late in the fourth quarter.

Elway not only couldn't put points on the board, but his mistake yielded the game's only touchdown. Bills lineman Jeff Wright swatted one of Elway's pass attempts, which floated in the air until linebacker Carlton Bailey pulled in the football. Bailey rumbled toward the goal line, knocking over Elway on his way to the end zone.

The play broke a scoreless tie late in the third period. Buffalo hung on to win 10-7, clinching the Bills' return trip to the world championship and giving Conway Bailey a second chance to see his son play in the Super Bowl.

Hours before the kickoff to Super Bowl XXV, Conway Bailey and the 260th Armored Division, Army Reserve Unit of Baltimore received new orders. They were to leave Saudi Arabia for a position twelve miles inside Iraq. As if marching further into enemy territory wasn't bad enough for the unit's ammunition technician, their destination was not within range of the Armed Forces Radio and Television Network: Bailey wouldn't be able to hear his son's team play that evening.

"When I was in Iraq, I thought it was a once-in-a-lifetime opportunity, that would never come around again," Bailey said.

Instead of watching or listening to the action, Conway had to wait until late Monday to hear the results of Buffalo's 20-19 loss on a BBC broadcast. He saw a video replay of the game once he came back to the United States on April 16, 1991. And although he watched the Bills' AFC Championship Game victory over Denver in his Baltimore home, Conway Bailey would be at Minneapolis' Hubert H. Humphrey Metrodome two weeks later to see, in person, the Bills battle Washington in the Super Bowl.

Against the Broncos, Bailey's touchdown helped the Bills overcome a woeful offensive performance. The league MVP and the other four Pro Bowlers could manage only 213 yards of total offense against the AFC's top-rated defense. And given the late touchdown Denver scored, Bailey's interception alone was not enough to guarantee Buffalo's berth in Super Bowl XXVI.

Midway through the final period, the Bills offense crossed midfield for just the second time, but the drive stalled at Denver's twenty-seven. Head coach Marv Levy never hesitated in sending out the field-goal unit—even though gusting winds that day in Orchard Park, New York, had already caused Denver's kicker, former all-pro David Treadwell, to miss three field goal attempts.

With 4:18 remaining, Scott Norwood lined up for a forty-four-yarder that would increase Buffalo's lead to 10-0.

"I believe in my abilities. I'm a positive person," Norwood said that day. "That's why I've played seven years in the NFL."

Norwood struggled in the season following his wide-right attempt that ended Super Bowl XXV. He missed five of his first ten attempts during the 1991 season. Norwood's overtime game-winner against the Raiders in early December notwithstanding, he continued to struggle toward the end of the year. (His three missed field goals and botched extra point in the game against Los Angeles were the reasons sudden death was necessary.) Two more unsuccessful attempts in the season finale helped Detroit defeat the Bills 17-14.

He connected on all three attempts during the playoff win against the Chiefs, including a clutch forty-seven-yarder. And the one time he was called upon in the AFC Championship Game against Denver, Norwood delivered. The kick sailed through and Buffalo hung on to win 10-7.

"I didn't have any doubts that I was going to make my kick. I was hoping to get the opportunity to come through for my teammates," Norwood said.

In the postgame press conference, Marv Levy wasn't nearly as modest on his kicker's behalf.

"Any Norwood questions, guys?" Levy sarcastically asked the press. "He deserves some credit for what was done. I hate to see him catch a lot of crap when it goes against him and then have you just shrug your shoulders when he's done something meaningful."

The meaningful kick earned Buffalo another Lamar Hunt Trophy, awarded to the champion of the American Football Conference. But for a second straight season, the Bills would not supplement the Rich Stadium display case with a Lombardi Trophy.

Washington pummeled the Bills in Super Bowl XXVI, 37-24. A costly unsportsmanlike-conduct penalty against Andre Reed (he slammed his helmet on the ground after an incompletion) and Thurman Thomas' infamous misplacing of his helmet were as much an embarrassment as the 24-0 deficit they faced in the third period.

The resilience of a franchise that overcame so much just to get to their first Super Bowl, continued to shine the next season. Three losses in the final five games of the 1992 regular season kept Buffalo from claiming another division title.

To return to a third-straight Super Bowl, they would have to do so as a wild-card team. Minutes into their opening-round home playoff game against Houston, there was little hope of that happening. Without Jim Kelly (sprained knee) and Cornelius Bennett (hamstring) heading up their respective units, the Bills fell behind 35-3. Thurman Thomas' reinjuring of his hip pointer early in the third quarter seemed to signal the end of Buffalo's season.

Inconceivably, however, the Bills came back. Replacing Kelly was backup Frank Reich. The former University of Maryland quarterback had already engineered the greatest comeback in the history of college football: in November 1984, his Terrapins trailed Miami 31-0 at halftime, then scored six touchdowns to win 42-40. Reich repeated the miracle eight years later.

"[Bills third-string quarterback Gale Gilbert] came up to me and told me what I needed to hear," said Reich. "He said, 'Hey, you did it in college, and there's no reason why you can't do it here.'"

The Bills scored five touchdowns in the span of twenty-one minutes to stun the Oilers with a 41-38 overtime victory. On the momentum of that historic win, Buffalo cruised through the remainder of the AFC playoffs, only to be pounded in Super Bowl XXVII by Dallas, 52-17.

Again, the Bills did not give up. And, as luck would have it, the first half of the 1993 regular season even afforded the Bills a special opportunity for redemption. In Week One, they crushed New England 38-14, spoiling Bill Parcells' Patriots debut. Nine weeks later, the Bills again bested Parcells and their AFC East rival.

In between those two victories over the head coach who narrowly defeated the Bills in Super Bowl XXV, Marv Levy's squad won five of six games. Three of those wins came against the Cowboys, Redskins, and Giants, the franchises to which Buffalo had lost Super Bowls in each of the three previous Januaries.

"We know nobody wants us to win," Jim Kelly said during that season. "We know nobody wants to see us go back to the Super Bowl again. Everybody is sick of us. And you know what? We love it."

The Bills went on to reclaim the AFC East crown later that year, earning a first-round bye and another playoff showdown with the Los Angeles Raiders.

"The last time was an embarrassment," said Raiders perennial Pro Bowl receiver Tim Brown. "I think a lot of the guys are looking forward to going up there and making up for it."

Despite losing to the Raiders at Rich Stadium earlier that season, the Bills were still favored by seven points. The wild-card Raiders had qualified for the playoffs only by edging out Denver 33-30 in overtime on the final Sunday of the regular season. A Raiders' victory amid huge obstacles—sub-zero temperatures and a raucous Buffalo crowd—was a tall order.

Fortunately for Los Angeles, under center that day was a gutsy, battle-hardened veteran who had once quarterbacked a touchdown underdog to a postseason victory over the favored Buffalo Bills: Jeff Hostetler.

Dan Reeves needed roughly a month to decide Phil Simms, not Hostetler, was the right choice for the job of starting Giants quarterback. Both men were free agents during the spring of 1993, and the Giants chose to sign Simms to a two-year $5.05 million deal in March. They did not re-sign Hostetler.

"It's an end to one stage of my life and the beginning of something else," he said. "I want a team that I think wants me, that respects the abilities I have, a team that wants to win. There are a lot of them out there."

One such team actually shared the exact same address as the Giants. The New York Jets showed a great deal of interest in signing Hostetler. Instead of jumping at that opportunity to remain in town and show the Giants the mistake they made, Hostetler inked a blockbuster deal with the Los Angeles Raiders: three years, $8 million. The day he was introduced as member of the Raiders, Hostetler heard words never uttered during his nine-year tenure in New York.

"This was the guy we wanted," said Steve Ortmayer, the Raiders' director of operations. "This was our first choice, the guy we went after."

Changing out a flat tire on the car that drove him from the airport to his workout for team officials showcased his versatility. But the Raiders courted Hostetler for his proven record as quarterback.

"He runs very well, takes few sacks and has a 70 percent winning percentage as a starter," owner Al Davis said.

The cross-country move liberated Hostetler. His multimillion-dollar salary proved they had faith in him, and he didn't have to worry about being promised playing time only to sit on the sidelines, waiting, begging for a chance to perform. In the Raiders' pass-oriented offense, Hostetler had considerable input and impact on the team's destiny, far more than he ever had in New York.

His first pass as a Raider, in Week One against Minnesota, went for a seventeen-yard touchdown to Tim Brown. Hostetler completed thirteen of his next fourteen attempts as the Raiders cruised to victory over the defending NFC East Champion Vikings.

"It is still a team game, I am only one part," he said. "They played back, so we could not go long. We just took what they gave us. I felt I was able to see the whole field today. Our offensive line did a great job of giving me time."

Hostetler's Raiders finished the 1993 season 10-6. Playing through a slew of injuries (swelling of both knees, sprained right ankle, bruised throwing shoulder and ribs), he racked up 3,242 yards passing. Seven days after a concussion knocked him out in a loss at Green Bay, Hostetler returned to start the regular season finale against Denver. The finest passing day of his career—twenty-five of forty-one, 310 yards, three touchdowns—sparked a seventeen-point second-half comeback. Los Angeles' 33-30 overtime victory clinched a home playoff game for the Raiders.

A week later, again versus the Broncos on a Wild Card Sunday, Hostetler threw three more touchdowns in the Raiders' 42-24 victory. Hostetler benefited that season from a tremendous corps of wide receivers—along with Tim Brown, the Raiders sported two of the league's fastest players, Raghib

"Rocket" Ismail and the aptly named former Olympic sprinter, James Jett. But the addition of Hostetler turned Los Angeles into a winner.

"People can talk all they want about the receivers, but to me, Jeff's the reason for the Raiders' success," noted Broncos offensive coordinator Jim Fassel, who witnessed Hostetler combine for 868 yards and eight touchdowns in three victories that season against Denver. "They finally have not only a guy who can throw but one who can move."

As the Giants quarterbacks coach and offensive coordinator in the two years after the Super Bowl XXV victory, Fassel knew his skills as well as anyone. He also knew that in order to be a success, in addition to a good running game, capable receivers, and a solid offensive line, Jeff Hostetler needed a change of scenery.

"I went to talk to him, and I could see it in his eyes," Fassel said after the Raiders' playoff victory. "I don't think he ever could have gotten that look in New York. His team, no questions asked. Even if Phil had gone instead of Jeff, there would still have been Phil's ghost. A bad game or two, people would've said they should've kept Phil. Who knows what that would've done? Chemistry is something you never can predict."

The wild-card victory advanced Los Angeles to the AFC divisional round and set up Hostetler's personal rematch with Buffalo. This time, however, instead of balmy west Florida weather, Hostetler would face the Bills on a much different stage.

As much as the Bills stout defense—still anchored by Bruce Smith, Darryl Talley, and Cornelius Bennett—and a thoroughly partisan crowd, Hostetler would have to contend with frigid temperatures and sixteen-mile-per-hour winds. Throwing the football was going to be extremely difficult.

"You've just got to go out there and play," receiver Don Beebe said. "Marv Levy says it all the time that championship teams have got to play in all the elements."

The forecast was so bad that, on game day, nearly one-quarter of the tickets went unused. Nevertheless, more than sixty thousand Bills fans roared when, early in the second period, the Bills scored to take a 6-3 lead. A pair of touchdowns by running back Napoleon McCallum gave Los Angeles a 17-6 edge, but Jim Kelly then marched Buffalo seventy-six yards in the final two minutes of the quarter. Thurman Thomas' eight-yard touchdown run cut the deficit and the Bills headed into halftime behind 17-13.

"It was very important," said Smith, who sacked Hostetler twice, although neither came in the end zone and produced a safety. "It was probably the most important drive in the game. There's a tremendous difference being down four points as opposed to 11 points. That motivated us to come out in the second half and achieve the things we did."

The first-half offensive malaise—the weather contributed to Buffalo totaling just 102 yards—did not carry over to the third quarter. Kelly tossed a touchdown to retake command of the game. Napoleon McCallum's fumble on the ensuing Raider drive produced three more points by way of a short field goal.

At that moment in the game, with three touchdowns and a field goal, the Bills expected to have twenty-four points on the scoreboard. But the minus-thirty-two-degree wind-chill factor and snow showers that covered western New York that day hindered more than just the passing game. The AstroTurf at Rich Stadium was extremely slick, making it nearly impossible for kickers to secure their plant foot. Each team's kicker missing forty-plus-yard field goals—which they did—should have been expected. What astounded football fans was the uncertainty that crept into the game's so-called easiest way to score: the point-after-touchdown.

Steve Christie—signed for the 1992 season to replace Scott Norwood—missed two of his three extra points that day. But Christie persevered and his twenty-nine-yarder late in the third period extended the Buffalo lead.

"You get in there and you're thinking, 'Well, I've had trouble today. I don't know where to line up. I don't know where my plant-foot is,'" Christie said. "I couldn't feel my kicking foot. So you just bear down, just keep swinging."

Now trailing 22-17, Hostetler broke the Raiders' huddle with under a minute to play in the third quarter. On second and ten from their own fourteen-yard line, Hostetler danced around the pocket, set his feet, and fired a pass over the middle. In between two Bills defenders, Tim Brown caught the ball and raced downfield for a crowd-silencing eighty-six-yard go-ahead touchdown. Given Hostetler's history of clutch completions in big games, the Bills should not have been surprised.

"I was hoping that would get the defense going," Brown said about the play, "and they would go three and out and we'd get the ball again and maybe get some more points."

But Brown's touchdown—the third-longest reception in postseason history—would be the last points Los Angeles accumulated that day. Raiders kicker Jeff Jaeger even missed the extra-point try in the face of the harsh winds. No kick in the postseason, it seems, is ever a gimme.

Behind by a single point in the final quarter, the Bills needed to respond. And in typical K-Gun fashion, they did. Within three minutes, Kelly put the Bills in scoring position. At the Raider twenty-two, he floated a perfect pass into the post, right into the grasp of Bill Brooks, capping a nine-play, seventy-one-yard drive.

"Jim put it right on the money," said Brooks, the free agent signed that season to replace James Lofton. "I wanted to make sure I looked it in; the play before, I dropped the ball. I'd never been in a game this big before. I drove my mom and dad and wife over and my dad said when we got out of the car, 'You've got to relax, you're too tense.'"

Los Angeles failed to pick up a first down on their next two drives, the second of which ended by way of Bruce Smith sacking Jeff Hostetler on third down. The Raiders were forced to punt with just under six minutes remaining in the game. Hostetler would not get another chance to score as Kelly and the K-Gun shortened the game, hoarding the remainder of the clock. The 29-23 victory sent Buffalo to a fifth AFC Championship Game in six years.

"We have a lot of experience in the playoffs, but most of all, we have a lot of character," running back Kenneth Davis said. "And character is what's carried us more than anything."

A week later, in the AFC Championship Game, the Bills faced Kansas City and another Super Bowl–winning quarterback acquired via free agency, Joe Montana. Once again, it was Thurman Thomas' incredible performance (thirty-three carries, 186 yards, three touchdowns) that put Buffalo on the verge of a world championship. The 30-13 win sent Buffalo to a record fourth-consecutive Super Bowl. At the Georgia Dome, the Bills led Dallas 13-6 through thirty minutes. But a scoreless effort from the Buffalo offense, two turnovers, and the legs of Cowboys running back Emmitt Smith, buried the Bills in the second half. Dallas repeated as world champions, 30-13.

The Bills quasi-dynasty came to an end that day. Buffalo missed the playoffs the following season and after nine postseason victories during the previous four years, scored just one more the rest of the decade.

Although the optimism that each Buffalo fan, player, and coach awoke with on those four consecutive last Sundays in January ultimately disintegrated into sadness and despair, the Bills run of the early 1990s produced something as historic as any one of the Lombardi Trophies handed out at the end of each season.

"I think if you look at the Bills during those four years, there were games that were won by the offense and there were games won by the defense," Darryl Talley said ten years after the Bills' final Super Bowl loss.

And there were a lot of times that we brought it all together and overwhelmed teams on both sides of the ball. The thing to remember about the Bills of the 1990s was the fact that leadership didn't come from just one player. It came from different guys each week. We took it game by game as far as leadership went.

We weren't always looking for one or two individuals to always make the big plays. It just seemed like somebody new always came up every week to come through for us. I think that's what made us so unique. Plus, the fact that we had so much depth on offense and defense.

We might suffer an injury or two, but always seemed to have a player on the sidelines that was willing to come in and do a great job. Depth is something you don't see that much of today, which again is another reason you won't see a team go to four straight Super Bowls again.

Epilogue: Super Bowl XLII

On January 20, 2008—exactly seventeen years after Matt Bahr's last-second field goal sailed through the Candlestick Park goalposts, ending the 49ers' bid for a three-peat—the New York Giants met the Green Bay Packers at Lambeau Field.

Although billed as a matchup between the Giants' unproven quarterback Eli Manning and aging, future Hall of Famer Brett Favre, defense decided the outcome of this NFC Championship Game.

New York's all-time career sack leader, Michael Strahan (his first sack of that 2007 season pushed him past Lawrence Taylor), and all-pro defensive end Osi Umenyiora completely shut down Green Bay's running game, yielding just twenty-eight yards. Still, after sixty minutes, the game remained tied, and sudden death was needed to determine the NFC's representative in Super Bowl XLII.

The Giants intercepted Favre—playing his final playoff game for the franchise he led to Super Bowl glory—on the second play of overtime. Three snaps later, head coach Tom Coughlin sent his kicking team out to attempt the game-winner. If his forty-seven-yard field goal was good, kicker Lawrence Tynes would complete an improbable upset victory over the seven-point-favorite home team.

Punter Jeff Feagles placed the ball from long-snapper Jay Alford—Zak DeOssie snapped for punts, not field goals—and Tynes nailed the kick through, sending New York back to the Super Bowl.

"The thing I'm most proud of is the way we hang together and the way we never say die," Coughlin said. "No matter what the odds are, we keep scrapping, we keep working and finding a way to win."

Eager Giants fans would have to wait fourteen days to see their team try and win its first world championship since January 1991. But the Giants coaching staff didn't complain about the extra week in between championship game and Super Bowl: it would give them more time to prepare for their opponent's incredibly explosive offense.

The New England Patriots won every game of the 2007 regular season, then won both of their home playoff games to claim the AFC's Super Bowl berth. As usual, head coach Bill Belichick's defense was fantastic that year, allowing just 17.1 points per game, fourth best in the league.

But it was the Pats offense that was historic. League Most Valuable Player Tom Brady, all-pro wide receiver Randy Moss, and a unit that set a new record for touchdowns, could seemingly score at will.

"It will be our job as an offense to try to hold the ball as long as we can," Eli Manning said. "You can't afford to have three-and-outs and get their offense back on the field. We have to move the ball, control the clock and when you get close to the end zone, you have to score touchdowns."

Although they represented different conferences, New England and New York were familiar with one another. The previous December, on a cold Saturday in the Meadowlands, the Patriots defeated the Giants 38-35. Giants Stadium was a familiar place for each team's head coach. Both Bill Belichick and Tom Coughlin had once been "whipping boys" there under Bill Parcells.

Five weeks later, the two Parcells protégés squared off again, this time with the Lombardi Trophy on the line.

"It makes me feel proud," said Parcells, who a month earlier ended his third retirement to become executive vice president of the Miami Dolphins. "But it's been a long time since I worked with them. They both have gone on and established themselves on their own merit."

The Patriots, a team chasing a perfect season, were naturally favored to win. As two-touchdown underdogs, a victory for Coughlin's Giants would qualify as one of the Super Bowl's greatest upsets.

"There is a way to win all of these games," Parcells said prior to the game. "I went into a Super Bowl against one of those (heavily favored) teams, and we won. It can happen."

Beneath the retractable roof at the University of Phoenix Stadium in Glendale, Arizona, the Patriots and Giants battled neck-and-neck before the largest Super Bowl television audience in history.

The game was so exciting that inside the White House, George W. Bush stayed up "later than [he] normally stays up to see the conclusion." The president had earned some R & R. That week he delivered a State of the Union Address centered around the two wars America was in the middle of fighting, one in Afghanistan, one in Iraq.

Late in the fourth quarter, the explosive Brady-to-Moss duo pushed New England into the lead 14-10. But via one of the most memorable drives in Super Bowl history, Manning and a receiving corps that showed a newfound knack for impossible plays retook the lead 17-14.

With under a minute to play, the Giants needed a stop.

"That offense is built to stay in rhythm," said defensive end Justin Tuck. "Some things we showed (Brady) up front and in the secondary threw him off rhythm. It's the culmination of pressure in his face and the secondary doing a good job of locking down receivers."

As they had all night, New York's defense came through. A sack and two incompletions by Brady brought the Giants to within one play of a stunning victory.

New York's sideline exploded when Brady's final attempt for Moss fell to the ground. Giants fullback Madison Hedgecock dumped the contents of a Gatorade cooler atop coach Coughlin's head and the celebration began.

"This is the greatest feeling in professional sports," Plaxico Burress said afterward. "For us to come out and win a world championship tonight—nobody gave us a shot."

When it comes to Super Bowls, history has a way of repeating itself.

Appendix 1

Super Bowl XXV Statistics

January 27, 1991, Tampa Stadium, Tampa, Florida

SCORE BY QUARTER

	1st	2nd	3rd	4th	Totals
Bills	3	9	0	7	19
Giants	3	7	7	3	20

TEAM SCORING

New York: 46-yard field goal by Matt Bahr
11 plays, 58 yards, time of possession: 6:15
New York 3, Buffalo 0; 7:14 remaining in 1st quarter

Buffalo: 23-yard field goal by Scott Norwood
6 plays, 66 yards, time of possession: 1:23
New York 3, Buffalo 3; 5:51 remaining in 1st quarter

Buffalo: 1-yard touchdown run by Don Smith (Norwood kick)
12 plays, 80 yards, time of possession: 4:27
Buffalo 10, New York 3, 12:30 remaining in 2nd quarter

Buffalo: safety by Bruce Smith, 7-yard sack of Jeff Hostetler
Buffalo 12, New York 3, 8:27 remaining in 2nd quarter

New York: 14-yard touchdown pass, Stephen Baker from Hostetler (Bahr kick)
10 plays, 87 yards, time of possession: 3:24
Buffalo 12, New York 10, 0:25 remaining in 2nd quarter

New York: 1-yard touchdown run by Ottis Anderson (Bahr kick)
14 plays, 75 yards, time of possession: 9:29
New York 17, Buffalo 12, 5:31 remaining in 3rd quarter

Buffalo: 31-yard touchdown run by Thurman Thomas (Norwood kick)
4 plays, 63 yards, time of possession: 1:27
Buffalo 19, New York 17, 14:52 remaining in 4th quarter

New York: 21-yard field goal by Bahr
7 plays, 74 yards, time of possession: 7:32
New York 20, Buffalo 19, 7:20 remaining in 4th quarter

Final Score: New York 20, Buffalo 19

TEAM STATISTICS

	BILLS	GIANTS
FIRST DOWNS	18	24
Rushing	8	10
Passing	9	13
Penalty	1	1
TOTAL NET YARDS	371	386
Total Offensive Plays	56	73
Average Gain	6.6	5.3
NET RUSHING YARDS	166	172
Attempts	25	39
Average Rush	6.6	4.4
NET PASSING YARDS	205	214
Completed Attempts	18-30	20-32
Average per Attempt	6.83	6.69
Times Sacked-Yards Lost	1-7	2-8
Interceptions	0	0
PUNTS-Yards	6-213	4-175

TOTAL RETURN YARDS	124	85
Punt Returns-Yards	1-33	2-37
Kickoff Returns-Yards	5-81	3-48
Interceptions-Yards	0-0	0-0
PENALTIES-Yards	6-35	5-31
FUMBLES-Lost	0-0	0-0
TIME OF POSSESSION	19:27	40:33

INDIVIDUAL STATISTICS

COMPLETIONS-ATTEMPTS-YARDS

Buffalo Bills: Jim Kelly: 18-30-212

New York Giants: Jeff Hostetler: 20-32-222

RUSHES-YARDS

Buffalo Bills: Thurman Thomas: 15-135; Jim Kelly: 6-23; Kenneth Davis: 2-4: Jamie Mueller: 1-3; Don Smith: 1-1

New York Giants: Ottis Anderson: 21-102; Dave Meggett: 9-48; Maurice Carthon: 3-12; Jeff Hostetler: 6-10

RECEPTIONS-YARDS

Buffalo Bills: Andre Reed: 8-62; Thurman Thomas: 5-55; Kenneth Davis: 2-23; Keith McKeller: 2-11; James Lofton: 1-61

New York Giants: Mark Ingram: 5-74; Mark Bavaro: 5-50; Howard Cross: 4-39: Stephen Baker: 2-31; Dave Meggett: 2-18; Ottis Anderson: 1-7; Maurice Carthon: 1-3

TACKLES-ASSISTS-SACKS

Buffalo Bills: Leonard Smith: 8-0-0; Shane Conlan: 8-0-0; Jeff Wright: 6-1-1; Nate Odomes: 5-0-0; Leon Seals: 5-0-0; Mark Kelso: 4-2-0; Cornelius Bennett: 4-1-0; Ray Bentley: 3-1-0; Bruce Smith: 3-0-1; Kirby Jackson: 2-1-0; Carlton Bailey: 2-1-0; Darryl Talley: 2-1-0; Mike Lodish: 2-0-0; Gary Baldinger: 2-0-0; Steve Tasker: 2-0-0; James Williams; 1-0-0; Dwight Drane: 1-0-0; Rick Tuten: 1-0-0; Carwell Gardner: 1-0-0; Jamie Mueller: 1-0-0; Don Smith: 1-0-0

New York Giants: Mark Collins: 6-0-0; Gary Reasons: 6-0-0; Erik Howard: 6-1-0; Reyna Thompson: 4-0-0; Greg Jackson: 4-0-0; Carl Banks: 3-1-0; Pepper Johnson: 3-0-0; Everson Walls: 2-1-0; Myron Guyton: 2-0-0; Lawrence Taylor: 2-0-0; Leonard Marshall: 2-0-1; Matt Bahr: 2-0-0; Lee Rouson: 2-0-0; John Washington: 1-0-0; Lewis Tillman: 1-0-0; Roger Brown: 1-0-0; Perry Williams: 0-1-0

KICKOFF RETURNS-YARDS
Buffalo Bills: Don Smith: 4-66; Al Edwards: 1-15
New York Giants: Dave Meggett: 2-26; Dave Duerson: 1-22
PUNT RETURNS-YARDS
Buffalo Bills: Al Edwards: 1-33
New York Giants: Dave Meggett: 2-37
PUNTS-YARDS
Buffalo Bills: Rick Tuten: 6-213
New York Giants: Sean Landeta: 4-175

ADDITIONAL PLAYERS
Buffalo Bills: Gale Gilbert, Frank Reich, John Hagy, Clifford Hicks, David
Pool, Jim Ritcher, Mitch Frerotte, Adam Lingner, John Davis, Kent Hull,
Will Wolford, Glenn Parker, Howard Ballard, Butch Rolle, Mark Pike, Hal
Garner, Pete Metzelaars
New York Giants: Matt Cavanaugh, David Whitmore, Bobby Abrams, Law-
rence McGrew, Brian Williams, Eric Moore, Bob Kratch, Tom Rehder,
Bart Oates, William Roberts, Doug Riesenberg, John (Jumbo) Elliott,
Eric Dorsey, Bob Mrosko, Stacy Robinson, Troy Kyles, Mike Fox, Johnie
Cooks, Steve DeOssie

OFFICIALS
Jerry Seeman, Referee
Art Demmas, Umpire
Sid Semon, Head Linesman
Dick McKennie, Line Judge
Banks Williams, Back Judge
Larry Nemmers, Side Judge
Jack Vaughan, Field Judge
Mark Burns, Replay

Attendance: 73,813
Time: 3:19

(Compiled from NFL.com; USAToday.com; and *The Capitol,* January 28,
1991)

Appendix 2
Original Interviews Conducted

Adm. Steve Abbott
Ernie Accorsi
Carlton Bailey
Stephen Baker
Mark Bavaro
Bill Belichick
Norm Bulaisch
Maurice Carton
Rear Adm. Ron Christenson
Jonnie Cooks
Bill Curry
Bob Daugherty
Bruce DeHaven
Tom Depolis
Clint Didier
Ray Didinger
Dan Dierdorf
Boyd Dowler
Ron Erhardt
James Farrior
Vince Ferragamo

Msg. Rick Fuller
Mark Gaughan
Don Gleisner
Hank Gola
Jeff Hostetler
Whitney Houston (via agent)
Erik Howard
Kent Hull
David Isby
Jim Kelly
Mark Kelso
Arthur Kent
John Kidd
Kim Kolbe
Lynn Larson
Marv Levy
Maestro Jahja Ling
Adam Lingner
Mike Lodish
James Lofton
Bob Long

Jack Maitland
Ted Marchibroda
Dr. Ricardo Martinez
Leigh Montville
Eric Moore
Earl Morrall
Bob Mrosko
Don Nehlen
Milt Northrop
Bart Oates
Jim O'Brien
Ernie Palladino
Bill Parcells
Bill Polian
Gary Reasons

Doug Riesenberg
Mark Rush
Howard Schnellenberger
Bruce Smith
Jim Steeg
Cheryl Stupar
Mike Sweatman
Darryl Talley
Steve Tasker
Lawrence Taylor
Lt. Tom Van Leunen
Everson Walls
Warren Welch
Will Wolford

Notes

PROLOGUE: NOVEMBER 9, 1986

6 "What it made"—Jeff Hostetler, author interview, January 26, 2010.

6 "I wanted desperately"—Jeff Hostetler with Ed Fitzgerald, *One Giant Leap* (New York: Putnam, 1991), 126.

6 "I knew they"—Frank Litsky, "Giants Put a Clamp on Eagles," *New York Times*, November 10, 1986.

6 "It gets boring"—Frank Litsky, "Hostetler Will Take Any Job He Can Get," *New York Times*, November 16, 1986.

7 "And I hope everyone"—Frank Litsky, "Hostetler Will Take Any Job He Can Get," *New York Times*, November 16, 1986.

7 "The Giants told me"—Ottis Anderson, "Super Bowl XXV: Ottis Anderson," in *Super Bowl: The Game of Their Lives*, ed. Danny Peary (New York: Macmillan, 1997), 347.

7 "This is like"—Frank Litsky, "Anderson Happy to Be a Giant," *New York Times*, October 10, 1986.

7 "Embarrassed. That's it"—Frank Litsky, "Giants' Anderson Learning a Blocking Role," *New York Times*, October 26, 1986.

8 "somewhat saddened"—Anderson, "Super Bowl XXV: Ottis Anderson," 347.

8 "To be honest"—Dave Anderson, "Anderson's 'Sweetest' Season," *New York Times*, December 25, 1989.

8 "There was a pretty"—Jeff Hostetler, author interview, January 26, 2010.

9   "I went through"—Malcolm Moran, "The Wait Is Over for Bills and Fans," *New York Times*, January 22, 1991.

9   "We felt that"—Michael Janofsky, "Bullough Dismissed by Bills," *New York Times*, November 4, 1986.

9   "I'm very excited"—Janofsky, "Bullough Dismissed by Bills." *New York Times*, November 4, 1986.

10   "I think defensively"—*Syracuse Post-Standard*, "New Turn in Direction," November 4, 1986.

10   "It's a young team"—Michael Janofsky, "Bullough Dismissed by Bills," *New York Times*, November 4, 1986.

10   "It's easy to lose"—Paul Zimmerman, "A New Namath, but with Knees," *Sports Illustrated*, September 15, 1986.

10   "I hate losing"—Bill Utterback, "Learning to Lose," *Pittsburgh Press*, November 9, 1986.

10   "Marv had an immediate"—Jim Kelly with Vic Carucci, *Armed & Dangerous* (New York: Doubleday, 1992), 96–97.

11   "I've seen hurricanes"—Scott Pitoniak, "A Winning Debut, 16-12," *Democrat & Chronicle*, November 10, 1986.

11   "They were mixing"—Steve Hubbard, "Intensity is Lacking in Defeat by Bills," *Pittsburgh Press*, November 10, 1986.

12   "No wonder"—Steve Tasker with Scott Pitoniak, *Steve Tasker's Tales from the Buffalo Bills* (Champaign, Ill.: Sports Publishing, 2006), xv.

12   "The ball was"—Ed Bouchette, "Steelers Swept to Defeat on Gusts of Bill Wind," *Pittsburgh Post-Gazette*, November 10, 1986.

12   "I kept saying"—Scott Pitoniak, "Bills Notebook," *Democrat & Chronicle*, November 10, 1986.

13   "Mark throws it"—Steve Tasker, author interview, June 17, 2010.

13   "We were relaxed"—Scott Pitoniak, "Bills Notebook," *Democrat & Chronicle*, November 10, 1986.

13   "Thank God"—Scott Pitoniak, "Bills Notebook," *Democrat & Chronicle*, November 10, 1986.

CHAPTER 1: EVERY PENNSYLVANIA BOY WANTS TO PLAY FOR JOEPA

15   "Mom and dad"—Ralph Bernstein, "Is Ron or Doug Best Linebacker," *Bradford Era*, August 18, 1977.

16 "I think he'll"—Bob Fulton, "Vikes Face Huge Yough," *Indiana Evening Gazette*, August 31, 1978.

16 "The fact that"—Hostetler, *One Giant Leap*, 28.

17 "It came down"—Hostetler, *One Giant Leap*, 43.

17 "This is great"—Hostetler, *One Giant Leap*, 44.

18 "I was in the locker room"—Bill Utterback, "Cultivating His Dreams Hostetler Learned Virtues of Work, Patience on Farm," *Pittsburgh Press*, January 20, 1991.

18 "We all learned to"—Kelly, *Armed & Dangerous*, 4.

18 "He had something"—Rick Telander, "Has Anybody Here Seen Kelly," *Sports Illustrated*, February 27, 1984.

18 "I always told"—NFL Films Presents, Show #10, 1996.

19 "Looking back now"—Rick Telander, "Has Anybody Here Seen Kelly," *Sports Illustrated*, February 27, 1984.

19 "[East Brady] was a small"—Jim Kelly, author interview, January 22, 2010.

19 "I wanted to"—Jim Kelly, author interview, January 22, 2010.

19 "Well, look at it"—Wilt Browning, "2007 ACC Football Legend: Miami's Jim Kelly," ACC.com, (November 13, 2007).

20 "Quarterback was the"—Kelly, *Armed & Dangerous*, 22.

20 "Lots of big linemen"—*Sports Illustrated*, "Scorecard," ed. John Papanek, April 2, 1979.

20 "Jeff only wanted"—Hostetler, *One Giant Leap*, 45.

21 "Jeff Hostetler isn't"—Terry Nau, "Paterno Eyes Future as Army Faces Lions," *Daily Intelligencer*, October 12, 1979.

21 "At this stage"—*Gettysburg Times*, "Hostetler Gets Nod," September 6, 1980.

21 "There's a lot"—*Altoona Mirror*, "Quotes about Freshman Often Scarce," October 22, 1980.

22 "I played extremely well"—Jeff Hostetler, author interview, January 26, 2010.

22 "For the bowl"—Jeff Hostetler, author interview, January 26, 2010.

22 "Joe had to"—Jack McCallum, "The Place Where He Belongs," *Sports Illustrated*, September 27, 1982.

22 "It was probably"—Jeff Hostetler, author interview, January 26, 2010.

23 "would constantly"—Kelly, *Armed & Dangerous*, 25.

23 "When I coached"—Howard Schnellenberger, author interview, December 9, 2009.

24 "We felt we had"—Joe Juliano, "Hurricanes Stop Penn State, 26-10," *Tyrone Daily Herald*, November 5, 1979.

24 "Just a few"—Jim Kelly, author interview, January 22, 2010.

25 "Schnellenberger was"—Mark Rush, author interview, January 8, 2010.

25 "We're not a real"—John Clayton, "Hurricanes Bury Penn State Hopes, 26-10," *Pittsburgh Press*, November 4, 1979.

25 "This day will"—Joe Juliano, "Hurricanes Stop Penn State, 26-10," *Tyrone Daily Herald*, November 5, 1979.

26 "Afterward, Paterno"—Kelly, *Armed & Dangerous*, 31.

26 "contagious"—Kelly, *Armed & Dangerous*, 35.

26 "something popped"—Arthur Daley, "The Injury Jinx," *New York Times*, November 13, 1968.

27 "It was awesome"—Jim Kelly, author interview, January 22, 2010.

27 "In order for us"—Gordon White Jr., "Miami Enhances Reputation," *New York Times*, November 2, 1981.

28 "People are going"—Gordon White Jr., "Miami Enhances Reputation," *New York Times*, November 2, 1981.

28 "Everywhere around"—*Sports Illustrated*, "College Football: The Top 20," September 1, 1982.

28 "Unfortunately, we"—Mark Rush, author interview, January 8, 2010.

29 "I would drag"—Mark Rush, author interview, January 8, 2010.

30 "I always wanted"—*Syracuse Herald-Journal*, "Draftees Bargaining," May 3, 1983.

30 "Buffalo would"—Kelly, *Armed & Dangerous*, 57.

31 "Jim and I always"—Mark Rush, author interview, January 8, 2010.

31 "His signing is"—Jim Achenbach, "Houston 'Gambles' on Kelly," *Sarasota Herald Tribune*, June 13, 1983.

31 "We had Jim Kelly"—*Palm Beach Post*, "Kelly and Rush Sign with USFL Gamblers," June 10, 1983.

31 "There are risks"—Gary Taylor, "Hurricane Kelly Inks Big Contract with USFL Gamblers," *Tyrone Daily Herald*, June 11, 1983.

32   "Our family had"—*Post-Gazette,* "Hostetler Decides to Leave Penn State; Cites Backup Role," January 7, 1981.

32   "My older brother"—Jeff Hostetler, author interview, January 26, 2010.

32   "It was a cold"—Jeff Hostetler, author interview, January 26, 2010.

32   "Jeff came in"—Darryl Talley, author interview, December 18, 2009.

33   "He was our"—Don Nehlen, author interview, April 22, 2010.

34   "The Oklahoma"—Don Nehlen, author interview, April 22, 2010.

34   "Jeff was a great"—Darryl Talley, author interview, December 18, 2009.

34   "Ole Hoss, Ole Hoss"—Sarajane Freligh, "When One Dream Died, Another Began for Hostetler," *Philadelphia Inquirer,* October 20, 1983.

34   "He is more handsome"—Sarajane Freligh, "When One Dream Died, Another Began for Hostetler," *Philadelphia Inquirer,* October 20, 1983.

35   "I still had friends"—Hostetler, *One Giant Leap,* 92.

36   "We had him"—Bob Duffy, "Penn St. Rips W. Va., 41-23," *Boston Globe,* October 23, 1983.

36   "Later my family"—Hostetler, *One Giant Leap,* 93.

36   "Nothing seemed to"—*Annapolis' The Capitol,* "'Believing' Pays Off," December 23, 1983.

37   "a great educational"—William Wallace, "Unsigned Giants in Camp," *New York Times,* May 23, 1984.

37   "I didn't know"—Jeff Hostetler, author interview, January 26, 2010.

37   "I thought that"—Jeff Hostetler, author interview, January 26, 2010.

37   "After all our changes"—Craig Wolff, "'Cutthroat Time' for Giants," *New York Times,* July 16, 1984.

38   "He's not ready"—William C. Rhoden, "Gray Quits Camp in Contract Dispute," *New York Times,* July 31, 1984.

38   "It was Penn State"—Hostetler, *One Giant Leap,* 112.

38   "Now he's doing real"—Frank Litsky, "Hostetler Will Take Any Job He Can Get," *New York Times,* November 16, 1986.

39   "I knew it was"—Hostetler, *One Giant Leap,* 136.

39   "If Hostetler plays"—Frank Litsky, "Simms's Status Still Not Clear," *New York Times,* November 26. 1988.

39 "The reason I"—Frank Litsky, "Giants Defeat Saints at Wire," *New York Times*, November 28, 1988.

40 "I'm hot"—Frank Litsky, "Giants Defeat Saints at Wire," *New York Times*, November 28, 1988.

40 "I'm through here"—George Willis, "QB Rutledge Gets the Call and Responds," *Newsday*, November 28, 1988.

40 "George asked me"—Bruce Lowitt, "Managing to Be Humble," *St. Petersburg Times*, January 25, 1991.

40 "The rule of"—Bruce Lowitt, "Managing to Be Humble," *St. Petersburg Times*, January 25, 1991.

40 "I went in and"—Jeff Hostetler, author interview, January 26, 2010.

40 "I thought he was"—Bill Parcells, author interview, July 16, 2010.

40 "the lowest point"—Hostetler, *One Giant Leap*, 139.

41 "gut feeling"—Hostetler, *One Giant Leap*, 138.

41 "I thought Jeff"—George Willis, "Hostetler Guides Giants," *Newsday*, November 6, 1989.

41 "I think our"—Frank Litsky, "Hostetler Accepts His Role As the No. 2 Quarterback," *New York Times*, November 8, 1989.

41 "I wanted him"—George Willis, "What's Not to Like," *Newsday*, October 1, 1990.

41 "I think [Parcells]"—NFL Films, America's Game, 1990 Giants.

42 "I thought it"—George Willis, "6-0, With a Little Luck Giants Rally in Final 3:21 to Beat Upstart Cards," *Newsday*, October 22, 1990.

42 "I didn't have"—Jeff Hostetler, author interview, January 26, 2010.

43 "Jeff is the"—Jeff Hostetler, author interview, January 26, 2010.

43 "Seven, eight weeks"—NFL Films, America's Game, 1990 Giants.

CHAPTER 2: QUARTERBACK LACK

46 "Each week"—Frank Litsky, "Eagles Keep Giants from Turning to the 49ers," *New York Times*, November 20, 1990.

47 "There's a lot"—Gerald Eskenazi, "Giants Need Remedy for Streaking Vikings," *New York Times*, December 6, 1990.

47 "[Parcells said to me]"—Gerald Eskenazi, "Parcells Is Ill but He's on Giants' Sideline," *New York Times*, December 10, 1990.

48   "He didn't make"—Gerald Eskenazi, "Parcells Is Ill but He's on Giants' Sideline," *New York Times*, December 10, 1990.

48   "We didn't tackle"—Frank Litsky, "Giants Awaken and Clinch Division," *New York Times*, December 10, 1990.

48   "We weren't"—Frank Litsky, "Giants Awaken and Clinch Division," *New York Times*, December 10, 1990.

48   "We're not physical"—Dave Anderson, "Cancel L. T.'s Rocking Chair," *New York Times*, December 10, 1990.

49   "He's a one-man"—*Syracuse Herald-Journal*, "'One-Man Wrecking Crew' Salvages Giants Win over Vikes," December 10, 1990.

49   "We'd gotten"—Dave Anderson, "Cancel L. T.'s Rocking Chair," *New York Times*, December 10, 1990.

49   "I just remember"—Kim Kolbe, author interview, October 6, 2010.

49   "We've taken"—George Willis, "A Giant Sigh of Relief," *Newsday*, December 10, 1990.

50   "I don't think"—George Willis, "Giants Preview: Conference Call?" *Newsday*, December 15, 1990.

51   "For a new league"—Rick Telander, "Life with Lord Jim," *Sports Illustrated*, July 21, 1986.

51   "they need more"—Gerald Eskenazi, "Bills Sign Kelly to Record Pact," *New York Times*, August 19, 1986.

51   "messiah"—Howard Schnellenberger, author interview, December 9, 2009.

51   "I can remember"—Kent Hull, author interview, December 11, 2009.

52   "It's all about the"—John Oeshser, "Indianapolis Colts President Bill Polian: Trading Out of First Round of 2010 NFL Draft a Possibility," *Indianapolis Colts Examiner*, April 22, 2010.

53   "He ended his career"—*Kerrville Times*, "OSU Wins Snowy Sun Bowl," December 27, 1987.

53   "This is the best"—Bill Polian, author interview, May 12, 2010.

54   "Thurman is the"—Ted Marchibroda, author interview, December 5, 2009.

54   "What would they"—Lindsay Kramer, "Wealth of Optimism, if Not Talent," *The Post-Standard*, September 3, 1988.

54   "Hopefully . . ."—Kevin Harmon, "Kelly Eager to Start Afresh," *Syracuse Post Standard*, September 8, 1990.

55 "No one had ever"—James Lofton, author interview, June 14, 2010.

56 "If you think"—Vic Carucci, "Kelly Lobbies For More 'Gun' Use," *The Buffalo News*, September 19, 1989.

56 "They chose not"—Bib Finnan, "Narrow Escape," *Elyria Chronicle Telegram*, January 7, 1990.

57 "There was an important"—Marv Levy, *Where Else Would You Rather Be?* (Champaign, Ill.: Sports Publishing, 2004), 330.

57 "We used it sparingly"—Ted Marchibroda, author interview, December 5, 2009.

58 "That's where"—Mark Kelso, author interview, May 26, 2010.

58 "Everybody liked it"—Ted Marchibroda, author interview, December 5, 2009.

58 "It was a miserable"—Frank Litsky, "A Tough Day for Giants and Quarterbacks," *New York Times*, December 16, 1990.

58 "I don't care"—NFL Films: New York Giants 1990 Video Year Book.

59 "On both drives"—Kelly, *Armed & Dangerous*, 180.

59 "We're not going"—Frank Litsky, "Bills' No-Huddle Offense Is No Big Deal, Giants Say," *New York Times*, December 14, 1990.

59 "I guess a lot"—Frank Litsky, "Bills' No-Huddle Offense Is No Big Deal, Giants Say," *New York Times*, December 14, 1990.

60 "I just turned"—Vic Carucci, *The Buffalo Bills and the Almost-Dream Season* (New York: Simon & Schuster,1991), 113.

60 "Jim's like the"—Carucci, *The Buffalo Bills and the Almost-Dream Season*, 109.

61 "That's when"—Dave Anderson, "Super Bowl Detour for X-Rays," *New York Times*, December 16, 1990.

61 "I was turning"—*Syracuse Herald-Journal*, "Simms May Be Lost for Rest of Year," December 17, 1990.

62 "It was a tough"—Gerald Eskanazi, "Day for Backups to Call Shots," *New York Times*, December 16, 1990.

62 "my hand was"—Frank Litsky, "A Tough Day for Giants and Quarterbacks," *New York Times*, December 16, 1990.

62 "We were moving"—Frank Litsky, "A Tough Day for Giants and Quarterbacks," *New York Times*, December 16, 1990.

62 "We were running"—Bob Glauber, "Hostetler Vows to Be Ready," *Newsday*, December 16, 1990.

62 "If you told"—Frank Litsky, "Another Loss for Giants: Simms Is Out Indefinitely," *New York Times*, December 17, 1990.

63 "Not making those"—Frank Litsky, "A Tough Day for Giants and Quarterbacks," *New York Times*, December 16, 1990.

63 "We've been pathetic"—Paul Zimmerman, "Rough Stuff," *Sports Illustrated*, December 24, 1990.

63 "After Jim was"—Carucci, *The Buffalo Bills and the Almost-Dream Season*, 118.

63 "I don't think"—Joe Gergen, "It's Simply De-Bill-itating," *Newsday*, December 16, 1990.

64 "looks significant"—Bob Glauber, "Hostetler Vows to Be Ready," *Newsday*, December 16, 1990.

64 "A lot of people"—NFL Films, America's Game, 1990 Giants.

64 "Anytime you lose"—Frank Litsky, "Another Loss for Giants: Simms Is Out Indefinitely," *New York Times*, December 17, 1990.

CHAPTER 3: SCUDS, PATRIOT MISSILES, AND THE K-GUN

66 "We haven't been"—Charles Anzalone, "Why We Love the Bills," *Buffalo News*, January 13, 1991.

66 "practice in three"—*Aiken Standard*, "Bills' Kelly Out Until at Least Playoffs," December 19, 1990.

66 "a near perfect game"—*Chicago Daily Herald*, "Bills Win AFC East, Clinch Home Field for Playoffs," December 24, 1990.

66 "[He] ran as"—Carucci, *The Buffalo Bills and the Almost-Dream Season*, 130.

67 "If we get complacent"—Milt Northrop, "Bills Turn Focus to Dolphins—Again," *The Buffalo News*, January 7, 1991.

67 "We simply came"—*Lawrence Journal World*, "Buffalo's Kelly Wins Snowy Duel, 44-34," January 13, 1991.

68 "Nobody was going"—Dan Herbeck, "Win Puts Bills One Game Away From Super Bowl," *The Buffalo News*, January 13, 1991.

68 "I've been watching"—Dan Herbeck, "Win Puts Bills One Game Away from Super Bowl," *The Buffalo News*, January 13, 1991.

68 "We have now"—*New York Times*, "Bush's Remarks after Congress Authorized War," January 13, 1991.

68 "This will not"—*New York Times*, "Questions and Answers," August 6, 1990.

69 "We don't underestimate"—Philip Shenon, "Defiant Iraqi President Declares He Is Ready for War against U.S.," *New York Times*, November 30, 1990.

69   "the mother of all"—*Syracuse Herald-Journal,* "U.S. 2nd Wave Attacks: Saddam Spits Defiance," January 17, 1991.

69   "of justice against"—*Hutchinson News,* "Bush: Desert Storm Attack 'Will Not Fail.'" January 17, 1991.

69   "We're using force"—Michael R. Gordon, "American Defenses Block Attack on Saudi Arabia," *New York Times,* January 18, 1991.

70   "I was a lot"—Ken Rosenthal, "Saddam Can't Scud-le Dad's Plans This Time," *Baltimore Evening Sun,* January 25, 1992.

70   "I knew that"—Carlton Bailey, author interview, January 15, 2010.

70   "He was always"—Hal Block, "Tough Times Won't Last," *Aiken Standard,* January 27, 1991.

70   "It's kind of"—Bill Ordine, "Bills' Bailey Battles to Keep Focus on Football," *Baltimore Sun,* January 17, 1991.

70   "He hasn't missed"—Bill Ordine, "Bills' Bailey Battles to Keep Focus on Football," *Baltimore Sun,* January 17, 1991.

71   "In one of"—Vic Carucci, "Bailey Thinking about Battlefields," *The Buffalo News,* January 16, 1991.

72   "was more suitable"—Marcus Hayes, "Bills Snow Dolphins, 44-34," *Syracuse Herald-American,* January 13, 1991.

72   "It was horrible"—Marcus Hayes, "Bills Snow Dolphins, 44-34," *Syracuse Herald-American,* January 13, 1991.

72   "He's doubtful"—*Doylestown Intelligencer,* "Bo Knows Injuries: Raiders' Jackson to be Sidelined Again," January 18, 1991.

73   "We're going to have"—Philip Shenon, "Long Wait Begins for Ground Forces," *New York Times,* January 20, 1991.

73   "There is a time"—Malcolm Moran, "Bills' Fans Attend Services as Rally Is Cancelled," *New York Times,* January 19, 1991.

73   "Once the game"—*Frederick News Post,* "War on the Minds of Most Athletes," January 19, 1991.

73   "I can't even"—*Buffalo News,* "Prayers to Replace Pep Rally," January 18, 1991.

74   "Our attitude is"—Gerald Eskenazi, "N.F.L. Decision Comes Down to Game Day," *New York Times,* January 20, 1991.

74   "could not win"—*Los Angeles Times,* "Charger Players Rap Kemp Trade," September 28, 1962.

74 "highest levels"—Ira Berkow, "A Man with a Lot on His Mind," *New York Times*, January 18, 1991.

74 "We can't be"—Ira Berkow, "A Man with a Lot on His Mind," *New York Times*, January 18, 1991.

75 "I really think"—Jerry Sullivan, "Bills' Arsenal of Weaponry Is Sparked by Thomas," *Buffalo News*, January 21, 1991.

75 "First I thought"—William N. Wallace, "Bills in a Hurry to Beat Raiders," *New York Times*, January 20, 1991.

75 "I was going"—Carucci, *The Buffalo Bills and the Almost-Dream Season*, 184.

75 "This is going"—NBC Sports, January 20, 1991.

76 "I don't think"—Darryl Talley, author interview, December 18, 2009.

76 "I was on everybody"—Darryl Talley, author interview, December 18, 2009.

76 "We understand"—NBC Sports, January 20, 1991.

78 "The Buffalo Bills"—NBC Sports, January 20, 1991.

79 "We had the kind"—*Frederick New Post*, "No-huddle Rips Raiders 51-3," January 21, 1991.

79 "With an insurmountable"—NBC Sports, January 20, 1991.

79 "They told me"—Carucci, *The Buffalo Bills and the Almost-Dream Season*, 184.

CHAPTER 4: A YOUNG MAN'S GAME

81 "When you've"—Anderson, "Super Bowl XXV: Ottis Anderson," 350.

82 "I hope he runs"—Steve Cady, "People In Sports," *New York Times*, December 29, 1976.

82 "He shows up"—Dan Dierdorf, author interview, July 30, 2010.

82 "booing, hissing"—*Ocala Star Banner*, "Anderson Won't Play for Just Anybody," May 2, 1979.

83 "He's a great"—Michael Katz, "Giants Fall; Jets Win," *New York Times*, December 10, 1979.

83 "I'd like to"—*Paris News*, "Anderson top NFL rookie," December 23, 1979.

84 "Every year"—Frank Litsky, "Giants' Anderson Is Defying Critics," *New York Times*, August 30, 1989.

84 "This was my"—Dave Anderson, "Anderson's 'Sweetest' Season," *New York Times*, December 25, 1989.

84   "I don't think"—Frank Litsky, "No Teams Showing Interest in Anderson," *New York Times*, March 7, 1990.

85   "The passing"—"O. J. Hits 10,000, Looks to Future," *Newsday*, Bob Glauber, December 10, 1990.

85   "Continued trust"—Bob Glauber, "Analysis: Tough Task for Hostetler," *Newsday*, December 18, 1990.

86   "The more time"—*Winchester Star*, "Waiting Game Finally Over for Hostetler," December 26, 1990.

86   "Two weeks"—Greg Logan, "Inside the NFL: Bills Win Backup Derby," *Newsday*, December 26, 1990.

87   "That was a real"—*Daily Intelligencer*, "Career day for Hostetler," January 14, 1991.

87   "All day"—*Daily Intelligencer*, "Career day for Hostetler," January 14, 1991.

87   "Hopefully, it would"—William N. Wallace, "Giants Defense Makes Just the Right Move," *New York Times*, January 14, 1991.

87   "They forced us"—William N. Wallace, "Giants Defense Makes Just the Right Move," *New York Times*, January 14, 1991.

88   "We're very predictable"—NFL Films: New York Giants 1990 Video Year Book.

88   "My leg felt numb"—Bob Glauber, "That's All for Hampton," *Newsday*, January 14, 1991.

88   "Ottis thought"—*Post-Standard*, "Hostetler, Giants' 'D' Dominate," January 14, 1991.

89   "I ain't throwing"—NFL Films: New York Giants 1990 Video Year Book.

90   "People talk about"—Jim Van Vliet, "Bradshaw, Madden Go for the 49ers," *Sacramento Bee*, January 17, 1991.

91   "There was just"—Bill Parcells, author interview, July 15, 2010.

91   "I was supposed"—Dave Anderson, "Chess Game in Shoulder Pads," *New York Times*, December 4, 1990.

92   "Each time I"—*Kokomo Tribune*, "Walls, Giants' 'game' is now," January 16, 1991.

92   "I went for the"—Mike Celizic, "Win Lifts a Weight from Walls," *Bergen County Record*, January 21, 1991.

92   "You can't blame"—*Sarasota Herald-Journal*, "Clark TD Sets Off Celebration," January 12, 1982.

93   "Everson Walls is"—CBS television broadcast, January 20, 1991.

93 "I thought"—Mike Celizic, "Win Lifts a Weight from Walls," *Bergen County Record,* January 21, 1991.

93 "It wasn't the first"—Everson Walls, author interview, June 17, 2010.

93 "Good luck"—Matt Bahr, author interview, July 29, 2010.

93 "I can't say enough"—*Chicago Tribune,* "Bahr Gives Boot to 49ers' Win Streak," November 16, 1981.

94 "I held for a lot"—Jeff Hostetler, author interview, January 26, 2010.

95 "That's the way"—Michael Martinez, "'Cheap Shot' Accusations Anger 49ers' Burt," *New York Times,* January 22, 1991.

96 "It was a clean lick"—Bruce Keidan, "Giants End 49ers' Quest to Threepeat," *Pittsburgh Post-Gazette,* January 21, 1991.

96 "After the second series"—Dan Pierson, "Giants Bahr Niners from 3rd Straight," *Syracuse Herald-Journal,* January 21, 1991.

97 "Coach Parcells"—Dan Moffett, "Bahr's FG on Last Play Denies 'Three-Peat' 15-13," *Palm Beach Post,* January 21, 1991.

97 "They were ready"—Rich Cimini, George Willis, and Greg Logan, "Super Bowl XXV Notebook," *Newsday,* January 22, 1991.

97 "I'm just looking"—Michael Martinez, "Bad Memory Erased with Three Big Plays," *New York Times,* January 21, 1991.

98 "I remember Mark"—NFL Films, America's Game, 1990 Giants.

98 "felt as good as"—CBS television broadcast, January 20, 1991.

98 "I knew we'd"—Michael Martinez, "Bad Memory Erased with Three Big Plays," *New York Times,* January 21, 1991.

98 "To me, it was like"—Jeff Hostetler, author interview, January 26, 2010.

99 "This might be"—Bob Glauber, "Analysis: Tough Tasks for Hostetler," *Newsday,* December 18,1990.

99 "The pass to Bavaro"—Dave Anderson, "The Hostetler Cow Pasture," *New York Times,* January 21, 1991.

100 "When they called"—Stephen Baker, author interview, May 13, 2010.

100 "Jeff scrambled"—Don Nehlen, author interview, April 22, 2010.

100 "We let Ottis take"—Ron Erhard, author interview, July 14, 2010.

101 "It could be an"—CBS television broadcast, January 20, 1991.

101   "Those last few"—George Willis, "Giants vs. 49ers: Here They Go Again!" *Newsday*, January 14, 1994.

101   "He's setting up"—Charles Bricker, "49ers Bahred from 3-Peat," *Florida Sun-Sentinel*, January 21, 1991.

101   "I didn't notice"—Ira Berkow, "Where the Kick Fits In," *New York Times*, January 25, 1991.

102   "I didn't want to look"—Charles Bricker, "49ers Bahred from 3-Peat," *Florida Sun-Sentinel*, January 21, 1991.

102   "When I saw it"—Ira Berkow, "Where the Kick Fits In," *New York Times*, January 25, 1991.

102   "I may not"—Scott Newman, "Cast-off Bahr Gets His Kicks," *Pittsburgh Press*, January 21, 1991.

102   "I just remember"—Stephen Baker, author interview, May 13, 2010.

102   "It was a good"—CBS television broadcast, January 20, 1991.

102   "I've been trying"—Mike Celizic, "Win Lifts a Weight from Walls," *Bergen County Record*, January 21, 1991.

102   "We had them"—Frank Litsky, "Fantastic Finish Puts Giants in Super Bowl vs. Bills," *New York Times*, January 21, 1991.

103   "It's better than—Frank Litsky, "Fantastic Finish Puts Giants in Super Bowl vs. Bills," *New York Times*, January 21, 1991.

103   "That's probably"—Bill Parcells, author interview, July 16, 2010.

103   "The decision was"—Gerald Eskenazi, "An Unusual Day for Football Fans," *New York Times*, January 21, 1991.

103   "Life has to"—Bob Glauber, "'It was a Big Shock': War Personally Touches Cooks," *Newsday*, January 18, 1991.

104   "This is for"—George Willis, "Giants vs. 49ers: Here They Go Again!" *Newsday*, January 14, 1994.

104   "The NFL didn't"—Jim Baumbach, "Where Are They Now? Matt Bahr," *Newsday*, January 30, 2008.

104   "This game, of course"—CBS television broadcast, January 20, 1991.

104   "Instead, the war"—*Kansas City Star*, "Sports and the Persian Gulf," January 21, 1991.

105   "Nobody forgot"—*New York Times*, "Fans Focus beyond Game Too," January 21, 1991.

105   "How many were"—*Frederick News Post*, "Service Members in Gulf Appreciate Title Games," January 22, 1991.

CHAPTER 5: RESPECT WEEK

107   "It was a good"—Vic Carucci, "Spirits High as Showdown Looms Sunday," *Buffalo News*, January 22, 1991.

107   "Showtime"—Vic Carucci, "Spirits High as Showdown Looms Sunday," *Buffalo News*, January 22, 1991.

107   "I want all"—Vic Carucci, "Spirits High as Showdown Looms Sunday," *Buffalo News*, January 22, 1991.

107   "I won't turn"—Darrell Fry, "Cornelius Bennett: A Rhapsodist in Blue," *St. Petersburg Times*, January 24, 1991.

107   "beauty contest"—Tim Kawakami, "Kelly-Taylor Wrestling Match Is a Beauty," *Los Angeles Times*, January 25, 1991.

108   "I'm going"—Thomas George, "Bills, in Loud Form, Demand Respect," *New York Times*, January 23, 1991.

108   "Joe, Joe"—*Sarasota Herald Tribune*, "Joe, Jim, It's All the Same," January 23, 1991.

108   "Our goal is"—*Newport News Daily Press*, "Report: Bills QB Almost Pulls a Namath," January 23, 1991.

108   "in the best"—*San Diego Union*, "Marv Levy Quits Cal Grid Position," December 12, 1963.

109   "I felt beyond"—Bill Polian, author interview, May 12, 2010.

109   "I've been coaching"—Gerald Eskenazi, "Levy Catching Up in Duel of Coaches," *New York Times*, January 24, 1991.

109   "When people talk"—Dan Moffett, "Varying Perspectives among Athletic Elite, with All Due Respect," *Palm Beach Post*, January 26, 1991.

109   "Kelly draws"—Peter King, "Great Gamble," *Sports Illustrated*, January 28, 1991.

110   "Evidently I'm"—*Post-Standard*, "Talley, Banks Play in Shadows on 'D,'" January 24, 1991.

110   "There's probably"—Dan Moffett, "Varying Perspectives among Athletic Elite, with All Due Respect," *Palm Beach Post*, January 26, 1991.

110   "I hope we're"—Paul Woody, "Smith Fills Role Bills Already Planned," *Richmond Times-Dispatch*, August 29, 1985.

110   "I just decided"—Len Pasquarelli, "Bills' Smith: Latest Model in Legends," *Atlanta Constitution*, January 23, 1991.

111   "Over the last"—George Willis, "Big Bad Bruce," *Newsday*, December 13, 1990.

111   "I still think"—Armando Salguero, "'I'm the Best': Smith Is Campaigning for Fame and Fortune beyond Buffalo," *Palm Beach Post,* January 24, 1991.

111   "I'd rather have"—Thomas George, "Bills, in Loud Form, Demand Respect," *New York Times,* January 23, 1991.

111   "I wish we could"—Thomas George, "Bills, in Loud Form, Demand Respect," *New York Times,* January 23, 1991.

111   "My reason for"—Armando Salguero, "'I'm the Best': Smith Is Campaigning for Fame and Fortune beyond Buffalo," *Palm Beach Post,* January 24, 1991.

112   "heavy"—"This LT Version as Good as Ever," *Newsday,* Joe Gergen, December 10, 1990.

112   "It doesn't bother"—Frank Litsky, "Bills' No-Huddle Offense Is No Big Deal, Giants Say," *New York Times,* December 14, 1990.

112   "Right now"—Frank Litsky, "Giants Take Understated Approach," *New York Times,* January 23, 1991.

112   "Can I jump"—Craig Dolch, "Ultimate Warriors," *Palm Beach Post,* January 24, 1991.

113   "They're cocky"—Frank Litsky, "Giants Take Understated Approach," *New York Times,* January 23, 1991.

113   "I think for"—Bill Parcells, author interview, July 16, 2010.

113   "best player"—*Hutchinson News,* "Taylor Freely Passes Mantle of Best Defender to Smith," January 23, 1991.

113   "Obviously, Bruce"—Hank Gola, author interview, October 15, 2010.

114   "The Bills have"—Frank Litsky, "Giants Take Understated Approach," *New York Times,* January 23, 1991.

114   "We get there"—Doug Riesenberg, author interview, May 12, 2010.

114   "I remember one"—Maurice Carthon, author interview, May 21, 2010.

115   "That's a testament"—Doug Riesenberg, author interview, May 12, 2010.

115   "We would have"—Ed Hilt, "Bills, Naturally, Should Win," *Press of Atlantic City,* January 27, 1991.

115   "Get it like"—Bill Parcells, author interview, July 15, 2010.

115   "I'd rather go"—Don Pierson and Fred Mitchell, "Lofton Says Green Bay's Goals Lower," *Chicago Tribune,* January 24, 1991.

116   "golf course"—Lawrence Taylor and David Falkner, *LT: Living on the Edge* (New York: Times Books, 1987), 175.

116   "There's a way to"—Jerry Izenberg, *No Medals for Trying* (New York: Ballantine Books, 1990), 166.

116   "Did you ever"—Kevin Mulligan, "For Giants, It's Think Fast or Sink Fast," *Philadelphia Daily News*, January 25, 1991.

116   "I don't think"—Vinny DiTrani, "Timing Is Everything," *Bergen County Record*, January 27, 1991.

117   "Our whole plan"—Ron Borges, "No-Huddle—and No-Kick: Giants Prevail over Bills as Norwood Field Goal Try Misfires with 0:08 Left," *Boston Globe*, January 28, 1991.

117   "There were stretches"—Dan Moffett, "Storied Strengths and Flaws, with One Most Telling," *Palm Beach Post*, January 27, 1991.

117   "Power football"—Craig Barnes, "Giants Respond to Hostetler's Leadership Play," *Sun Sentinel*, January 28, 1991.

117   "It's always been"—Paul Zimmerman, "High and Mighty," *Sports Illustrated*, February 4, 1991.

117   "You've got to"—George Willis, "O. J. a Big Key to That Perfect Ending," *Newsday*, January 26, 1991.

118   "It would be like"—Steve Serby, "Bahr: 1950 U.S. Win Like High School Team Beating Yankees," *New York Post*, June 12, 2010.

119   "If the better"—Matt Bahr, author interview, July 29, 2010.

119   "[Growing up]"—Gary Mihoces, "A Kicker's Anguish: Bahr Is Ecstatic, but Says 'I Feel for Scott,'" *USA Today*, January 28, 1991.

119   "I can remember"—Len Pasquarelli, "Just for Kicks, the Giants Took Other Brother," *Atlanta Journal*, January 23, 1991.

119   "Because it was"—Matt Bahr, author interview, July 29, 2010.

120   "[Football] wasn't"—John McClain, "Norwood's Dream Would be a Giant Nightmare," *Houston Chronicle*, January 27, 1991.

120   "I gave up"—*Winchester Star*, "Norwood Gives JMU Kick," October 7, 1980.

121   "He's capable"—Bob Morgan, "JMU Football Begins Move to Division I," *Harrisonburg Daily News-Record*, August 29, 1979.

121   "I really began"—*Winchester Star*, "Norwood Gives JMU Kick," October 7, 1980.

121   "Scott was just"—John Kidd, author interview, August 5, 2010.

122   "In 1988"—Bruce DeHaven, author interview, July 19, 2010.

122   "You set yourself"—Carucci, *The Buffalo Bills and the Almost-Dream Season*, 62.

123   "He's always right"—Darrell Fry, "Norwood's Quest for Perfection." *St. Petersburg Times*, January 27, 1991.

123   "He's very picky"—Darrell Fry, "Norwood's Quest for Perfection." *St. Petersburg Times*, January 27, 1991.

123   "If I had to"—Carucci, *The Buffalo Bills and the Almost-Dream Season*, 62–63.

123   "He had the"—Bruce DeHaven, author interview, July 19, 2010.

124   "I was in a little"—John McClain, "Norwood's Dream Would be a Giant Nightmare," *Houston Chronicle*, January 27, 1991.

124   "It was never"—Darrell Fry, "Norwood's Quest for Perfection." *St. Petersburg Times*, January 27, 1991.

124   "Now that I'm"—John McClain, "Norwood's Dream Would be a Giant Nightmare," *Houston Chronicle*, January 27, 1991.

CHAPTER 6: SUPER SUNDAY

125   "My name is"—Stephen Baker, author interview, May 12, 2010.

125   "That video game"—Stephen Baker, author interview, May 12, 2010.

125   "It just makes you"—Stephen Baker, author interview, May 12, 2010.

126   "I hate waiting"—Dave Anderson, "Parcells Always Has a Plan," *New York Times*, January 28, 1991.

126   "spaghetti, baked"—Carucci, *The Buffalo Bills and the Almost-Dream Season*, 216.

126   "The ride to the"—Bill Polian, author interview, May 12, 2010.

126   "I told Charlie"—NFL Films, viewed at the NFL Films offices in Mt. Laurel, N.J., on June 29, 2010.

127   "First of all"—Ira Kaufman, "Silver Team Huddles Upset," *Tampa Tribune*, January 25, 1991.

127   "I was moved"—Ira Kaufman, "Silver Team Huddles Upset," *Tampa Tribune*, January 25, 1991.

128   "I did not think"—NFL Films, America's Game, 1975 Steelers.

129   "I never had"—Dave Anderson, "Swann's 4 Timely Receptions Result of a Timely Recovery," *New York Times*, January 19, 1976.

130   "I think it took"—Roger Fischer, "ABC Unveils Super Game Plan," *St. Petersburg Times*, January 27, 1991.

130 "I'm having a"—Leonard Shapiro, "ABC Realizes That This Time Around, 'Super' Really Is a Misnomer," *Washington Post,* January 25, 1991.

131 "[The] game"—Mary Jo Melone, "Let's Call the Whole Thing off Series," *St. Petersburg Times,* January 23, 1991.

131 "Somebody asked"—*New York Times,* "Excerpts from Bush's Remarks on Moves in Gulf," January 26, 1991.

131 "I don't think"—Rick Fuller, author interview, July 26, 2010.

132 "Saddam has a"—ABC broadcast (halftime), January 27, 1991.

133 "various terrorist"—*Pacific Stars & Stripes,* "FBI Checking on Terrorist Backers," January 26, 1991.

133 "At the time"—David Isby, author interview, July 13, 2010.

134 "Probably not"—Robert Reinhold, "Threats, Real or Not, Still Fears across U.S.," *New York Times,* January 24, 1991.

134 "very concerned"—Robert Reinhold, "Threats, Real or Not, Still Fears across U.S.," *New York Times,* January 24, 1991.

134 "We really didn't"—Jim Steeg, author interview, July 19, 2010.

134 "A black helicopter" Jim Steeg, author interview, July 19, 2010.

135 "The three of us"—Dan Dierdorf, author interview, July 30, 2010.

135 "They proceed"—Dan Dierdorf, author interview, July 30, 2010.

135 "It was pretty hard"—Dr. Ricardo Martinez, author interview, August 20, 2010.

136 "That area of"—Dr. Ricardo Martinez, author interview, August 20, 2010.

136 "We tend to forget"—Dr. Ricardo Martinez, author interview, August 20, 2010.

136 "That Super Bowl"—Jerry Anderson, author interview, August 23, 2010.

137 "We've always had"—Jerry Anderson, author interview, August 23, 2010.

137 "Usually, Americans"—*Toronto Star,* "Bowl Security Fails to Faze Football Fans," January 28, 1991.

137 "I'm real glad"—*Toronto Star,* "Bowl Security Fails to Faze Football Fans," January 28, 1991.

137 "It's just taking"—Gerald Eskenazi, "Security: Security Slows Crowd Entry," *New York Times,* January 28, 1991.

138 "Running out"—Michael Wilbon, "For Parcells, Euphoria and Now a Seller's Market," January 29, 1991, *Washington Post.*

138　"And now to"—ABC television broadcast, January 27, 1991.

138　"It was the most"—ABC's *Television's Greatest Performances*, hosted by Jimmy Smits, 1995.

139　"I keep pride inside"—ABC's *Television's Greatest Performances*, hosted by Jimmy Smits, 1995.

139　"We were in white"—Steve Tasker, author interview, June 17, 2010.

139　"Here we are"—Stephen Baker, author interview, May 13, 2010.

CHAPTER 7: THE FIRST THIRTY MINUTES

142　"No name is"—Armando Salguero, "Tampa Drops Discord for Super Bowl," *Palm Beach Post*, January 22, 1991.

142　"It has been"—*San Diego Union*, "NFL Fans Blast Decision to Play," November 24, 1963.

142　"Playing the"—Michael Wilbon, "Rozelle Grew into His Job, and NFL Grew into a Giant," *Washington Post*, March 26, 1989.

142　"President Roosevelt"—Gerald Eskenazi, "N.F.L. Says It Will Play, with Tight Security," *New York Times*, January 18, 1991.

142　"the Super Bowl is"—Ken McKee, "Parcells: 'A Mad-Dog Coach,'" *Toronto Star*, January 26, 1991.

143　"It'd be like"—Nancy Imperiale, "Party Mood Pierces Shadow of Gulf War," *Pittsburgh Press*, January 28, 1991.

143　"Commissioner Rozelle"—ABC television broadcast, January 27, 1991.

143　"Don't be off-sides"—NFL Films, viewed at the NFL Films offices in Mt. Laurel, N.J., on June 29, 2010.

144　"He did not want"—David Halberstam, *The Education of a Coach* (New York: Hyperion, 2005), 172.

144　"We went into the game"—Bill Belichick, author interview, May 11, 2011.

144　"They were used"—Erik Howard, author interview, July 21, 2010.

145　"Supposedly"—Bill Ordine, "From Kutztown to Super Bowl," *Philadelphia Inquirer*, January 22, 1991.

145　"Everybody talks"—Bill Ordine, "From Kutztown to Super Bowl," *Philadelphia Inquirer*, January 22, 1991.

146　"I don't think"—NFL Films, "The Wild Ride to Super Bowl I."

147　"There were a few"—NFL Films, "The Wild Ride to Super Bowl I."

147   "He didn't come"—NFL Films, "The Wild Ride to Super Bowl I."

147   "I was rooming"—NFL Films, "The Wild Ride to Super Bowl I."

148   "Men, if you bust—NFL Films, "The Wild Ride to Super Bowl I."

148   "They had these little"—Boyd Dowler, author interview, June 21, 2010.

148   "Here's McGee"—Bob Long, author interview, August 27, 2010.

149   "A lot of guys"—Bill Curry, author interview, June 12, 2010.

149   "Max took"—Bob Long, author interview, August 27, 2010.

149   "[Willie] Mitchell"—Bill Curry, author interview, June 12, 2010.

150   "He thought he"—Bill Curry, author interview, June 12, 2010.

150   "I was just a kid"—Malcolm Moran, "The Wait Is Over for Bills and Fans," *New York Times*, January 22, 1991.

150   "I really didn't"—Malcolm Moran, "The Wait Is Over for Bills and Fans," *New York Times*, January 22, 1991.

151   "I talked to those"—James Lofton, author interview, June 14, 2010.

151   "[Playing the Super"—Glenn Sheeley, "Lofton Knows He's Not Bills' Speed-Burner," *Atlanta Constitution*, January 24, 1991.

151   "The ball was"—James Lofton, author interview, June 14, 2010.

152   "He got a lot"—James Lofton, author interview, June 14, 2010.

152   "I played safety"—Everson Walls, author interview, June 12, 2010.

153   "I've never"—Paul Zimmerman, "High and Mighty," *Sports Illustrated*, February 4, 1991.

153   "They were sagging"—Paul Zimmerman, "High and Mighty," *Sports Illustrated*, February 4, 1991.

154   "It was really"—Darrell Fry, "Smith Returns to Glory," *St. Petersburg Times*, January 28, 1991.

154   "Seals is a big"—Hostetler, *One Giant Leap*, 206.

154   "I couldn't even"—Bill Millsaps, "Super Sub Hostetler Set Off Mettle-Detector," *Richmond Times-Dispatch*, January 28, 1991.

155   "In the tapes"—Craig Barnes, "Confusion and Contusions Beat Bills," *Fort Lauderdale, Sun-Sentinel*, January 28, 1991.

155   "I remember the"—Jeff Hostetler, author interview, January 26, 2010.

156 "[All] of a sudden"—Bob Glauber, Rich Cimini, and Jon Pessah, "Super Bowl XXV: Notebook," *Newsday*, January 28, 1991.

156 "If I lost the"—Jeff Hostetler, author interview, January 26, 2010.

156 "That was a"—Bruce Smith, interviewed by John Murphy, WKBW-TV, 2006 .

156 "[Parcells] said it multiple"—Bob Mrosko, author interview, July 28, 2010.

157 "He runs so big"—ABC television broadcast, January 27, 1991.

157 "It's up to Thomas"—ABC television broadcast, January 27, 1991.

157 "Thurman was"—Bill Parcells, author interview, July 15, 2010.

158 "I had seen so"—Ray Didinger, author interview, July 13, 2010.

158 "I told them"—Craig Barnes, "Giants Respond to Hostetler's Leadership, Play," *Fort-Lauderdale Sun-Sentinel*, January 28, 1991.

159 "Hostetler has"—ABC television broadcast, January 27, 1991.

159 "I was mad"—Hostetler, *One Giant Leap*, 208.

159 "When he threw"—Stephen Baker, author interview, May 13, 2010.

160 "When we got back"—Stephen Baker, author interview, May 13, 2010.

160 "back green X flag"—Official Postgame Quotes from Super Bowl XXV.

160 "The line blocked"—Stephen Baker, author interview, May 13, 2010.

160 "That was a very"—Stephen Baker, author interview, May 13, 2010.

160 "They're not used"—*Aikens Standard*, "Finally, a Super Bowl Truly Worth Watching," January 28, 1991.

CHAPTER 8: WHIPPING BOYS

161 "Today we should"—ABC broadcast, January 27, 1991.

163 "Baseball was my"—Bill Parcells, author interview, July 16, 2010.

163 "At that game"—*Winnipeg Free Press*, "Long-Time Dream Realized," December 16, 1982.

163 "10 minutes after"—*New York Times*, "Giants Hire a Linebacker Coach," March 2, 1979,

163 "We won the"—Bob Long, author interview, August 27, 2010.

164 "It's called 'Pizza Hut'"—Bill Parcells, author interview, July 16, 2010.

164 "He wound up"—Bill Parcells, author interview, July 16, 2010.

164 "I didn't think"—Bob Long, author interview, August 27, 2010.

165   "We are the same" Frank Litsky, "Parcells Sidelines New Role," *New York Times*, December 20, 1982.

165   "If you understand"—Jack Magruder, "Parcells Outlines Future," *Colorado Springs Gazette-Telegraph*, December 14, 1977.

165   "He's a typical guy"—Rich Hofmann, "Just a Guy from Jersey," *Winnipeg Free Press*, January 26, 1991.

165   "If you're sensitive"—Rich Hofmann, "Just a Guy from Jersey," *Winnipeg Free Press*, January 26, 1991.

165   "His personality"—Rich Hofmann, "Just a Guy from Jersey," *Winnipeg Free Press*, January 26, 1991.

166   "He really wasn't"—Bill Parcells, author interview, July 16, 2010.

166   "A lot of people"—Bob Long, author interview, August 27, 2010.

167   "Very few people"—*New York Times*, "A Friendly Coach," December 16, 1982.

167   "I think he'll"—*Winnipeg Free Press*, "Long-Time Dream Realized," December 16, 1982,

167   "Dear coach"—*Los Angeles Times*, "Parcells Credits Power Football, and Amazing Good Lucky Towel," January 28, 1991.

168   "Augie from the"—Frank Litsky, "On Top of Clouds, Giants Dance to Tampa," *New York Times*, January 22, 1991.

168   "We had a lot"—Bill Parcells, author interview, July 16, 2010.

169   "towel boy"—*Hamilton Daily News Journal*, "Draft Towel Boy to Play Fullback," October 15, 1941.

169   "He was a lot"—Don Gleisner, author interview, July 29, 2010.

169   "There was a real"—Eric Lincoln, "Sports World Specials," *New York Times*, October 27, 1980.

169   "This guy"—Ernie Accorsi, author interview, July 19, 2010.

170   "That's when I hired"—Ted Marchibroda, author interview, December 5, 2009.

170   "A lot of my"—Eric Lincoln, "Sports World Specials," *New York Times*, October 27, 1980.

171   "In the rain"—Frank Litsky, "Simms of Giants Is Out for Season," *New York Times*, November 17, 1981.

171   "He's always given"—George Willis, "Belichick's Record Needs No Defending," *Newsday*, December 31, 1989.

171   "a terrible bedside"—Christine Brennan, "Belichick Provides Giants' Diagram for Domination," *Washington Post*, January 24, 1987.

171   "Doom"—Hank Gola, author interview, October 15, 2010.

171   "They talked about"—Don Gleisner, author interview, July 29, 2010.

172   "Parcells would challenge"—Mary Kay Cabot, "Friends and Rivals," *Cleveland Plain Dealer*, January 1, 1995.

172   "I'm not going"—Gerald Eskenazi, "Parcells Resigns as Jets' Coach; Belichick Assumes the Top Role," *New York Times*, January 4, 2000.

172   "Most of the"—Bill Parcells, author interview, July 16, 2010.

173   "We're just two different people"—Bill Belichick, author interview, May 11, 2011.

173   "Charlie was"—Tim Layden, "Charlie In Charge," *Sports Illustrated*, April 25, 2005.

173   "I always laugh"—Bill Parcells, author interview, July 16, 2010.

CHAPTER 9: GRINDING OUT A CHAMPIONSHIP

175   "The first drive"—Tim Looney, "Q & A with Giants Coach Bill Parcells," *St. Petersburg Times*, January 28, 1991.

175   "Parcells said"—NFL Films, America's Game, 1990 Giants.

176   "I understood we"—Mark Bavaro, author interview, January 19, 1991.

177   "We went 13-3"—Bob Glauber, *Newsday*, January 13, 1991.

177   "It's always frustrating"—Bob Glauber, *Newsday*, January 13, 1991.

177   "Our offensive linemen"—Chris Dufresne, "Giants Have It Under Control," *Los Angeles Times*, January 28, 1991.

178   "half-right"—Peter King, "A Career Move at a Key Time," *Sports Illustrated*, February 4, 1991.

178   "Here we go!"—Peter King, "A Career Move at a Key Time," *Sports Illustrated*, February 4, 1991.

178   "All I saw was"—Official Post Game Quotes from Super Bowl XXV.

179   "We played a"—Mark Kelso, author interview, May 26, 2010.

179   "When I fell"—Official Post Game Quotes from Super Bowl XXV.

179   "Every now"—ABC broadcast, January 27, 1991.

179   "Except for a"—Frank Litsky, "Giants Start Adjusting to Life without Simms," *New York Times*, December 21, 1990.

180   "[On] those bootlegs"—Frank Litsky, "Giants Are Deflecting the Big Question," *New York Times*, January 30, 1991.

180   "He kept trying"—*Seattle Times*, "Bennett's Advice Helps Wrong Team," January 28, 1991.

181   "I always had"—NFL Films Greatest Games: 1992 NFC Championship Game.

182   "Bill Belichick is a"—Kent Hull, author interview, December 11, 2009.

182   "We were on"—Bob Glauber, Rich Cimini, and Jon Pessah, "Super Bowl XXV," *Newsday*, January 28, 1991.

182   "We weren't used"—Chuck Mulling, "Bills Feel Heartache of Defeat," *Tampa Tribune*, January 29, 1991.

183   "We had a lot"—Mark Bavaro, author interview, January 19, 1991.

183   "I'm bored"—*Hutchinson News*, "Riggins Returns," June 12, 1981.

184   "the New Yorkers'"—Gerald Eskenazi, "Riggins to Shop for Best Deal," *New York Times*, April 29, 1976.

184   "[I] never had a"—*Free Lance Star*, "Fullback Riggins Optimistic over Redskins' 'New' Offense," July 27, 1978.

184   "When I got the job"—The Mike Wise Show with Holden Kushner, June 23, 2010.

185   "I'm out here"—*Hutchinson News*, "Bored and Broke, Riggins Back," June 12, 1981.

186   "I thought it was"—Ray Didinger, author interview, July 13, 2010.

186   "In our first"—Joe Jacoby, "Super Bowl XVII: Joe Jacoby," in *Super Bowl: The Game of Their Lives*, ed. Danny Peary (New York: Macmillan, 1997), 238.

187   "I almost swallowed"—Ira Rosenfeld, "Wait Is Finally Over for Butz," *Kokomo Tribune*, January 31, 1983.

187   "Nobody panicked"—Ira Rosenfeld, "Wait Is Finally Over for Butz," *Kokomo Tribune*, January 31, 1983.

187   "Joe [Jacoby]"—John Clayton, "Stop Fancy Stuff, Hogs Told Coach," *Pittsburgh Press*, January 31, 1983.

187   "He's our bread"—*Kokomo Tribune*, "Hogs Magnificent, Riggins Even Better," January 31, 1983.

188   "We were on"—Clint Didier, author interview, June 23, 2010.

188   "Goal line"—Clint Didier, author interview, June 23, 2010.

188   "[Redskins offensive"—Ray Didinger, author interview, July 13, 2010.

189   "I can remember"—Clint Didier, author interview, June 23, 2010.

189   "It was amazing"—Ray Didinger, author interview, July 13, 2010.

189   "I hope when"—Bruce Lowitt, "Redskins 'Super' over Dolphins," *Gettysburg Times*, January 31, 1983.

189   "Ron is the"—*Miami Herald*, "Reagan, Riggins," January 31, 1983.

190   "I felt like"—Ray Didinger, "Big John Smash Hit in Drummer Boy Role," *Reading Eagle*, January 31, 1983.

191   "We contributed"—Bill Parcells, author interview, June 15, 2010.

191   "Any time you're"—Official Post Game Quotes from Super Bowl XXV.

CHAPTER 10: BUFFALO'S BICKERING BILLS

193   "There are moments"—Ira Berkow, "How the Bills Build Their Vocabulary," *New York Times*, January 23, 1991.

193–4 "extrapolate, salient"—Ira Berkow, "How the Bills Build Their Vocabulary," *New York Times*, January 23, 1991.

194   "That kinda came"—Steve Tasker, author interview, June 17, 2010.

194   "One More River to Cross"—NFL Films, America's Game: Missing Rings, 1990 Bills.

194   "He's a better"—*Colorado Springs-Gazette Telegraph*, "Just like Brown Bomber, Levy Plans to Be on Time," January 27, 1991.

194   "I wondered if"—Levy, *Where Else Would You Rather Be?* 338.

195   "I know exactly"—*Syracuse Herald Journal*, "Bills' Thrills," September 11, 1989.

195   "The 'Bickering Bills'"—Darryl Talley, author interview, December 18, 2009.

195   "I knew, the"—Kelly, *Armed & Dangerous*, 137.

196   "It should have"—Vic Carucci, "Kelly Says Hit Ballard's Fault," *Buffalo News*, October 10, 1989.

196   "I told him"—*Syracuse Herald Journal*, "Bills' Thomas Exchanges Fire with Critical Kelly," October 14, 1989.

196   "unhappy with"—Will Hampton, "Big play Oilers to Meet Bickering Bills Next," *Galveston Daily News*, December 25, 1988.

196 "rammed his"—Vic Carucci, "Bills Admit Fight, Say Case Closed," *Buffalo News*, October 25, 1989.

197 "only allowed"—Vic Carucci, "New Leaders Emerging As Bills Become Team Harmony," *Buffalo News*, September 6, 1990.

197 "It wasn't so"—Steve Tasker, author interview, June 17, 2010.

197 "Ronnie came back"—Gerald Eskenazi, "Browns Hold Off Bills in Playoff Shootout," *New York Times*, January 7, 1990.

198 "I was open"—Gerald Eskenazi, "Browns Hold Off Bills in Playoff Shootout," *New York Times*, January 7, 1990.

198 "If you don't"—NFL Films Presents, Show #1, 1997.

198 "troublemakers"—Levy, *Where Else Would You Rather Be?* 339.

198 "Joe Devlin"—Steve Tasker, author interview, June 17, 2010.

198 "I told the team"—Don Williams, "Bickering Bills Change Name, Not Attitude," *Newark Star Ledger*, September 20, 1990.

199 "I think they"—Vic Carucci, author interview, August 19, 2010.

199 "we just fuckin'"—Carucci, *The Buffalo Bills and the Almost-Dream Season*, 12.

199 "The harmony has"—*Chicago Daily Herald*, "'Bickering Bills' Say They'll be Ready for New-Look Jets," September 24, 1990.

199 "It was Jim too"—Vic Carucci, author interview, August 19, 2010.

200 "I told Vic [Carucci]"—Steve Tasker, author interview, June 17, 2010.

CHAPTER 11: THE IRRESISTIBLE FORCE VS. THE IMMOVABLE OBJECT

201 "Bobby Layne"—Pro Football Hall of Fame Official, http://www.profootballhof.com/hof/member.aspx?PlayerId=126.

202 "That was a freakin'"—Everson Walls, author interview, June 10, 2010.

202 "It would be hard"—Dan Dierdorf, author interview, July 30, 2010.

202 "Anytime, whether"—Ron Erhard, author interview, July 14, 2010.

203 "There was no"—John Romano, "Giants' Motto: Don't Worry, be Methodical," *St. Petersburg Times*, January 28, 1991.

203 "He is a money"—ABC broadcast, January 27, 1991.

203 "He's the toughest"—Mike Freeman, "Bavaro out of His Shell: Neither Shy Nor Retiring," *Washington Post*, January 24, 1991.

203   "I saw a few"—Official Postgame Quotes from Super Bowl XXV.

205   "the air out"—Jim Donaldson, "Super Bowl XXV New York Giants: 1991 Super Bowl
       Champions," *Providence Journal,* January 28, 1991.

205   "We had had"—Bill Parcells, author interview, July 15, 2010.

206   "The two guys"—Steve Tasker, author interview, June 17, 2010.

207   "Dave Meggett had a"—ABC broadcast, January 27, 1991.

207   "We really didn't"—Bill Parcells, author interview, July 15, 2010.

207   "What do you think"—ABC broadcast, January 27, 1991.

208   "the irresistible force"—Bob Glauber, "A Closer Look at a Real Thriller," *Newsday,*
       January 29, 1991.

208   "Two minutes to go"—Jim Kelly, author interview, January 22, 1991.

209   "We're going to have"—NFL Films, Top Ten Nicknames.

209   "I really think"—Sam Huff and Leonard Shapiro, *Tough Stuff* (New York: St. Martin's
       Press, 1988), 40.

209   "He hated rookies"—Doug Kennedy, "Andy Russell: The Silver Fox," SteelersLIVE
       'Xtra, October 12, 2005.

209   "Super Bowl III"—NFL Films, America's Game, 1970 Colts.

210   "It was one"—NFL Films, America's Game, 1970 Colts.

210   "They weren't"—NFL Films, America's Game, 1970 Colts.

210   "A couple guys"—Jim O'Brien, author interview, July 19, 2010.

210   "We were debating"—Jack Maitland, author interview, July 21, 2010.

211   "To my recollection"—NFL Films, America's Game, 1970 Colts.

211   "I didn't have"—Jim O'Brien, author interview, July 19, 2010.

211   "According to the"—Arthur Daley, "Sports of the Times: Not Very Super," *New York
       Times,* January 18, 1971.

212   "A lot of"—Ernie Accorsi, author interview, July 20, 2010.

212   "I think [Cowboys"—Norman Bulaich, author interview, July 21, 2010.

212   "just don't fumble"—Norman Bulaich, author interview, July 21, 2010.

212   "Earl Morrall"—Jim O'Brien, author interview, July 19, 2010.

213   "Billy Ray Smith"—Jim O'Brien, author interview, July 19, 2010.

213   "It was such"—Ray Didinger, author interview, July 13, 2010.

213   "Keep your head"—Jim O'Brien, author interview, July 21, 2010.

214   "I remember Cornelius"—Jack Maitland, author interview, July 21, 2010.

214   "He wasn't any star"—Ernie Accorsi, author interview, July 20, 2010.

215   "Counting my"—Ray Grody, "Quotable Quotes," *Milwaukee Sentinel*, July 22, 1971.

215   "People don't"—Jim O'Brien, author interview, July 21, 2010.

216   "I remember Jim"—Will Wolford, author interview, December 14, 2009.

217   "We came in there"—Everson Walls author interview, June 12, 2010.

217   "I was gonna pass"—Erik Howard, author interview, July 21, 2010.

218   "as good an"—NFL Films, Top 10 Linebacking Corps.

219   "Bill [Belichick] said"—Bill Parcells, author interview, July 15, 2010.

219   "I thought about"—Official Postgame Quotes from Super Bowl XXV.

219   "It's an emotional"—Erik Howard, author interview, July 21, 2010.

220   "Out of the corner"—Mike Sweatman, author interview with July 15, 2010.

221   "When they were"—Bill Parcells, author interview, July 15, 2010.

221   "The quiet man"—NFL Films, Highlight Video of Super Bowl XXV.

222   "He absolutely crushed"—Vic Carucci, "Norwood Kept Composure before, after His Failed Kick," *Buffalo News*, January 28, 1991.

222   "As the ball was"—Bill Polian, author interview, May 12, 2010.

222   "I left it out right"—Bob Harig, "Kick Is Hard to Forget for Bills' Norwood," *St. Petersburg Times*, January 28, 1991.

222   "That was the most"—Kent Hull, author interview, December 11, 2009.

222   "Take me for a ride"—NFL Films, Special Roll of Super Bowl XXV, Part 3.

223   "We got you two"—NFL Films, Special Roll of Super Bowl XXV, Part 3.

223   "six tight diamond"—Hostetler, *One Giant Leap*, 213.

223   "I remember looking"—Hostetler, *One Giant Leap*, 212–13.

223   "I was drunk"—Hostetler, *One Giant Leap*, 213.

224   "That's the best"—NFL Films, Special Roll of Super Bowl XXV, Part 3.

224   "We heard all"—Paul Daugherty, "Nation Puts Sports in Perspective," *Syracuse Herald Journal*, January 28, 1991.

232   "Hostetler, of course"—John Markon, "Super Bowl XXV Erred in MVP Pick,"
       Richmond Times-Dispatch, January 29, 1991.

232   "He's going to"—Tim Looney, "Q & A with Coach Bill Parcells," *St. Petersburg Times*,
       January 28, 1991.

233   "They brought Parcells"—Ray Didinger, author interview, July 13, 2010.

233   "The third floor"—Frank Litsky, "Giants Go without Sleep but Nobody's Complaining,"
       New York Times, January 29, 1991.

234   "My elbow is"—George Willis, "Super Bowl XXV: A Super Sensation Giants Savoring
       Triumph," *Newsday*, January 28, 1991.

234   "A couple of us"—Ernie Palladino, author interview, July 14, 2010.

234   "You'd think"—Jay Mariotti, "Little to Cheer at Giants' Homecoming," *The National*,
       January 29, 1991.

234   "What they did"—Jay Mariotti, "Little to Cheer at Giants' Homecoming," *The National*,
       January 29, 1991.

234   "do something"—Rita Delfiner, "Dinkins Says City Will Stage Celebration," *New York
       Post*, January 22, 1991.

234   "Let Moonachie"—Richard Justice, "Notebook; Cuomo Makes Giant Reversal,"
       Washington Post, January 22, 1991.

235   "They may"—Rita Delfiner, "Dinkins Says City Will Stage Celebration," *New York Post*,
       January 22, 1991.

235   "You have to"—Everson Walls, author interview, June 10, 2010.

235   "There wasn't"—Erik Howard, author interview, July 21, 2010.

235   "There were some"—Bill Gutman, *Parcells: A Biography* (New York: Carroll & Graf
       Publishers, 2000), 155.

235   "It would have"—Bill Parcells, author interview, July 15, 2010.

236   "Bill is bright"—Tom Skernivitz, "Browns Hope Belichick 'Super Coach,'" *Elyria
       Chronicle Telegram*, February 6, 1991.

236   "I've been"—Dan Coughlin, "Belichick Next Shula? Super Coach," *Elyria Chronicle
       Telegram*, February 6, 1991.

236   "Belichick is probably"—*Marysville Journal Tribune*, "New Coach Is Man of Detail,"
       February 11, 1991.

237   "The last time"—Official Post Game Quotes from Super Bowl XXV.

237   "The way I"—Jerry Izenberg, *No Medals for Trying* (New York: Ballantine Books, 1990), 190.

237   "Any of us"—Dave Anderson, "Parcells Feels Ditka's Pain," *New York Times*, November 3, 1988.

237   "It's tough to"—Gerald Eskenazi, "Parcells Is Expected to Step Down Today," *New York Times*, May 15, 1991.

237   "It's becoming"—Rich Hofmann, "Just a Guy from Jersey," *Winnipeg Free Press*, January 26, 1991.

238   "Everything that's"—Craig Dolch, "Parcells Looking Ahead, QB, Plan B Talks Quiet Rumors," *Palm Beach Post*, January 29, 1991.

238   "The fans made"—Robert McG. Thomas, "A Super Good Night for a Happy Parcells," *New York Times*, January 30, 1991.

238   "He'll be coaching"—Vinny DiTrani, "Parcells Shall Make Triumphant Return," *Bergen County Record*, January 29, 1991.

238   "would be the"—Bob Glauber, "Bavaro Down to One Knee," *Newsday*, January 11, 1991.

239   "I think he saw"—Hank Gola, author interview, October 15, 2010.

239   "No way, I'm"—ABC television broadcast, January 27, 1991.

239   "It's the player"—Malcolm Moran, "Anderson Is Most Venerable and Most Valuable," *New York Times*, January 28, 1991.

240   "would be insulted"—Dave George, "Man for the Ages," *Palm Beach Post*, January 29, 1991.

240   "Jeff Hostetler is"—*Orlando Sentinel*, "Parcells' Promise: There Won't Be Any Controversy," January 28, 1991.

240   "[It] doesn't matter"—Hostetler, *One Giant Leap*, 233.

240   "I've got two pretty"—Craig Dolch, "Parcells Looking Ahead," *Palm Beach Post*, January 29, 1991.

241   "I like Phil Simms"—Hostetler, *One Giant Leap*, 233.

241   "For more than"—Dave Anderson, "Giants Not a Dynasty, Just Champs," *New York Times*, January 29, 1991.

242   "I recalled a"—Ken Leiker and Craig Ellenport, eds., *The Super Bowl: An Official Retrospective* (New York: Ballantine Books, 2005), 27.

242   "I've got to"—*The Capitol*, "Giants Savor Title; Bills Savor Warmth," January 29, 1991.

242   "The reception"—Bill Polian, author interview, May 12, 2010.

243   "[We] get back"—Everson Walls, author interview, June 10, 2010.

243   "It was a great"—*New York Post,* "Gov Shuffled Off to Buffalo to Cheer Bills," January 29, 1991.

243   "Buffalo Bills"—Barbara O'Brien, "30,000 Fans Shower Bills with Welcome," *Buffalo News,* January 29, 1991.

243   "It was off the"—Carlton Bailey, author interview, January 15, 2010.

CHAPTER 13: JANUARY 15, 1994

246   "I just think"—George Willis, "It Was Time for a Move," *Newsday,* May 16, 1991.

246   "It's been a great"—Joe Gergen, "Parcells Goes Out on Top." *Newsday,* May 16, 1991.

246   "I was just in"—Frank Litsky, "Retirement's Timing Is Biggest Surprise," *New York Times,* May 16, 1991.

246   "I had a pretty"—Kim Kolbe, author interview, October 6, 2010.

247   "I knew something"—Bill Parcells, author interview, July 15, 2010.

247   "When the [1991]"—Stephen Baker, author interview, May 13, 2010.

248   "When Ray Handley"—Bob Mrosko, author interview, July 28, 2010.

248   "In my mind"—Bob Mrosko, author interview, July 28, 2010.

249   "[1991 and 1992]—Ernie Palladino, author interview, July 14, 2010.

249   "I started my"—Bob Dick, "Patriots Tap Parcells to be Savior," *Providence Journal,* January 22, 1993.

249   "I didn't need"—Vinny DiTrani, "Reeves Answers Questions," *Bergen County Record,* May 13, 1993.

249   "Maybe we're not"—Michael Mayo, "Giants Aren't Jazzy, but Tune-Up Went Well," *Sun Sentinel,* January 10, 1994.

250   "Some of the guys"—Mike Freeman, "Giants' Season Ends in a Million Pieces," *New York Times,* January 16, 1994.

251   "Maybe the key"—*Pacific Stars and Stripes,* "49ers Dwarf Giants 44-3." January 17, 1994.

251   "They were just"—*Alton Telegraph,* "Bills Shade Raiders, San Francisco Rips Giants," January 16, 1993.

251   "I think it's time"—Dave Anderson, "L.T. Decides 'It's Time for Me to Go," *New York Times,* January 16, 1994.

251   "I'm fortunate the"—Dave Anderson, "L.T. Decides 'It's Time for Me to Go," *New York Times*, January 16, 1994.

252   "When I was"—Milton Kent, "This Time, Gulf War Veteran Gets Closer Seat for Son's Super Bowl," *Baltimore Sun*, January 14, 1992.

253   "I believe in my"—Mike Harris, "Positive Look: Norwood Takes on 'The Miss,'" *Richmond Times-Dispatch*, January 13, 1992.

253   "I didn't have"—Kevin Mannix, "Norwood Gets Kickback," *Boston Herald*, January 13, 1992.

254   "Any Norwood"—Bud Poliquin, "One Little Field Goal Can Make Us Forget," *Syracuse Herald Journal*, January 13, 1992.

254   "[Bills third"—Terry Blount, "Reich Reprises Roles as Clutch QB," *Houston Chronicle*, January 4, 1993.

255   "We know"—Bill Plaschke, "No More Apologies Bills Won't Give Up, and They're Driven to Make Critics Shut Up," *Los Angeles Times*, September 26, 1993.

255   "The last time"—Chris Dufresne, "Wiping Out Memory of Wipeout," *Los Angeles Times*, January 13, 1994.

255   "It's an end"—Vito Stellino, "Two Quick Changes Wipe Out Redskins' Big Advantages," *The Sun*, March 7, 1993.

255   "I want a team"—Frank Litsky, "Simms Signs On; Hostetler Signs Off," *New York Times*, March 6, 1993.

256   "This was the"—Don Amore, "Hostetler Becomes a Raider, Signs 3-Year Deal for $7.5 Million," *Hartford Courant*, March 25, 1993.

256   "He runs very"—Frank Litsky, "Add Hostetler and Bavaro to New Millionaires' Club," *New York Times*, March 26, 1993.

256   "It is still a team"—Ed McNamara, "NFL '93 Riding the Big Hoss," *Newsday*, September 6, 1993.

257   "People can talk"—Harvey Araton, "Examining Reeves's Reasoning," *New York Times*, January 12, 1994.

257   "I went to talk"—Harvey Araton, "Examining Reeves's Reasoning," *New York Times*, January 12, 1994.

257   "You've just got"—Vic Carucci and Mark Gaughan, "Players Must Find Ways to Conquer Cold," *Buffalo News*, January 15, 1994.

258   "It was very"—Vic Carucci, "Bounce-Back Bills Land in Title Game," *Buffalo News*, January 16, 1994.

258 "You get in"—Jim Thomas, "Buffalo Zeroes In, but It Was Really Hot Stuff," *St. Louis Post-Dispatch*, January 16, 1994.

258 "I was hoping"—Chris Dufresne, "The Raiders Don't Need Brown-and-Out Pattern," *Los Angeles Times*, January 16, 1994.

259 "Jim put it right"—*Syracuse Herald American*, "Bills Thrill As Buffalo Chills," January 16, 1994.

259 "We have a lot"—Vic Carucci, "Bounce-Back Bills Land in Title Game," *Buffalo News*, January 16, 1994.

260 "I think if you"— Randy Schultz, "A Run for the Ages," *Football Digest*, December 2004.

EPILOGUE: SUPER BOWL XLII

262 "The thing I'm"—Arthur Staple, "Third Thynes a Charm," *Newsday*, January 21, 2008.

262 "It will be our"—Ira Kaufman, "Keeping Ball a Giant Part of Game Plan," *Tampa Tribune*, January 28, 2008.

262 "It makes me"—Vinny DiTrani, "Parcells Proud of Former Aides Coughlin, Belichick," *The Record*, January 24, 2008.

262 "There is a way"—Vinny DiTrani, "Parcells Proud of Former Aides Coughlin, Belichick," *The Record*, January 24, 2008.

263 "later than"—Peter Yoon, "Morning Briefing; Fan Gets Mickelson and More," *Los Angeles Times*, February 5, 2008.

263 "That offense"—George Willis, "Un-'D'-Lievable-Giant Defense Turns Juggernaut into Patsies," *New York Post*, February 4, 2008.

263 "This is the"—Vinny DiTrani, "One Giant Jolt; Last-Minute Rally Denies New England Immortal Status," *Burlington Times-News*, February 4, 2008.

Acknowledgments

I spent a great deal of time thinking about what I wanted my second (first solo-authored) book to be about. One day, I accompanied my then-fiancé, Sarah, to Coffee Tree Roasters on Walnut Street in the Shadyside section of Pittsburgh, where she would study for the next of an endless string of medical school exams: Step-II if you know that sort of thing.

After a few weeks and a few failed ideas, Super Bowl XXV popped into my head in the summer of 2008. A handful of Hall of Fame participants, the quarter-century milestone, Whitney Houston's national anthem, and the closest game in Super Bowl history rendered the idea viable. But it was the lesson taught to me by graduate-school mentor, Tom O'Boyle—that if you try hard enough and do it right, you can write an exceptional story about almost anything—that clinched the January 27, 1991, championship game as ideal.

Jim Kelly, Jeff Hostetler, Lawrence Taylor, Thurman Thomas, and Bill Parcells are naturally the foundation of this story. But the inclusion of many lesser-explored tales—Carlton Bailey, Stephen Baker's love for key lime pie, a young James Lofton watching Super Bowl I with his father, and Captain Steve Abbot's Super Bowl party—were directly the result of Tom O'Boyle's guidance.

As the idea and the structure unfolded during the remainder of that year and the three years that followed, a large group of people contributed to both the book's viability and research.

First, I want to thank all the people who granted me interviews that were so vital to the retelling of this story (see appendix 2). Many people helped me contact these interviewees. Thanks to Jim Neville, Billy Watkins, Mark Lepselter, Cynthia Winters, Frank "Digger" Dawson, Jill Fritzo, Ralph Cindrich, Don Jay Smith (executive director of the New Jersey Hall of Fame), Craig Kelley with the Indianapolis Colts, Pete Moris with the Kansas City Chiefs, Pat Hanlon with the New York Giants, and Andy Major and Chris Jenkins with the Buffalo Bills. And to the gracious people who provided back-jacket blurbs, I am equally grateful.

Quite obviously, Lynn Swann deserves special thanks as well. For *this* particular book—not only a time capsule of the 1991 NFL Championship Game but also a selective anthology of the Super Bowl's history—the foreword could not have come from a more perfect candidate. Credit Sylvan Holzer with a game-changing assist there.

In terms of pure football counsel, University of New Hampshire running backs coach Mike Ferzoco—who happens to have been my college roommate and fellow Kenyon College Lords football player—provided key insights on the so-called X's and O's. And my former head coach at Shaker Heights High School, Dave Sedmak, did a wonderful job breaking down game film and reading portions of the manuscript to validate my observations.

For verification of the facts I found regarding the Persian Gulf War, much thanks is due Professor Glenn McNair at Kenyon College, who put me in touch with Richard S. Faulkner, the associate supervisory professor of military history at the U.S. Army Command and General Staff College. During Operation Desert Storm in the Gulf War, Professor Faulkner was an army captain and tank commander in the Third Battalion, Thirty-fifth Regiment, First Armored Division, stationed in Saudi Arabia.

For the vast research conducted for this book—and the notes section portrays only a portion of the archives collected—I have one person to thank. Steve Schlossman, my coauthor of *Chasing Greatness: Johnny Miller, Arnold Palmer, and the Miracle at Oakmont,* my first book, about the 1973 U.S. Open, taught me how to "break the back" of the research phase. Without his training and diligence on that earlier project, I would never have pursued the finer details that make this book so rich.

There were a few rough bumps on the road to finishing this project, and for that, Don Van Natta Jr., Flo Conway, and my uncle, Jim Siegelman, gave wonderful counsel on many "off-the-field" issues.

Peter Burford also deserves my endless gratitude, as do his colleagues at Taylor Trade: Rick Rinehart, Flannery Scott, Gene Margaritondo, Alden Perkins, Kalen Landow, and everyone who worked on *Super Bowl Monday*. My thanks also go to Cathy L. Gonzalez and Reuben Canales at the Associated Press, Brooke Thomas at Getty Images, and David Valenzuela at the *Buffalo News*.

My two-part June 2010 research adventure was also vital to the book. I visited the NFL Films offices in Mt. Laurel, New Jersey. Chris Willis and Linda Endres deserve great thanks. The next leg of the trip was at the Pro Football Hall of Fame in Canton, Ohio. Jason Aikens and Jon Kendle were a tremendous help, pulling archives and microfiche, as well as yielding control of the copy machine for quite a while. My "research assistant-ish" on this fruitful journey, Dr. Hillard Lazarus, was tremendous assistance.

And a very special thanks to Colleen Smith-Grubb at NFL Films. Without her enthusiastic and exceptional kindness, this book would not have turned out as well as I had hoped.

Index